THE SCHOOL PSYCHOLOGY PRACTICUM AND INTERNSHIP HANDBOOK

Diana Joyce-Beaulieu, PhD, NCSP, is a faculty member of the National Association of School Psychologists (NASP)-approved and American Psychological Association (APA)-accredited School Psychology Program at the University of Florida. She has taught 75 graduate courses, including psychopathology, diagnosis, and behavioral/social–emotional disabilities. As a licensed psychologist and nationally certified school psychologist, she is the coordinator of the practica program and supervises practica placements across four county school districts and nine clinical sites (e.g., hospital adolescent psychiatric unit, university Americans with Disabilities Act [ADA] office for college students with disabilities, and a child forensics law clinic). Her research interests include behavioral assessment, social–emotional wellness, and implementation of multitiered systems of support (MTSS) or response-to-intervention (RtI) as applied to school behavioral intervention. Her publications include three books and numerous chapters and peer-referred articles. As coprincipal investigator, she has been awarded $830,000 in professional development grants to research school-based behavioral and mental health components of MTSS/RtI.

Eric Rossen, PhD, NCSP, is a nationally certified school psychologist and licensed psychologist in the state of Maryland. He has experience working in public schools as well as independent practice, and is currently the director of professional development and standards for the National Association of School Psychologists (NASP). Within his role, Dr. Rossen supports the implementation of NASP standards related to credentialing, graduate preparation, professional ethics, and practice. His publications include two books, numerous chapters and peer-refereed articles, and policy briefs on issues related to bullying, crisis response, school safety, trauma, and school psychological practices. He also has served as a college instructor and adjunct faculty at the University of Missouri and Prince George's Community College in Maryland.

THE SCHOOL PSYCHOLOGY PRACTICUM AND INTERNSHIP HANDBOOK

Diana Joyce-Beaulieu, PhD, NCSP, and
Eric Rossen, PhD, NCSP

SPRINGER PUBLISHING COMPANY
NEW YORK

Copyright © 2016 Springer Publishing Company, LLC

All rights reserved.

No part of this publication may be reproduced, stored in a retrieval system, or transmitted in any form or by any means, electronic, mechanical, photocopying, recording, or otherwise, without the prior permission of Springer Publishing Company, LLC, or authorization through payment of the appropriate fees to the Copyright Clearance Center, Inc., 222 Rosewood Drive, Danvers, MA 01923, 978-750-8400, fax 978-646-8600, info@copyright.com or on the Web at www.copyright.com.

Springer Publishing Company, LLC
11 West 42nd Street
New York, NY 10036
www.springerpub.com

Acquisitions Editor: Nancy S. Hale
Composition: diacriTech

ISBN: 978-0-8261-1931-5
e-book ISBN: 978-0-8261-1932-2
Student Resources ISBN: 978-0-8261-3187-4

Student Resources are available from *www.springerpub.com/school-psychology-practicum*

15 16 17 18 19 / 5 4 3 2 1

The author and the publisher of this Work have made every effort to use sources believed to be reliable to provide information that is accurate and compatible with the standards generally accepted at the time of publication. The author and publisher shall not be liable for any special, consequential, or exemplary damages resulting, in whole or in part, from the readers' use of, or reliance on, the information contained in this book. The publisher has no responsibility for the persistence or accuracy of URLs for external or third-party Internet websites referred to in this publication and does not guarantee that any content on such websites is, or will remain, accurate or appropriate.

Library of Congress Cataloging-in-Publication Data
Joyce-Beaulieu, Diana.
The school psychology practicum and internship handbook / by Diana Joyce-Beaulieu, PhD, NCSP, and Eric Rossen, PhD, NCSP.
    pages cm
Includes bibliographical references and index.
ISBN 978-0-8261-1931-5
1. Clinical psychology—Study and teaching (Internship)—United States. 2. Clinical psychologists—Training of—United States. 3. Practicums—United States. I. Rossen, Eric A. II. Title.
RC467.7.J69 2016
616.890076—dc23

2015014932

Special discounts on bulk quantities of our books are available to corporations, professional associations, pharmaceutical companies, health care organizations, and other qualifying groups. If you are interested in a custom book, including chapters from more than one of our titles, we can provide that service as well.

For details, please contact:
Special Sales Department, Springer Publishing Company, LLC
11 West 42nd Street, 15th Floor, New York, NY 10036-8002
Phone: 877-687-7476 or 212-431-4370; Fax: 212-941-7842
E-mail: sales@springerpub.com

Printed in the United States of America by Gasch Printing.

This book is dedicated to my mother, Caroline Ann Joyce, a woman who believed in the abilities of her children long before they could even conceptualize their own aspirations. She facilitated success by encouraging a love of reading, frequently reiterating the importance of an education, always encouraging our own unique dreams, cultivating our strengths, and ever moving us forward with optimism and compassion. She is a prodigious contributor to the opportunity I now have for a rewarding career in the field of school psychology. I am also immensely grateful to my husband, David Beaulieu, for his intellect that challenges me to aspire higher, as well as his steadfast encouragement and marvelous sense of humor during the creation of this text.

—Diana Joyce-Beaulieu

I dedicate this book to my wife, Lauren, and my daughters Emily and Nora, who offer daily reminders that I still have much to learn. More importantly, they offer me the important conditions for happiness: unconditional love, support, laughter, and distraction. I also thank my entire family for always standing shoulder to shoulder with me throughout my personal and professional growth. Lastly, I am lucky and grateful to have surrounded myself with colleagues and friends that possess such extraordinary talents, skills, and abilities that force me to grow alongside them.

—Eric Rossen

Lastly, we dedicate this book to our colleague and friend, Dr. Thomas Oakland. His positive and profound impact on the profession, and on our lives personally, will never be forgotten.

—Diana Joyce-Beaulieu and Eric Rossen

Contents

Contributors ix
Foreword by Alex Thomas xi
Preface xiii
Acknowledgments xv

SECTION I: PRACTICUM 1

1: Practicum 101—Preparing for Practicum *3*
Practica Program Structure *4*
Surviving and Thriving in Grad School *8*
Security Procedures *13*
Student Liability Insurance *15*
Professional-Issues Vignettes *17*
Chapter Review *18*

2: Orientation to Practicum *21*
Entry Procedures Considerations *21*
Direct Student, Patient, and Client Contact Considerations *24*
Professional Practice Considerations *29*
Orientation to Practica Vignettes *36*
Chapter Review *37*

3: Portfolios and Competency-Based Evaluation *39*
Demonstrating Acquisition of Knowledge and Skills *39*
Conflict Between Supervisor Evaluation and Students *44*
Performance Competency Vignettes *48*
Chapter Review *50*

4: Peer Mentoring and Peer Supervision *53*
(*Olivia Soutullo, coauthor*)
Roles and Responsibilities *54*
Levels of Support *55*
Facilitating Positive Interactions *56*
Models of Supervision *57*
Critiquing Test Administration *58*
Scoring Protocols *63*
Proofing Common Writing Errors *64*
Peer Supervision Vignettes *65*
Chapter Review *67*

5: Advanced Practica *69*
(*Sally Grapin, coauthor*)
Transition and College Student Evaluations *70*

vii

viii • CONTENTS

Advanced Practica Vignettes   *77*
Forensic Psychology   *79*
Research Considerations Through Practicum   *82*
Mental Health Settings   *85*
Classification Models Beyond the *DSM*   *87*
Chapter Review   *88*

SECTION II: INTERNSHIP   93

6: Preparing for Internship   95
Writing a Winning Curriculum Vita   *95*
Selecting Internship Sites   *99*
Application Process   *105*
Statement of Interest   *106*
Interview   *107*
Letters of Recommendation   *112*
No Offers—Now What?   *113*
Final Considerations   *113*
Chapter Review   *115*

7: Internship 101   *117*
(*Olivia Soutullo, coauthor*)
Documentation, Logs, and Record Keeping   *117*
Time Management for Interns   *122*
Setting Boundaries and Expectations   *125*
Transitioning to the Role of Professional   *126*
Internship Evaluation Measures and Competencies   *130*
Chapter Review   *131*

8: Ethical and Professional Practice: Potential Conflicts   133
School Psychology Interns' Obligations to the Ethics Code   *133*
Internship Contract   *138*
Conflicts With Supervisors   *140*
Conflicts in Laws and Agency Rules or Policies   *143*
Chapter Review   *149*

9: Psychological Case Reports   151
Report-Writing Principles   *152*
Report-Writing Vignettes   *152*
Report-Writing Basics   *157*
Chapter Review 184

10: Preparing for Career Positions   185
(*Janise Parker, coauthor*)
Is a Postdoc in Your Future?   *185*
Career Listing Resources   *189*
Writing a Career Cover Letter and Vita   *191*
Career Interviews   *194*
Chapter Review   *202*

APPENDICES
  Appendix A: Resources: Professional Organizations and Standards   205
  Appendix B: Chapter Exhibits   209
Index   225

Contributors

Sally Grapin, PhD Assistant Professor, Department of Psychology, Montclair State University, Montclair, New Jersey

Diana Joyce-Beaulieu, PhD, NCSP School of Special Education, School Psychology, and Early Childhood Studies, College of Education, University of Florida, Gainesville, Florida

Janise Parker, MEd, PhD University of South Florida, Tampa, Florida

Eric Rossen, PhD, NCSP NASP Director Professional Development and Standards, Silver Spring, Maryland

Olivia Soutullo, MEd School of Special Education, School Psychology, and Early Childhood Studies, College of Education, University of Florida, Gainesville, Florida

Foreword

Drs. Joyce-Beaulieu and Rossen, where were you when I needed you? Yours is the book that should have been ready for reference during my four decades as a school psychologist, time about evenly divided between school-based practitioner and teaching school psychology students at a university. During my practitioner time, I fondly recall the many yearlong stints as an intern's sole/primary/only field-based supervisor and the many short-term visits by practicum students from area universities. As university-based faculty, I have a more immediate memory of the thousands of questions asked by the hundreds of students who received program supervision from me during practicum and/or internship experiences. In both roles, school and university based, I winged it well using whatever diverse resources were at hand. It would have been most helpful to have a single resource containing the detailed guidance for practicum and internship this text offers. I could have benefited from a reference containing the national picture of where such experiences fit into the scope of training (professional standards, accreditation and program approval guidelines, etc.) along with the plethora of details associated with day-to-day functioning (how to get fingerprinted, developing a résumé, finding a job, resolving conflicts, etc.).

Having been both practitioner and trainer, I was confident in knowing that the quality of real-world experiences and the supervision the students receive are the most important contributors in providing practical interactions that give substance and confidence to their future professional practice. You may be able to recite every article ever published in the *School Psychology Review*, *Journal of School Psychology*, or *School Psychology Quarterly*, be able to memorize all the articles in the most recent *Best Practices in School Psychology*, and adeptly recite every lecture heard and textbook read from preparation courses, but that would not guarantee that you would become a successful professional. Content knowledge is necessary but not sufficient to be a competent school psychologist. Successful application of that content through supervised practice is essential to become a competent professional.

School psychologist training is a large and essential enterprise in our country. During the 2013–2014 academic year, 9,613 students were enrolled in school psychology graduate education programs leading, at a minimum, to state certification/licensure as a school psychologist. These students were spread across 240 universities providing 313 programs (142 universities provided specialist-only programs, 25 provided doctoral-only programs, and 73 provided both specialist and doctoral programs). Most of those students receive practicum experience during each year of their program, and, during the last decade, approximately 2,500 interns spent an entire school year as a culmination of their formal training (2,578 during the 2013–2014 year).

In one volume, this is an "Everything you ever needed to know about school psychology practica and internship" resource that can be used by university programs to evaluate the structure and organization involved in their own program, used by aspiring school psychology students to ensure they are obtaining the experiences they need to guarantee professional competencies, and used by field-based facilitators who can use this broad-based resource to place their most important supervisory role in a larger context. Though we may like to think that providing practicum/internship experiences is relatively straightforward, these experiences are embedded in a complex web of state and federal law, ensuing regulations, and school district procedures, and then folded in with national program accreditation and approval processes. I am pleased that this resource provides the overarching big picture along with the nuanced details of training for professional competencies. The big picture includes program approval/accreditation, doctoral/specialist issues, performance assessment procedures, and so forth. The little picture includes topics such as professional dress, surviving graduate school, liability insurance, time management, interviewing skills, and a host of other issues that contribute to the inside and outside boundaries within which professional preparation in school psychology resides. Many topics may seem to be on the periphery in developing competent practitioners but are nonetheless important considerations in the achievement of that goal, particularly from a student viewpoint. This is a comprehensive resource on the topic and useful from a university, practice, or student perspective.

School psychology is an important endeavor and excellent training is the heart and soul of the profession's future, with quality supervised practical experience the heart and soul of training. I laud the comprehensiveness in breadth and depth of this excellent resource and believe it can serve as an essential foundation on which to augment one's own background and experiences to enrich the training of future school psychologists. Drs. Joyce-Beaulieu and Rossen, where were you when I needed you?

Alex Thomas, PhD
Professor Emeritus
Miami University
Oxford, Ohio

Preface

Approximately 2,800 new students enroll in school psychology programs in the United States each year (Rossen & von der Embse, 2014). These students regularly enter the program with expectations to engage in supervised field-based experiences within the first year, and sometimes within the first semester of graduate school. As these same students progress through their programs and field-based experiences evolve, new expectations and challenges emerge related to ethical dilemmas, supervisory relationships, meeting program requirements and national standards, selecting internships, meeting certification and licensure requirements, and applying for jobs to begin a career path.

In *The School Psychology Practicum and Internship Handbook*, we have attempted to provide a guided curriculum that introduces school psychology graduate students to a range of professional issues that may be faced within the context of supervised field-based experiences. Topics addressed in the book span entry-level practica through advanced clinical applications, the culminating internship year, and transitioning to professional practice.

The intention of the *Handbook*, in part, is to give students a single resource that can help them anticipate and navigate the various experiences throughout the graduate school experience from program entry to career entry. With that intention in mind, we gave significant attention to providing recommendations on developing CVs, interviewing, writing personal statements, considerations for certification and licensure, and applying to jobs—tasks often beyond the scope of what a program may offer through formal course work or seminars. Other core competencies essential to developing professionals in the context of field supervision also are addressed.

Additionally, our intention is to offer faculty a ready resource and text for use across a range of practicum and internship seminars. Graduate preparation programs in school psychology offer such seminars and formal university-based supervision to provide guidance to students as they traverse these experiences. Practica and internships remain among the most ubiquitous components of every school psychology program in the United States. Despite this long-standing requirement, however, a single, comprehensive, and practical text for practica and internships did not exist.

xiii

The *Handbook* can easily be adopted by most programs and emphasizes applied examples including vignettes to help facilitate discussion. To assist programs working to further develop their own processes, the *Handbook* includes various tools and templates (e.g., contracts, evaluations, record-keeping forms, logs) that represent actual forms utilized by National Association of School Psychologists (NASP)-approved and American Psychological Association (APA)-accredited programs across the country. **A Student Resources ancillary is available for download from Springer Publishing Company's website: www.springerpub.com/school-psychology-practicum.** Related issues associated with best practices in supervision are addressed, along with recommendations on how to effectively meet the supervision needs of students in a variety of settings and formats.

Notably, the *Handbook* is not intended to provide a comprehensive curriculum on issues such as professional ethics, assessment and evaluation, intervention, or consultation, as those topics are extensively addressed through core program course work. However, these topics are discussed within the context of related issues typically encountered during field-based experiences. Rather, the book serves as a guide to both faculty and students to support growth during field-based experiences.

REFERENCE

Rossen, E., & von der Embse, N. (2014). The status of school psychology graduate education in the United States. In P. L. Harrison & A. Thomas (Eds.), *Best practices in school psychology: Foundations* (pp. 503–512). Bethesda, MD: National Association of School Psychologists.

Acknowledgments

The foundational knowledge, research, and clinical expertise reviewed in this book are an invaluable gift from past and present visionaries who have dedicated their lives to meeting the needs of children and adolescents in our country's school. Their research, legacy of scholarship, and wealth of applied expertise have provided the foundation for best practices in this field and built the infrastructure that keeps the quality of services provided among the best in the world. Thus, we are grateful and ever cognizant of their contributions.

We are especially appreciative of the dedicated and scholarly contributions to this manuscript from Olivia Soutullo (who coauthored Chapters 4 and 7), Sally Grapin (who coauthored Chapter 5), and Janise Parker (who coauthored Chapter 10). It also has been a pleasure to work with Nancy S. Hale, who is the editorial director of social sciences at Springer Publishing Company. Her personal warmth and professional support from guiding the original proposal to facilitating the final publication have brought this project to fruition. Thank you!

SECTION I

Practicum

CHAPTER 1

Practicum 101—Preparing for Practicum

LEARNING OBJECTIVES

At the conclusion of this chapter, readers should be able to:

1. Acquire a basic knowledge of the professional attributes required to thrive in practica

2. Understand the sequence, structure, and training purposes of practica requirements

3. Describe the security processes and procedures required for accessing schools and clients as well as providing direct service to youth

Practicum is a training requirement for school psychology programs with approval from the National Association of School Psychologists (NASP) and the American Psychological Association (APA) accreditation (APA, 2006; NASP, 2010). The practica experience supports a scientist–practitioner model. Originally introduced in 1949, the model combines a dual emphasis on science and practice (Petersen, 2007). This training paradigm has a long-standing tradition in the disciplines of medicine, psychology, and education emphasizing close integration of theoretical knowledge and applied clinical skills.

Practica are based on an applied clinical science orientation and are considered to have a reciprocal nature whereby science guides practice and applied research data in turn inform science. Thus, the acquisition of applied clinical skills through practicum experiences serves multiple purposes. They provide a socialization process into the career setting for preprofessionals and ensure that applied expertise is acquired within an authentic context. The coinciding core curriculum also provides a broad scientific spectrum of theoretical knowledge that teaches an empirical foundation for supporting best practices in service delivery. In addition, the scientific inquiry method is taught to foster a philosophical approach to practice based on critical thinking skills. Diagnostic and intervention decisions in the practica site occur with collaborative problem-solving techniques informed by data to generate hypotheses, and then intervention or treatment goals are designed from this information. Following implementation of an intervention, outcome data measures are utilized to determine intervention effectiveness. The process of learning applied skills within a practica scientist–practitioner model requires sophisticated knowledge, well-practiced skills, a collaborative orientation, and analytical reasoning. These are all competencies you will acquire as you participate in practica and internship experiences, and our goal for this text is to offer a student-friendly guide for navigating the intricate context of developing applied professional practice skills.

PRACTICA PROGRAM STRUCTURE

To facilitate professional development within the scientist–practitioner model, school psychology practica requirements are juxtaposed with core curriculum (see sample multiyear practica sequence in Figure 1.1; additionally, sample practica syllabi [Exhibits 1.1 and 1.2] are also available from www.springerpub.com/school-psychology-practicum). The experiences include carefully orchestrated assignments that increase in complexity and levels of independence over time. The sequence, duration, and content of assignments correspond to academic knowledge acquired in course work with progressively greater individual responsibility for application in the practica site. As best practices and ethical guidelines require, all field-based practica activities are supervised by appropriately credentialed school psychologists or psychologists so there is on-site guidance as graduate students learn new skills and acquire competencies. Personalized supervision and multiple progress monitoring measures are utilized to evaluate the practica student's professional development and to inform areas for further growth. The short-term goal of these experiences is to develop students' applied clinical skills. The long-term goals include preparation for the internship and ultimately a career in the field of school psychology as a practitioner, researcher, administrator, or through child advocacy appointments.

Practicum placement matches are typically decided in collaboration with faculty and site supervisors and the practica sequence of the program may be administered by a practica coordinator. For some programs, practica placements will begin during the first semester in the program and be available throughout the duration of training. Other programs may offer shorter practica sequences or practica that begin during the latter portions of the training sequence. While NASP (2010) Standards for Graduate Preparation of School Psychologists identify a requirement for a practica experience that is distinct from and precedes internship, the standards do not describe a specific minimum hour requirement, leading to the potential for significant variability

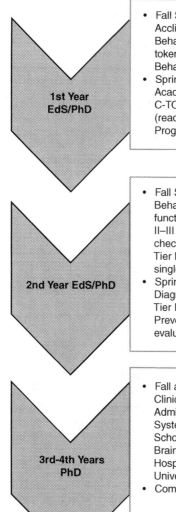

FIGURE 1.1 Sample multiyear practica curricula sequence.
BASC-3, Behavioral Assessment System for Children, Third Edition; BASC-2-PM, Behavioral Assessment System for Children, Second Edition–Progress Monitor; BESS, Behavioral and Emotional Screening System; CBMs, curriculum-based measures; CTOPP-2, Comprehensive Test of Phonological Processing–Second Edition; DIBELS, Dynamic Indicators of Basic Early Literacy Skills; GORT-5, Gray Oral Reading Tests, Fifth Edition; K-ABC, Kaufman Assessment Battery for Children; WIAT-III, Wechsler Individual Achievement Test, Third Edition; WISC, Wechsler Intelligence Scale for Children; WJ-IV, Woodcock–Johnson Battery, Fourth Edition.

across programs. The faculty within a particular institution and the program's graduate handbook will provide detailed information on the design of practica for training. The role of practica coordinators may include:

- Recruitment and retention of high-quality practica placement training sites and credentialed supervisors

- Direct supervision and administration of university-based clinics
- Site visits to off-campus practica sites
- Coordination and administration of program test lab facilities and assessment/intervention resources
- Monitoring evaluation data of sites and student performance to ensure continued high performance as well as facilitate accreditation outcome data requirements. Often evaluations are facilitated through student ratings of sites/supervisors and supervisor ratings of practica student performance
- Keeping site supervisors informed of program course and assignment requirements that will be facilitated through the practica experience
- Providing continuing professional development to site supervisors (often through semiannual meetings, in-service workshops, or invitations to join program seminars and attend guest speaker topics)
- Teaching university-based practica supervision seminars and courses
- Facilitating student/site matches that best serve training and research access needs

Practica Site Placements

Student experiences prior to enrollment in the graduate school program as well as personal career goals are often primary considerations in the practica matching process. Once the placement match is finalized, it is time to begin preparing for entry into the school district, agency, or institution, and the new preprofessional service role.

The options for practica placements will vary significantly by institution based on the training focus, resources, and needs of the program. For example, master's and specialist-level programs will have students who complete their course work in a very short period of time (often 2 years); thus, practica settings preparing school psychologists will need a strong concentration on school-based experiences to ensure that all competencies for practice are met. They may rely heavily on local surrounding districts for practica supervision with an emphasis on offering a range of exposure to differing age levels (i.e., elementary school, middle school, high school) and disability needs. Opportunities to work with youth from diverse socioeconomic, linguistic, and ethnicity backgrounds also is part of the design of practica so that graduate students are well prepared to provide services to a wide range of students and families. For institutions that have the resources for university lab schools or program clinics, assessment and intervention opportunities also may be acquired on campus in these facilities, often supervised by program faculty. Additionally, programs can develop practica experiences through local community mental health agencies and private practitioners.

In larger university settings, there may be on-campus hospitals, outpatient clinics, and nationally funded research centers that offer a variety of specialization opportunities (e.g., spectrum clinics, attention deficit hyperactivity disorder [ADHD] clinics, eating disorders, or addiction clinics). For programs offering PhD or PsyD degrees, practica training may range from 3 to 5 years, thus extending the number of differing practica opportunities a student may have time to acquire. A doctoral program in school psychology may begin the first couple of years of practica in school-based settings as core practice competencies are secured, and then offer specialization sites (e.g., hospital clinics) or research-based practica settings to facilitate dissertations. For research-intensive programs, faculty also will often have research grants and projects that may facilitate practica experiences. Figure 1.2 provides a sample of one university's practica program options.

Given the range of practica opportunities available, it will be important to begin discussions with one's faculty advisor early in the program to plan experiences that best match one's individual career goals. Practica experiences are particularly important in preparing a strong vita for internship applications for accredited and/or nationally competitive sites. This chapter provides practical and procedural information for students beginning practicum and the journey toward entry-level professional competency.

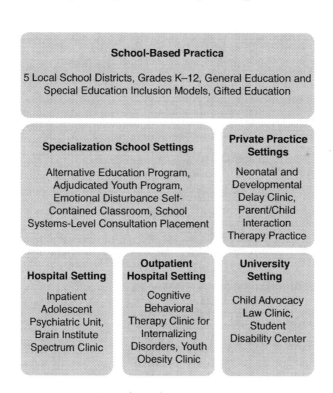

FIGURE 1.2 Sample multiyear practica placement options.

SURVIVING AND THRIVING IN GRAD SCHOOL

If you are reading this text in class, congratulations! Acceptance into a graduate school psychology program is a commendable accomplishment. It reflects the skills and knowledge to have successfully completed an undergraduate degree and to have navigated the recruitment process of graduate school. Individuals selected have demonstrated high scores on national entrance exams and a strong vita reflecting prior experiences that may include research, mental health agency service or employment, conference presentations, and possibly publications.

You have embarked on an exciting journey toward becoming an accomplished professional school psychologist. At the end of this odyssey lies a fulfilling and rewarding career with a wide range of opportunities. Immense consideration has already been given to the quality of your training through state and national approval and accreditations standards and procedures. These mandates safeguard the integrity of the professional development that you will receive and ensure that core competencies are acquired. In addition to the institutional foundations of your program, there are a number of personal strategies you also can apply to optimize the graduate school experience. Four factors for success include:

- Establish a strong mentor relationship with a faculty member who can guide your progress and direct your activities to best prepare you for your ultimate career goal. Faculty have already successfully navigated graduate school and acquired professional credentials and achievements. They have a wealth of valuable guidance to offer. Additionally, they can inform students of assistantship and research opportunities, offer to copresent at conferences, facilitate coauthoring opportunities, and provide references; additionally, many faculty maintain collegial friendships with former students throughout their careers.
- Keep a laser-sharp focus on your short- and long-term goals to avoid less important activities that detract from a timely graduation. Graduate school will offer many opportunities, especially as your skills increase; therefore, it is important to discern which experiences help move you toward your goals and which may only delay goals.
- Become immersed in your training to ensure an in-depth and inspiring process. The acquisition of knowledge can have an exponential effect in that concepts build upon each other and interconnect to quickly expand understanding. Consistently reading the literature in the field, participating in classroom discussion, attending conferences and professional workshops, and engaging in program teaching, practica, and research opportunities over time will result in a coalescence of expertise.

- And last, but not least, keep a balanced perspective. Graduate school will be challenging, time-consuming, require great energy, and push you to grow; therefore, it is important to stay aware of your own personal care needs, including health and social support networks. Remember to set aside some time for the hobbies, interests, and extracurricular activities that you personally find rejuvenating. Some graduate students find it helpful to write down five or six stress-relieving strategies (e.g., walking, running, playing sports, watching movies, dining out, talking with a friend, drawing, reading, listening to music) and keep the list at their desks as a reminder of techniques to incorporate when the pressures of graduate school begin escalating.

The rest of this chapter offers a number of practical tips on managing the graduate school experience successfully from professional dress and time management to compliance with federal mandates and practica log documentation procedures.

Professional Dress

The foundational psychology knowledge you have acquired as an undergraduate in combination with the school psychology graduate course work you are now acquiring will provide substantial academic knowledge upon which to build qualifications for clinical work. However, in addition to knowledge, a professional demeanor and dress also can have a significant impact on fostering credibility when you enter schools or clinics. Both are important forms of nonverbal communication regarding an individual's perceived authority and roles.

A professional demeanor in practicum can serve to establish trust and confidence in one's abilities. Attributes, such as self-assurance, maturity, sound judgment, and experience, are often discerned from the quality of voice tone, mannerisms, and posture. In addition, there are therapeutic implications for demeanor in rapport building with clients and families. Characteristics, such as facial expressions, gestures, and attentiveness, can be interpreted as approachability, caring, and empathy. The assumptions of parents and children, colleagues and peers also are influenced by demeanor. A large body of research on school consultation confirms the need for a professional disposition in establishing more effective collaboration with other professionals (Brown, Pryzwanski, & Schulte, 2006). These skills also are important to acquiring an open and receptive rapport that will foster supervision effectiveness between the practicum student and his or her supervisors (Freedheim & Overholser, 1998).

The assigned workspace for practicum students in schools is often in the administrative offices or student services buildings. Office space within clinics or hospitals tends to be located in treatment corridors of the facility. Although, in many circumstances practicum is an unpaid position, it is still considered a workplace assignment and thus appropriate attire is expected. Research from the early classic work of Malloy (1975) on business attire for success noted the importance of clothing choices to acceptance within organizations. More recent discussions of the business casual dress perspective also acknowledge the effect of aesthetic responses to appearance (Bixler & Nix-Rice, 1997). Just as demeanor is thought to impact rapport with families and students receiving services, professional dress also may influence their level of trust and confidence in the service provider. A survey of psychiatrists and their clients found both groups reported professional dress to be an important factor in the client/care provider relationship (Nihalani, Kunwar, Staller, & Lamberti, 2006). Zur (2007) proposes that dress is one factor of several nonverbal social language components that help define interpersonal boundaries in therapy with clients.

The expectation for dress at a practicum site is considerably different from typical student apparel for classes or lab work. Professional dress is often described as conservative, modest, clean, polished, and sophisticated. As a form of nonverbal communication, professional wear should communicate competency and reflect a well-educated persona. There is an emphasis on simple lines in clothing rather than decorative, and slogans, icons, or pictures on apparel are avoided. Items fit well, are pressed, and cloth patterns are nondistracting (e.g., solids, small patterns, or stripes). Casual and formal wear fabrics, as well as ornate trims, are typically avoided (e.g., denim, satins, metallic, and fur). Schools often provide very specific guidelines for both faculty and students that may include prohibitions for items, such as t-shirts, team sportswear, hoods, caps, or transparent clothing; or conversely, requirements, such as a button-down shirt and ties for all male employees. Exceptions are sometimes made for school logos and polo shirts. In addition, some schools with a history of gang participation may prohibit certain colors and clothing combinations (e.g., red/black with cap) that are indicative of gang membership. Other schools with uniform regulations may ask faculty and practicum students to also abide by the school's accepted colors. Makeup for workplace standards is typically minimal or natural in appearance. Jewelry that is not overly ornate or cumbersome can add a distinct personal style. When considering the inclusion of expensive jewelry or accessories, it is important to also be sensitive to the circumstances of poverty that many children and families face.

Schools, like other organizations, also have site-specific cultures that vary. In particular, school board administrative offices and urban settings tend to be more formal than alternative education offices or rural settings. For practica in clinics or hospitals, dress is usually more formal and may require a lab coat in psychiatric units. Participating in a setting as a practicum student can be conceptualized as being a guest and it is incumbent upon the visitor to know the customs and expectations of the environment. Therefore, it is important to obtain a copy of each school's or clinic's employee dress guidelines. A discussion regarding appropriate attire with the site supervisor prior to the first day on site can also be valuable when establishing this aspect of one's professional identity.

Organization and Time Management

Organization and time management are core skills for any professional career. This is particularly true for graduate study with ever-increasing demands in program standards and rigor. Graduate students typically enroll in 12 credit hours of classes per semester, which is considered a full-time load. In addition, practicum may be required one full day per week. Other responsibilities can include assistantships, fellowships, research projects, or part-time employment. Developing organizational and time-management skills will also be important to long-term career goals as a school psychologist or in an academic position as those roles impose many competing demands.

Strong organizational skills include self-discipline, foresight, and the ability to prioritize needs so the more important tasks are completed first. Self-awareness of one's own working style and habits can be very helpful in anticipating the pace of work, most suitable environmental factors (e.g., with music, good lighting), and motivational issues (e.g., time of day, reinforcement structure for accomplishments). Other organizational strategies include delegating nonessential tasks, starting projects early, and the ability to break large demanding projects into smaller and more manageable stages. Simple solutions such as a well-equipped workspace and an efficient filing system also can improve organization. In addition, there are a host of clerical supplies available for modest budgets (e.g., color-coded file folders, clipboards, sticky notes) that will help organize work. An often-neglected component of organizational skills is an awareness of personal stress management strategies. Ensuring adequate time for rest, relaxation, and recreation into a busy graduate schedule can ease much of the anxiety, frustration, and confusion that exacerbate poor self-management.

There are basics of time-management skills applicable to all business or achievement environments. The more obvious ones include setting a schedule, keeping a daily calendar, and planning appointments or deadlines well in advance (Kenny, 2005). Common errors in planning include underestimating the time commitments required for a project, overcommitted schedules that are easily foiled, and the neglect of time allowances for projects that must be coordinated with the schedules of others. Together, these characteristics can suggest a lack of realistic and careful preplanning.

Fortunately, there are simple strategies that can assist. Because graduate school is a new endeavor and more rigorous than undergraduate studies, students do not have this prior experience to compare in estimating time demands. An effective solution for underestimation can be as simple as asking faculty and more advanced graduate students what they think reasonable time frames for projects and particular commitments should be. For example, it might be good to inquire how long a comprehensive psychoeducational report typically takes to complete or how many hours one should need for preparing class lectures if you accept a teaching assistantship. There also is a particular personality temperament type (e.g., intuitive or imaginative) that is prone to prefer grand ideas with a propensity to underestimate the time required to complete them (Jung, 1971; Oakland & Joyce, 2006). If underestimation is the result of a long-standing personality characteristic, self-awareness and compensatory strategies (e.g., extending time estimations by half) may be required.

Overcommitted schedules may also be a result of the inability to say no to requests or an abundance of opportunities without discernment as to which are most appropriate. Learning to say no can be especially problematic for those who are passive or place a strong emphasis on pleasing others. A lack of positive assertiveness skills can result in unrealistic demands on one's time and have a host of negative implications for personal stress as well (Smith, 2002). In one study of 1,200 novice nurses, job burnout was greater for those with low assertiveness skills (Suzuki, Kanoya, Katsuki, & Sato, 2006). Persons with a feeling temperament style (approximately 60% of females and 40% of males) have enduring traits toward avoiding conflict and pleasing others (Jung, 1971; Oakland & Joyce, 2006). This combination may benefit from both assertiveness strategies and self-awareness in recognizing the behavioral patterns.

The neglect of time allowances for projects that must be coordinated with the schedules of others is primarily a result of perspective taking and a lack of information. It is often easier to anticipate one's own needs than those of others. This dilemma can be easily remedied by a specific discussion of resources and availability of others when collaborating on projects. The discussion may also include talking about personal work style as some prefer a steady consistent pace whereas others work in spurts of inspiration.

Even given the best of time-management and organizational skills, there are inevitable unforeseen events in life. This is particularly true when working with schoolchildren who may move during an evaluation, be out sick, have an important test to take, or just not wish to cooperate on a particular day. The ability to change plans and adapt will also be important in clinic and hospital practica as patients are more likely to struggle with mental health issues and sometimes compliance or attendance is

SECURITY PROCEDURES

To safeguard children, most school systems and mental health providers have implemented security-screening procedures that must occur prior to the first day in a practica setting. These may be as simple as an application with references or providing identification from a state agency (e.g., a driver's license) or they may be more comprehensive, such as fingerprinting and drug screening. The impetus behind these procedures is often based on protecting children and youth from care providers who have a history of inappropriate conduct with children, drug misuse, or criminal incidents. In addition, the security and identification measures can help protect participants of the building as identification badges provide law enforcement with a ready method for distinguishing employees from outsiders in the event of an emergency. Security screenings also serve to limit access to sensitive information (e.g., medical records) just to those persons approved.

A number of high profile criminal cases over the past few decades have resulted in the enactment of several laws to heighten security for children. These provisions provide safeguards for parents ensuring notification when convicted child sex offenders or predators are released into the community. In addition, restrictions ensure prior offenders are not employed by or in close proximity to child-care centers or schools. In 1990, Washington State was the first to enact mandates requiring that sex offenders register (Klasskids Foundation, 2007). Following the death of Megan Kanka, a 7-year-old girl murdered by a prior offender, Megan's Law was signed and provided requirements for registration and community notification (Walsh, 1998). The Klasskids Foundation provides a national website with extensive information on state contacts and criteria as well as offender database information (www.klaaskids.org/pg-legmeg.htm). Prior to this time, personal privacy rights had restricted such information from general distribution. The Adam Walsh Child Protection and Safety Act of 2006 (H.R. 4472) extended the national offenders registry, required background checks for adoptive and foster parents, and increased penalties for sex offender crimes involving children (U.S. Congress, 2007). The U.S. Department of Justice maintains this site at www.nsopr.gov.

The Jessica Lunsford Act is an example of state legislation that directly governs aspects of school personnel and visitor security clearance. The law was initiated following the abduction and murder of a 9-year-old girl. In 2005, the state of Florida passed legislation mandating that all school

14 • SECTION I: PRACTICUM

personnel and students in preparation programs who participate in field experiences in the schools provide fingerprints for criminal background checks (Florida State Senate, 2005).

Fingerprinting and Background Checks

Practicum site supervisors will be most familiar with their school board district's or agency's guidelines and procedures. The typical process includes providing a form of official photo identification, often one issued by another state agency such as a driver's license. Consent forms are also required in order for the processing agent to access confidential records. Once the records are obtained, a decision is made based on state or local criteria, as to whether the individual may have access to work directly with children. A history of offenses does not always preclude clearance. The severity of the incident (e.g., infraction, misdemeanor, or felony), the age of the incident, and whether that action endangered children are considerations. For example, a misdemeanor offense as a youngster for trespassing to swim in a neighbor's pool would be viewed quite differently from a drug possession charge. Interpretations of offenses may also differ by state whereby one state considers running a red light to be an infraction and another views this action as a misdemeanor. Some jurisdictions also change the level of offense in consideration of the outcome of the incident. Therefore, a minor traffic ticket infraction may become a misdemeanor or felony if there is injury or property damage. Another complexity in considering legal history is the question of sealed and expunged records. A sealed record still exists but has a high level of restricted access and an expunged record can be removed from general state files. However, there are exemptions from the requirements to either divulge or access sealed and expunged records. Exemptions may include employment checks or services with agencies and schools serving children (Florida Department of Law Enforcement, 2007). Specific laws and implementation guidelines will vary by state; thus, if you have questions, inquiring through the local agency may be helpful.

Processing can take several days and graduate students are usually not permitted direct contact with children until the process is successfully completed; therefore, it is important to apply as soon as the semester starts. Many school districts make this service available prior to the first day of class during their teacher preplanning days. School psychology programs may require a copy of security clearance for their records as well. This is a certificate simply noting "cleared" rather than details of an individual's history as that information is restricted. The agency processing the information will decide if an individual is cleared rather than training program personnel. It is important to note that most universities also have a self-disclosure statement included in their application process. The forms often ask questions regarding prior criminal record and convictions. In some circumstances, if offenses emerge during practica screening where clearance is denied and no incidents were disclosed on the required university application form, it is considered grounds for disciplinary action or dismissal from the program. Consultation with the program faculty regarding questions may help resolve these issues, especially if the conversations are held prior to a decision to prohibit security clearance. Often agencies will require background clearing processing to be updated and renewed periodically (e.g., annually) throughout practica to review any incidents that may have occurred during the interim between security checks.

Drug Testing

In addition to fingerprinting and background criminal records checks, some practicum sites also may require drug testing. Participants are often required to sign consent for release of information to the processing agent, which may be a lab that is subcontracted by the school or clinic for this service.

Identification

Most agencies and schools will require their own picture identification cards emphasizing that they be worn by all personnel and staff. Identification is a preventive safety measure serving to monitor who is entering buildings or working with children. In an emergency, identification lanyards and badges can help law enforcement discern which persons are personnel or visitors. More restrictive settings such as inpatient psychiatric units at hospitals may include an encoded film on the ID card that permits access to secure areas within the facility, often in combination with a keypad code. Some agencies and schools will permit use of a university ID card. The site supervisor will be able to provide guidance on this issue.

STUDENT LIABILITY INSURANCE

Liability insurance is typically a requirement in both practica and internship training and serves to protect the interests of graduate students and clients alike. Proof of liability insurance is often required prior to entering a practica site where children and youth are served. Insurance also should be a strong consideration during an individual's professional career. Some agencies such as school districts may offer this coverage through employee and union benefits, whereas other entities require the insurance be acquired by individual employees at their own expense.

Professional Liability Insurance

Lawsuits involving graduate students in school or clinical practicum cases are unusual; however, in the event of a suit, liability insurance may provide some individual protection for legal fees associated with defending against a claim or accusation. Student liability insurance is required beginning with the first semester of enrollment and must be renewed annually throughout the practicum sequence. Through membership in one of the national professional organizations, liability insurance can be obtained at a markedly reduced rate. Often a copy of the confirmation of insurance must be provided to the school psychology program and the practicum site to ensure coverage is current. Even if the program and practicum site do not require proof of insurance, graduate students may obtain a policy by following these simple steps:

- Apply for membership to either the NASP (www.nasponline.org) or the APA (www.apa.org).
- Membership in NASP or APA will entitle students to apply for a student liability insurance policy at a reduced rate. Insurance companies require an application and will notify students when the policy is approved. NASP members receive discounted insurance through Forest T. Jones (www.ftj.com, 1-800-821-7303) or the American Professional Agency (www.americanprofessional.com, 1-800-421-6694). APA members may apply to the APA Insurance Trust (www.apait.com/products/studentliability, 1-800-477-1200).
- Companies typically take 2 to 4 weeks to process and approve applications. Once the policy is accepted, coverage is effective for exactly 1 year from the policy start date; therefore, programs may require proof of annual renewals.

Personal Liability Insurance

School psychology graduate students are often responsible for any personal injuries they may sustain while participating in practicum assignments. The schools, school district, clinics, hospitals, and university may not provide workers' compensation coverage for students while engaged in required or voluntary field experience practica. Therefore, some college/university programs recommend that students maintain personal injury and health insurance coverage.

PROFESSIONAL-ISSUES VIGNETTES

All theory remains dormant until applied. Thus, this section and other chapters throughout the book provide professional-issues vignettes with the goal of fostering discussion on issues reviewed in the chapters. It is acknowledged that short descriptive scenarios do not explain all contingencies or have formulaic right or wrong answers. Therefore, these may be best viewed as a catalyst for critical thinking—the opportunity to connect knowledge with personal experience and reason to derive one's own conclusions.

Vignette 1.1

Sheila is a first-semester school psychology graduate student from another state. She is very bright and has worked hard to build a vita of nationally competitive achievements and secure acceptance into a Tier I research university. She is passionate about pursuing a career advocating for empirically based intervention services for children with spectrum disorder (i.e., autism) and knows a degree in school psychology will permit her to accomplish this goal. You are her peer, thus she has approached you with a dilemma. She has a misdemeanor infraction on her record from her home state for a driving accident that resulted in moderately damaging someone else's car. In her state, this is not considered a big deal and so she did not report it on her graduate school application questions regarding a prior record. She knows she will have a security check and hopes it will not show up.

Discussion Questions:

1. What is your advice to her?
2. What are the possible ramifications of not disclosing a prior criminal offense?

Generally, a misdemeanor that does not involve harm to others, especially a traffic violation that is fairly common, will not result in being denied entry into a practica site. Sites that utilize state databases to check for prior infraction history will yield a list of arrests, charges, and traffic violations. However, the site will have criteria that determine if those incidents constitute a danger to others and determine if the individual should be permitted to work with vulnerable populations (e.g., children, hospitalized, disabled). Most likely this matter would not be considered significant enough to bar entry to a practica placement. However, failure to disclose requested information on an application can result in a university discipline charge. The best advice is to encourage the student to discuss the oversight with an advisor or practica coordinator promptly.

18 • SECTION I: PRACTICUM

Vignette 1.2

Alima is an entering first-year practica student with a nose piercing and tongue stud that are part of her cultural tradition. Following a discussion in the first university practica seminar, the professor indicated that the nose ring is contrary to the local school dress code rules and there is concern regarding her pronunciation of some words when administering tests with the large tongue stud. The advisor has asked Alima to please remove the items when she attends the practica site.

Discussion Questions:

1. As a peer, what is your advice to Alima?
2. If she removes the items, how might she still express her traditions within the context of the schools?

Often in professional work there is a balance between personal expression and guidelines or rules within the institutions, some of which are flexible and some of which are not. In this case, Alima might obtain a copy of the school dress code rules for her site and verify what the adornment expectations and limitations are. Secondly, she may wish to discuss with her advisor the implications of clear pronunciation during test administrations and the impact that could have on children's scores. Additionally, she could explore ways to maintain her personal expressions of tradition and share those with others while staying within the workplace parameters (e.g., culturally traditional dress or jewelry).

CHAPTER REVIEW

This chapter has provided an overview of practical and procedural information for students beginning practicum and the journey toward entry-level professional competency. The practice of school psychology is a complex and challenging career that offers tremendous opportunity to affect positive outcomes for children and youth. Practica provides the initial experiences into this profession and a glimpse of the many possible career choices within the field. It is hoped that this chapter has provided advance-planning insights that make the preprofessional transition highly productive and personally rewarding.

A review of professional demeanor and appearance characteristics noted the impact of these nonverbal cues that can define professional identity from the very first day of practicum. Many important attributes, such as competency and sound judgment, are assumed by others based on aesthetic factors. The variation in expectations for appropriate attire and the importance of close supervisor discussion to determine institutional norms were also acknowledged. Site supervisors and faculty can also be an important resource in advising on organizational and time-management techniques that ease the stress of multiple time demands. Simple strategies in planning ahead for assignments, guarding against acquiring too many projects, and setting realistic timelines can be helpful.

Several topics related to security procedures and liability insurance also were reviewed. Some of these guidelines are intended for the protection of the practicum student and others to ensure the safety of children and youth receiving services. In preparation for entry into public school systems or restrictive clinical sites, background checks and identification documents are important and are common practices in preparing for practica work.

REFERENCES

American Psychological Association. (2006). *Guidelines and principles for accreditation of programs in professional psychology*. Washington, DC: Author.

Bixler, S., & Nix-Rice, N. (1997). *The new professional image: From business casual to the ultimate power look*. Cincinnati, OH: Adams Media Corporation.

Brown, D., Pryzwanski, W. B., & Schulte, A. C. (2006). *Psychological consultation and collaboration: Introduction to theory and practice* (6th ed.). Boston: Allyn and Bacon.

Florida Department of Law Enforcement. (2007). *Entities that get sealed and expunged records*. Retrieved from http://www.fdle.state.fl.us/expunge/agencies_allowed.html

Florida State Senate. (2005). *Jessica Lunsford Act: House 1877*. Retrieved from http://www.flsenate.gov

Freedheim, D. K., & Overholser, J. C. (1998). Training in psychotherapy during graduate school. *Psychotherapy in Private Practice, 17*(1), 3–18.

Jung, C. G. (1971). *Psychological types* (R. F. C. Hull, Revision of Trans. by H. G. Baynes). Princeton, NJ: Princeton University Press. (Original work published 1921)

Kenny, B. (2005). De-stressing in graduate school. *Communiqué, 33*(6), 32.

Klasskids Foundation. (2007). *Legislation: Megan's law by states: Victim's rights by states*. Retrieved from http://www.klaaskids.org/pg-legmeg.htm

Malloy, J. T. (1975). *Dress for success*. New York, NY: Warner Books.

National Association of School Psychologists. (2010). *Standards for graduate preparation of school psychologists*. Bethesda, MD: Author.

Nihalani, N. D., Kunwar, A., Staller, J., & Lamberti, J. S. (2006). How should psychiatrists dress? A survey. *Community Mental Health Journal, 42*(3), 291–302.

Oakland, T., & Joyce, D. (2006). Temperament-based learning styles and school-based applications. *Canadian Journal of School Psychology, 19*(1–2), 59–74.

Petersen, C. A. (2007). A historical look at psychology and the scientist-practitioner model. *American Behavioral Scientist, 50*(6), 758–765.

Smith, J. C. (2002). *Stress management: A comprehensive handbook of techniques and strategies*. New York, NY: Springer Publishing Company.

Suzuki, E., Kanoya, Y., Katsuki, T., & Sato, C. (2006). Assertiveness affecting burnout of novice nurses at university hospitals. *Japan Journal of Nursing Science, 3*(2), 93–105.

U.S. Congress. (2007). *Adam Walsh Child Protection and Safety Act of 2006: Pub. L. No. 109–248 (HR 4472)*. Washington, DC: Author.

Walsh, E. R. (1998). *Sex offender registration and community notification: A Megan's Law sourcebook*. Kingston, NJ: Civic Research Institute.

Zur, O. (2007). *Boundaries in psychotherapy: Clinical and ethical explorations*. Washington, DC: American Psychological Association.

CHAPTER 2

Orientation to Practicum

LEARNING OBJECTIVES

At the conclusion of this chapter, readers should be able to:

1. Acquire strategies for successful acclimation to school cultures
2. Understand the federal mandates for confidentiality and abuse reporting
3. Gain knowledge of Individuals With Disabilities Education Improvement Act (IDEIA) and Special Education Classifications

ENTRY PROCEDURES CONSIDERATIONS

Chapter 1 discussed the overarching purposes and structure of practica experiences and directed readers to sample syllabi that reflected general assignments. Preparation for clearance to participate in practica by obtaining professional liability insurance, completing security clearance procedures, and acquiring identification also were reviewed. Once these tasks are completed, graduate students are usually ready to enter into the practice setting and begin learning the nuances of service delivery. Each site will be unique and have differing orientation processes; however, they do share some common aspects.

Building Rapport

Typically, practica begin with introductions to the supervisor and key school personnel as well as a tour of the facilities. In the last chapter, the role of professional dress and a well-groomed appearance in making first impressions was noted. Another important strategy to facilitating a good start is to be prepared for introductions with knowledge of the names, roles, and backgrounds of the key individuals you will work with (e.g., the supervisor, school principal or lead psychologist, front desk office personnel). Most of this information, including personnel bios, educational background, and job titles, can be found on the school's or clinic's website, as well as professional networking websites. This information also is a great way to identify common experiences or interests to start conversations. For example, knowing a supervisor is an alumnus of your institution or noting his or her recent conference presentations can facilitate a collegial bond. Additionally, arriving with an idea of the overall infrastructure, including the leadership of the setting, the school or clinic philosophy, and general demographics, can provide you with a foundation for astute questions that guide the discussion about your future role in the site. Thus, a little homework prior to the first day can serve to quickly demonstrate your engagement and consideration in taking the time to learn about your future colleagues' work. Supervisors often are volunteering their time and expertise to mentor young professionals and any efforts to communicate respect for and a genuine interest in their career contributions will assist in building rapport.

Other ways to quickly acclimate to a setting are to acquire a copy of any clinic or school rules, building layout maps so you know your way around, and schedules to increase awareness of the daily logistics of the school or clinic and to assist in building familiarity with your new surroundings.

Setting Expectations and Boundaries

Initial supervision discussions are a good opportunity to review the parameters of your role in the practica site, the expectations the supervisor may have for your work, and also establish what title you will use (e.g., practica graduate student, practica extern). It is helpful to share the program syllabi with the supervisor so he or she has a copy of the assignment requirements. Often the early practica experiences will be observational and an opportunity to become familiar with the schedules, meetings, and activities of your supervisor. Following this adjustment period, you will most likely be asked to begin providing services while being observed and critiqued by the supervisor to ensure that skills are developing correctly. As skills are demonstrated, responsibilities will become more independent and self-directed, although a supervisor should also be accessible. It is acceptable during the initial meetings with the supervisor to discuss her or his thoughts and expectations regarding your progression of participation in service delivery. Generally, office space, supplies, and professional resources (e.g., test kits, protocols, and curricula) will be provided, but if not, this could be a point of discussion with program faculty. Important boundaries to inquire about include security measures for student records and general personnel conduct policies that are often available by acquiring a copy of the school's or clinic's handbook.

Acclimation to the Hierarchy and Culture Within Schools/Clinics

Each institution will have a hierarchical structure for decision making and division of responsibilities, as well as processes to organize the vital operations of its mission. Part of the acclimation to the profession of school psychology will include learning these systems-level procedures. If time permits, it often is helpful to conduct a series of short interviews with key personnel (e.g., school principal, clinic director, counselors, problem-solving team members, behavioral specialists, interventionist, and deans) as a way of understanding their roles within the system in which you will have practica. Other opportunities to garner a broad understanding of the institution include purposefully scheduling attendance at a variety of meetings where decisions are made (e.g., problem-solving team meetings, leadership meetings, Section 504 or special education eligibility meetings, parent–teacher association meetings, teacher/faculty meetings). Additionally, the practica experience can be enhanced by proactively seeking experiences working with children from differing grade levels with a variety of disabilities, and ensuring interactions with persons from diverse backgrounds. Once good rapport and confidence in your abilities are established at the site, the practica supervisor and other personnel are often very helpful in facilitating these additional opportunities upon request.

IDEIA and State Classification Systems and Local Programs

Practica work can include a number of school-wide service opportunities, such as participation in screening data reviews, implementation of prevention initiatives, and codelivering teacher professional development workshops. Given the skills set of school psychologists in assessment and interventions, a significant portion of the work may also be related to special education eligibility needs. Therefore, it will be helpful for practica students to have an awareness of the disability classifications systems utilized, eligibility criteria required, and any local programs offered. IDEIA (2004) delineates 13 disability classifications: Specific Learning Disability, Speech or Language Impairments, Mental Retardation (i.e., Intellectual Disability), Emotional Disturbance, Multiple Disabilities, Hearing Impairments, Orthopedic Impairments, Other Health Impairments, Visual Impairments, Autism, Deaf–Blindness, Traumatic Brain Injury, and Developmental Delay. An electronic copy of IDEIA can be accessed at the U.S. Department of Education website (idea.ed.gov) and familiarity with this law will be important to understanding classification systems in school. Additionally, although states cannot dismiss or supersede federal law, they do vary somewhat in their specific disability titles and documentation for eligibility criteria. Thus, it will be helpful to also be knowledgeable regarding state statutes and regulations for special education placements. State statutes also should be available online. Lastly, school districts will all serve the student needs within all IDEIA categories; however, there is some flexibility in how specific intensive intervention programs are administered. The practica site supervisor within a school district will be able to provide a copy of district program options and their alignment with both state and federal requirements.

DIRECT STUDENT, PATIENT, AND CLIENT CONTACT CONSIDERATIONS

As practica progresses, the role of the practica student will expand to include direct service delivery through a variety of activities, including assessment, intervention, and consultation. Working with children and youth as they demonstrate progress in response to an academic remediation strategy you have implemented or providing a functional behavioral assessment that yields definitive answers to behavioral problems can be inspiring. In most circumstances, practica experiences will be positive. However, in some circumstances, practical safety precautions are warranted, especially when working with children in restrictive settings that may include conduct disorders or debilitating emotional disturbance.

Personal Safety

Utilizing common sense is the overarching guideline to ensuring personal safety in most practica-related situations. This can be as simple as wearing clothing that is comfortable and provides easy movement. If the practica site specializes in working with very young children, there will be occasions when they try to hide under a table or perhaps run from a room. Both situations will require the examiner to have comfortable clothing and shoes that are safe to move in briskly. For inpatient settings that may serve children with psychotic features or conduct disorders, additional preventive dress strategies may be helpful. These include avoiding dangling earrings that could be pulled out or long necklaces, lanyards, and neckties that could be misused. In settings with these risk factors, supervisors and administration should provide guidelines on preventive dress and response training at orientation sessions.

Theft also is a consideration as schools and clinics are public institutions and, therefore, subject to crime just as any other domain. The risk for theft may be greater in some settings such as juvenile justice or inpatient treatment programs for conduct disorders. Avoiding wearing expensive jewelry and keeping items such as laptops and cell phones out of sight are simple solutions to lower risk. The exhibition of luxury items also is an important consideration when working with impoverished children and youth who may find these displays counterproductive to good rapport building.

Another safety issue is the access to medications. Most schools and hospital settings will require stringent safeguards on all medicines, including those in the possession of faculty, staff, and practica graduate students. Although it is expected that personnel will occasionally need medications for personal use and even may require them for serious health issues (e.g., insulin), secure locked storage is typically required. Even innocuous items, such as cough syrups, throat lozenges, and aspirin, can be hazardous to children.

Personal safety considerations also can be extended to the assessment or counseling environment when working directly with children and adolescents in an office setting. The first principle of individual work with children for the sake of propriety and safety is to ensure this does not occur in an isolated area or a place that does not permit visibility. Often testing rooms have one-way mirrors, door windows, or adjacent offices occupied by personnel that ensure visibility. If appropriate office space is not available, this should be discussed with the site supervisor and practica faculty promptly.

Practica students beginning their training will typically not be placed in settings that service students with significant behavioral disorders. However, more advanced practica placements may include such settings. When working in an office or therapy room environment with persons who may have significant emotional reactions, additional safety measures can be addressed through structuring the environment. Commonsense actions include removing target objects that can cause harm (e.g., fragile glass vases, sharp objects), arranging for an observer, and arranging the office furniture in configurations that allow easy access to the door for both the examiner and client (Florida Diagnostic & Learning Resources System, 2007). It is possible for persons who perceive themselves to be under duress or who have poor emotional regulation to demonstrate a fight-or-flight response. By structuring the room with a clear path to the door, a client does have the option of leaving without perceiving the examiner as an obstacle or becoming physically aggressive with the examiner. In this unusual event, the examiner can still call for assistance but is not harmed. The diagram in Figure 2.1 illustrates

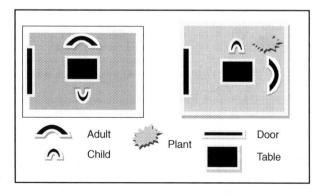

FIGURE 2.1 Practica evaluation/counseling room setting diagrams.

Health Issues

It is not uncommon for practicum students and interns beginning daily interactions with children to acquire an unusually high number of colds or influenzas the first year. All human interactions present risk for exposure to illness. However, large clusters of children, especially very young children, may have additional risks in that they share close contact, handle the same materials, and may have immature hygiene habits (e.g., washing hands). Risk factors tend to be elevated for educational settings that serve medically fragile students, developmental disabilities, immunocompromised students, low cognitive function students in toilet training or diaper change routines, students with frequent bodily fluid exposure (e.g., drooling with seizure disorders), or children with contagious diseases (Communicable Disease Epidemiology Program, 2004). Health precautions are important to practicum students for two reasons; self-care to avoid exposure and care for the children with whom we work to avoid spreading risk from one child to another.

Infectious disease exposure can occur in several ways, including contact with bodily fluids, biting, spitting, and airborne transmission, which varies by illness (Table 2.1). Bacteria, viruses, and parasites are the organisms responsible (Communicable Disease Epidemiology Program, 2004).

A number of practical precautions are recommended when working with children in schools. They include frequent hand washing, keeping immunizations current, monitoring appropriate use of antibiotics, and use of antiseptic wipes for shared test kit materials, especially if items were placed in a child's mouth (Communicable Disease Epidemiology Program, 2004).

TABLE 2.1 Illness and Transmission Mechanisms

TRANSMISSION MECHANISM	ILLNESS
Droplets	Chickenpox, colds, influenza, mumps, pink eye, strep throat, rubella (German measles)
Airborne	Measles (rubeola), tuberculosis
Fecal/Oral Spread	Hepatitis A, meningitis (viral), salmonellosis
Bodily Fluids	Hepatitis B, hepatitis C, HIV, AIDS, mononucleosis
Parasite Contact	Lice

Source: Communicable Disease Epidemiology Program, 2004.

Recognizing symptoms of illnesses early and avoiding contact with children or personnel when sick can be very helpful in eliminating exposure.

When working with high-risk children (e.g., medically fragile) it may also be informative to discuss care regimens with the school nurse. One important safety guideline is to treat all fluids as if they were contaminated and avoid any direct contact with them (e.g., use gloves for clean up).

Reporting Suspicion of Abuse and Neglect

In 2012, a total of 686,000 children were victimized by abuse or neglect. Most fatalities were under the age of 3 (70%) and the majority were boys. The majority of abusers were parents (80%) and women (53.3%). Among child fatalities due to maltreatment, 70% were caused solely by neglect, 43% were the result of abuse. Ratios range by state from zero cases to 2.28% per 100,000 children (Child Welfare Information Gateway, 2014). A number of state and national definitions of abuse exist with some variations. However, the national Child Abuse Prevention and Treatment Act is a commonly accepted definition. It states that abuse is:

> Any recent act or failure to act on the part of a parent or caretaker, which results in death, serious physical or emotional harm, sexual abuse, or exploitation, or an act or failure to act, which presents an imminent risk of serious harm. (Child Welfare Information Gateway, 2014)

All states within the United States mandate that specific institutions and professionals who know of, or have cause to suspect, abuse or neglect of a child must report the incident. Mental health care providers and educators are among those professionals required to report. In 2012, there were approximately 6 million suspected abuse cases reported. The majority of reports (three of five) were made by professionals (i.e., educators, police, lawyers, and social services) and 17.7% were substantiated. Based on these statistics and the vast number of hours per week that educators interact with children, educators are a critical source of protection for children through reporting suspected incidents. In the event that abuse or neglect is suspected, the site supervisor and practicum faculty should be notified. As the original witness, the graduate student may be required to file the report, but a supervisor can assist with the correct procedures (Child Welfare Information Gateway, 2014).

Emergencies and Crisis Intervention

There are a range of incidents that can occur in public schools that require an emergency response protocol or crisis intervention services. Most will be innocuous, such as fire or tornado drills, and have routine procedures to which children are accustomed. Faculty is notified in advance of drills and thus can plan accordingly. As part of the orientation to a site, the site supervisor will often provide a faculty/staff handbook with written procedures for emergencies and evacuation routes. Emergency procedures and evacuation maps also are typically laminated and posted in classrooms by the exit door.

The primarily responsibility as a practicum student is to be aware of procedures and take responsibility to ensure that children in your care are accompanied at all times and are safe. Other types of events that require emergency procedures include lock-downs or lock-ins. These are usually precipitated by unauthorized persons on or near campus. Examples include a hostile, noncustodial parent who is trying to pick up a child and a suspicious or armed person on or near school premises. In addition, law enforcement officials may call a school and ask that the campus be secured if they are pursuing an incident in the neighborhood and are unsure whether an assailant could be in the area. In these cases, the school procedure is not to evacuate the building, as this poses a greater risk for children. The protocol is typically to stay in a secure area, lock the outside entrance doors, and stay informed. These situations are signaled with a coded message typically given over the intercom system so as not to alarm students. Each type of emergency has a different message so adults know which response protocol to use. For example, the signal for a lock-in may be, "Teachers, the Cooper bookstore representative is now on campus." A different phrase may be used for lock-downs that involve a weapon or suspected weapon. The separate signal notifies personnel to secure the room and also move children away from windows, much like a teacher does in a tornado drill. Once the emergency has subsided, another code is issued to indicate all is clear. If a code occurs while a practicum student is testing or working with a child outside the classroom setting, it will be important to inform the teacher of the child's whereabouts as soon as possible, as teachers must account for all of their students in an emergency. It may be possible to contact the teacher by cell phone/e-mail or school phone/intercom.

Crisis intervention services differ from emergency management in that they are provided after an incident has occurred. School psychologists are often part of the response team and, in large counties, there may be specialized teams of school psychologists who rally to assist schools. Some incident responses are based on the aftermath of weather events, such as hurricanes, tornadoes, or ice storms that have devastated a particular area and had a stressful impact on both students and perhaps teachers as well. More common crisis interventions are a result of the serious injury or death of a teacher or child due to accident or illness. In rare cases, the crisis intervention is directed to provide care after a suicide or violent incident. As a member of the National Association of School Psychologists (NASP), there are several online resources and handouts instantly available to provide parents and teachers with suggestions on how to best approach a variety of crisis issues with children (www.nasplonline.org). There are also several in-depth training curriculum programs on crisis intervention (e.g., PREPaRE), and school psychology programs include training on crisis response for students as part of the NASP competency standards (Ysseldyke et al., 2006). A variety of services may be provided that vary by the crisis model utilized. Responses may require media management skills, informational announcements to control inaccurate rumors, affirmations of safety, counseling, evaluation of stress-related symptoms, and referrals for short-term care. During the early practicum stage, graduate students participating in a crisis response will most likely have an observational or assistive role with close supervision from the site supervisor rather than a direct service role.

PROFESSIONAL PRACTICE CONSIDERATIONS

Within the fields of education, the practice of psychology, and professional employment, there are a number of federal mandates regarding appropriate procedures. The principles behind these laws help to safeguard the security of personal information and protect persons in the workplace from inappropriate behaviors exercised toward them. The mandates also are pertinent to the services that practica students will provide within their field placement settings, and thus are briefly reviewed in this section.

Health Insurance Portability and Accountability Act

Many practicum requirements, including psychological evaluations, intervention design, and counseling services, will require a review of student records. This information can be extremely helpful in understanding a child's history and needs; however, the information is also sensitive and requires rigorous safeguards. Students' cumulative files can include immunization records, medical records, court custody or abuse/neglect documents, adoption verification, Social Security numbers, criminal judgments, prior psychological reports, grades, attendance, and academic scores. Records for children in a clinical setting may also contain therapy notes, treatment progress monitoring data, and psychological evaluation protocols. These files are typically kept in locked cabinets and practicum students are provided access only as needed.

The Health Insurance Portability and Accountability Act of 1996 (HIPAA) was enacted to provide guidelines that would ensure greater privacy for health records, especially the electronic transfer of records (Office for Civil Rights, 2003). These national standards apply to Internet, extranet, disk files, faxes, and even private computer network transmission of personally identifiable health care data. Personally identifiable health information is called Protected Health Information (PHI). Examples of personally identifiable data include demographic information (e.g., age, address), mental health conditions, and services provided (including past, present, and future), as well as payment records. There are no restrictions on data that have all personal identifiers removed and are compiled in aggregate form. Therefore, research data that are aggregated without identifiers are not restricted under this provision (Office for Civil Rights, 2003).

Patient or guardian consent must be obtained before disclosing any personal information for treatment, payment billing, or health care, which includes mental health services. Once consent is obtained, the PHI may be used for treatment, payment, health care, training, or to defend legal actions from the client. Due care to protect confidentiality and security of the records is still required. The privacy rule applies to a number of groups, including health care plans (e.g., insurance companies), health care providers, health care clearinghouses, and business entities who contract services for health care providers.

Mandates for HIPAA are relevant to school psychologists in several situations. School psychologists in private practice, working in clinics or hospitals, and employed by many federal programs have access to PHI and are billing health care insurance companies for evaluations or treatment. Many school districts also bill Medicaid for psychological services for children. In addition to having access to records, school psychologists and practicum students also generate psychological reports, which are individually identifiable and may contain mental health diagnosis or treatment information. Therefore, it is important to be cognizant of HIPAA standards and safeguards for PHI. Several commonsense precautions should be followed when accessing or creating PHIs. These include securing computers, disk files, and written records at all times and restricting access to information to authorized persons only. Each agency should have a written procedure for consent and securing files, as well as staff training procedures and a complaint process for individuals when records are compromised.

When the standards of HIPAA are breached, there are a number of fines and penalties that can be imposed. Noncompliance can be fined $100 to $50,000 penalty per infraction with an annual total of $1,500,000 per person, per year, per standard. Wrongful disclosure fines can be imposed up to $50,000 and up to one year in prison. If the wrongful disclosure incident includes false pretense ($100,000 and up to 5 years in prison) or selling information for a profit ($250,000 and up to 10 years in prison), the sanctions are more severe (Office for Civil Rights, 2003).

Family Educational Rights and Privacy Act

Another important privacy act that applies to working within schools is the Family Educational Rights and Privacy Act (FERPA, 2009; 20 U.S.C. § 1232g; 34 CFR Part 99). This law ensures families' rights to inspect, dispute, amend, or expunge student records following certain guidelines. Schools that receive federal funding must inform parents of these rights and cannot disclose identifiable student information outside the school without parental consent. A written policy for security and disposal of student records is required and this provision applies to all media forms (e.g., printed or electronic files, tape recordings). FERPA does have several exceptions, including the records of law enforcement, which are particularly pertinent to school psychologists who work within juvenile justice or alternative education programs. There will be many occasions when a discussion with the child's pediatrician or therapist can help inform school intervention planning. In order to share protected information with outside professionals, parental consent still must be obtained.

As a practicum student, an awareness of FERPA mandates and conscientious efforts to safeguard record security are important professional development standards. An in-depth discussion of HIPAA and FERPA is typically included in advanced school psychology curricula through ethics course work.

Sexual Harassment

Sexual harassment in workplace environments is a serious and often costly issue, because of emotional distress and financial penalties for offenses. Title VII of the Civil Rights Act of 1964 prohibits sex discrimination related to employment and the Equal Employment Opportunity Commission (EEOC) is authorized to enforce sexual harassment provisions under Title 29 of the Code of Federal Regulations, Section 1604.11 (Civil Rights Act, 1964; EEOC, 2007). The EEOC definition of sexual harassment follows:

> Unwelcome sexual advances, requests for sexual favors, and other verbal or physical conduct of a sexual nature constitute sexual harassment when: (1) submission to such conduct is made either explicitly or implicitly a term or condition of an individual's employment, (2) submission to or rejection of such conduct by an individual is used as the basis for employment decisions affecting such individual, (3) or such conduct has the purpose or effect of unreasonably interfering with an individual's work performance or creating an intimidating,

> hostile, or offensive working environment. (EEOC, 2007; Title
> 29 Code of Federal Regulations, Section 1604.11)

The EEOC and the Fair Employment Practice Agency provide national data on workplace complaints related to race, age, sex, religion, and other discrimination complaints. In 2013, they recorded over 7,256 complaints specific to sexual harassment. Other categories of complaints included race (35%), religion (4%), age (23%), and disability (28%) discrimination. The majority of complaints for sexual harassment were females (82.4%) although males (17.6%) also reported victimization. Monetary payouts totaled $44.6 million dollars (EEOC, 2015).

Victimization is not limited to just career employment and can also be experienced by postsecondary students. A survey of college students indicated 62% of females and 61% of males say they have been sexually harassed by others. In turn, 31% of females and 51% of males noted they had participated in sexual harassment of others. All postsecondary students involved in programs and activities at federally funded institutions are entitled to safeguards from sex discrimination based on Title IX of the Education Amendments of 1972 and, in cases of sexual harassment, may be entitled to damages (Hill & Silvia, 2005; *Franklin v. Gwinett County Public Schools*, 1992). Universities and agencies will typically offer guidelines and contact numbers to report incidents in their handbooks and during orientation. Some authors endorse a modified version of the EEOC sexual harassment definition that more specifically addresses academic situations to be utilized by educational institutions. For example, Hill and Silvia (2005) offer a definition that includes harassment that alludes to a conditional impact on academic achievement, academic advancement decisions, or interference with academic work. In contrast to other definitions that focus on the workplace, they also note that a hostile environment can be created in learning or social domains (Sandler & Shoop, 1997).

Students can also be liable for personal actions that constitute sexual harassment of others and the law prohibits student-to-student offenses or failure to act when a professional has knowledge of student-to-student harassment (Weiner & Weiner, 1999). When harassment involves a graduate student and a minor, depending on the behaviors, it may constitute abuse and be subject to both disciplinary action and criminal consequences. Therefore, it is important for graduate students to be cognizant of behaviors that could be considered sexual harassment when engaging in student/youth services, when providing peer mentoring or peer supervision, and when interacting with other personnel in the context of practica and/or teaching/research assistantships.

There are two primary types of harassment: hostile work environment and *quid pro quo*. Creating hostile circumstances includes behavior and comments that interfere with work or the academic environment. The principle of *quid pro quo* refers to suggestions that a trade of services will result in a preferred outcome (EEOC, 2007). Examples of behaviors that can be interpreted as sexual harassment include sexual jokes, gestures, pictures, comments, or cartoons. Actions such as impeding one's path (e.g., blocking a doorway), brushing up against another person, or spying in a sexual manner (e.g., restrooms) can also qualify as harassment. With the ubiquitous use of the Internet, sexual harassment may also occur electronically, creating broad dissemination, and negative impact of inappropriate information.

If any of these situations are encountered through the practicum setting, graduate students have a number of options. First, there are provisions within all state and federal agencies to file formal complaints (e.g., the EEOC website has information on filing complaints) and site supervisors as well as faculty should be able to assist in providing these contacts. Additionally, most universities will offer a process for filing a grievance within the department and the institution at large. A victim may approach the offender but is not under obligation to do so. There are circumstances where victims are too intimidated or are fearful of retaliation to directly approach the topic in a constructive manner. Keeping a written record of events may be especially helpful in documenting details for the complaint.

Record Keeping

Documentation of practicum activities is often structured through recording services in a practicum log. Practicum logs may also be utilized as part of an agency's service record for insurance reimbursements or graduate student stipend payroll justification, if the practicum is a paid position. The log is designed to serve several purposes. It provides monitoring data for the program's NASP or American Psychological Association (APA) reviews; it documents acquired competencies for individual students; and it provides data that can be utilized later by students for their internship and employment applications.

The log provides accountability for students and supervisors to ensure the supervisor is aware of all of the student's activities. It also verifies the diversity of experiences and range of opportunities that are being offered across service domains. Program data are acquired through the logs and then reviewed by type and ratio of activities for alignment with program curriculum and goals for skill development. In addition, the data are reviewed to compare activities by site, by supervisor, and by year in the program. Data may be reviewed annually or semiannually by faculty in lieu of national competencies standards and overall program evaluation to ensure the integrity and quality of practicum training. If structured

34 • SECTION I: PRACTICUM

correctly, logs can track supervision contact hours for individuals or record total number of hours for course requirements. As a monitoring tool, logs can also provide quick feedback on skill areas that require more or less time investment and thus allow students and supervisors to make adjustments in activities.

Logs

Log records may be submitted electronically through a program web file or manually utilizing data spreadsheets. There are a wide variety of forms available (see Appendix B, Exhibit B.1). Entries are often maintained on a daily or hourly basis and must accurately reflect interactions with students and other professionals. Typically logs are reviewed and signed by the site supervisor and/or practicum faculty for verification.

Log Data and Implications for Internships

Although the internship process is discussed in later chapters, it is important to note here that ultimately these practicum logs become a source of documentation of learning experiences for the internship applications. The practicum log is also important to students personally in aggregating data for later career position applications. Many school districts, hospitals, and community mental health agencies request information on prior practica experiences, including the number of direct student-contact hours, specific assessment instruments administered, types of interventions applied, and experience with diverse students (see Table 2.2 for possible data categories). The data requested are often specific to the population served at the application site. For example, an internship specialization in pre-K would desire data on services provided through practicum for preschool

TABLE 2.2 Possible Internship and Career Application Data Categories

TYPICAL SCHOOL-BASED ACTIVITIES	TYPICAL OTHER SITE ACTIVITIES
Intervention and Assessment Experiences	
Individual Therapy (by age)	Career Counseling
Group Counseling (by age)	Family Therapy
School Counseling Interventions	Couples Therapy
School Consultation	Other Psychological Interventions (Sports Psychology, Medical, Substance Abuse, Treatment Planning)
School Direct Intervention	
Other Psychological Intervention (Structured Interviews)	

(continued)

TABLE 2.2 Possible Internship and Career Application Data Categories (*continued*)

TYPICAL SCHOOL-BASED ACTIVITIES	TYPICAL OTHER SITE ACTIVITIES
Psychological Assessment	
(Including name and number of each test administered as well as number of reports written utilizing that particular test and the age range of examinee)	
Sensory/Motor Assessment	Neuropsychological Assessment
Psychodiagnostic Assessments/Tests (IQ, Achievement, Rating Scales, Personality, Projectives)	Career Assessments
	Program Development/Outreach
	Systems/Organizational Consultation
	Outcomes Assessment of Programs
Supervision	
(Supervision of other students performing assessments or interventions supervision [Total hours one-to-one, group, and peer])	
Support Activities	
Case Conferences	Progress Notes
Case Management/Consultations	Video Session Reviews
Didactic Training Seminars	Grand Rounds
Records Review	Chart Review
Test Scoring/Interpretation	Audio/Digital Reviews
Report Writing	Clinical Writing
Experience in Sites and Treatment Settings	
Child Guidance Clinics	Community Mental Health
Department Clinics	Medical Clinic/Hospital
Schools	Inpatient/Outpatient Psychiatric
Juvenile Justice	Forensics, Jail, Prison
University Counseling Center	Veteran's Counseling Center
Client Demographics	
For all clients: Race, ethnicity, gender, sexual orientation, disabilities (e.g., SLD), mental health diagnoses (e.g., depression, ADHD)	

ADHD, attention deficit hyperactivity disorder; SLD, special learning disability.

children. With astute planning, a well-designed log will delineate most of these data and thus provide an easy reference when preparing application packets later.

For doctoral-level students who plan to apply to nationally competitive internship sites with accreditation from the APA, these data are critical. The Association of Psychology Postdoctoral and Internship Centers (APPIC) provides a clearinghouse for APA approved internship opportunities across the United States. One general application form is utilized that requires extensive information on practicum experiences. This form changes periodically and is available online (www.appic.org).

36 • SECTION I: PRACTICUM

ORIENTATION TO PRACTICA VIGNETTES

Vignette 2.1

Taneka's career goal is to be a school psychologist specializing in working with children who have low-incidence disabilities. She is in her second year of practicum and is ready to gain experience working with this population. An opening is available in a self-contained classroom with children who have low cognitive abilities and are medically fragile, often requiring assistance with basic bodily functions. Many have compromised immune systems.

Discussion Questions:

1. What considerations should Taneka be aware of in order to best protect these children while she provides services?
2. What additional sources of information should she review to enhance her work with these children?

There are a number of practical precautions Taneka can take to safeguard the children she will work with. First, basic considerations for frequent handwashing, use of gloves if she is assisting with behavioral training for teaching hygiene habits, and antiseptic cleaning of materials that are shared between children (e.g., test materials, learning aids, and curricula materials) will be helpful. She also may wish to discuss additional precautions with the teachers and school nurse. In some school districts, professionals who have direct contact with medically at-risk students are provided additional health training, thus it may be helpful to inquire if such training is available.

Vignette 2.2

Jacob is completing his fall-semester, first-year practicum. In reviewing his log, he notices that he has acquired many valuable experiences that have helped him meet all program assignment requirements and also has learned a great deal about the operations of the school system through numerous opportunities to attend leadership meetings and eligibility staffings. However, his supervisor's referrals have been primarily to grades 1 to 3 and related to reading difficulties. In planning for the spring semester, he would like to broaden his experiences to include work with a wider age group and more diverse disabilities.

Discussion Questions:

1. What are Jacob's options in planning for the spring semester?
2. How should he approach such a discussion with his site supervisor?

First, Jacob is to be commended for his awareness and monitoring of his own practicum activities and planning ahead to be proactive in acquiring a broad range of experience. He has a number of options in preparing to discuss this issue with his site supervisor. First, it may be helpful to review the spring practica requirements and determine if they define work with other age groups and disabilities. If not, he may inquire with his practica seminar instructor, faculty advisor, and/or practica coordinator regarding strategies and suggestions on appropriate ways to expand his exposure to a wider variety of opportunities at the practica site. The practica coordinator may be especially helpful in this conversation as he or she will be familiar with the site's resources and programs and also have a rapport with the site supervisor in encouraging broader experiences. Ultimately, a conversation between the graduate student and site supervisor can easily address this need. The conversation may be opened with an expression of appreciation for the experiences that have already been facilitated, a desire to learn even more about services within the site, and a solicitation of the site supervisor's thoughts on additional opportunities that are available.

CHAPTER REVIEW

This chapter has discussed a number of strategies for building rapport when entering a new practica setting and also acclimating to the infrastructure within the site. Additionally, a number of federal mandates, including safeguarding confidentiality of records, required abuse or neglect reporting, and workplace harassment behaviors, were reviewed. Preparedness for handling emergency incidents from evacuation procedures during a fire drill to crisis intervention services also were noted. The final section in this chapter reviewed the important task of documenting practica activities in a manner that will meet program requirements. The log records also serve the purpose of providing aggregate data for internship and career applications as well as training program accreditation reviews. Awareness of the components in this chapter should serve to enhance entry into the rewarding endeavors that can be found as individuals begin their applied clinical training through practica experiences.

REFERENCES

Child Welfare Information Gateway. (2014). *Child maltreatment 2012: Summary of key findings*. Washington, DC: U.S. Department of Health and Human Services, Children's Bureau.

Civil Rights Act of 1964, Pub. L. No. 88–352, 78 Stat. 241 (1964).

Communicable Disease Epidemiology Program. (2004). *Infectious disease in school settings: Guidelines for school nurses and personnel*. Denver, CO: Colorado Department of Public Health and Environment.

Equal Employment Opportunity Commission. (2007). *Sexual harassment* (29 C.F.R. § 1604.11). Retrieved from http://www.eeoc.gov/

Equal Employment Opportunity Commission. (2015). *EEOC Charge receipts by state (includes U.S. Territories) and bases for 2013.* Retrieved from http://www1.eeoc.gov/eeoc/statistics/enforcement/state_13.cfm

Family Educational Rights and Privacy Act, 20 U.S.C. § 1232g; 34 CFR Part 99 (2009).

Florida Diagnostic & Learning Resources System. (2007). *Aggression control training.* Retrieved from http://www.paec.org/fdlrsweb/index.htm

Franklin v. Gwinett County Public Schools, 503 U.S. 60 (1992).

Hill, C., & Silvia, E. (2005). *Drawing the line: Sexual harassment on campus.* Washington, DC: American Association of University Women Educational Foundation.

Individuals With Disabilities Education Improvement Act, 20 U.S.C. § 1400 (2004).

Office for Civil Rights. (2003). *Summary of the HIPAA privacy rule: HIPAA compliance assistance.* Washington, DC: U.S. Department of Health and Human Services.

Sandler, B. R., & Shoop, R. J. (1997). *Sexual harassment on campus: A guide for administrators, faculty, and students.* Needham Heights, MA: Allyn & Bacon.

Weiner, R. L., & Weiner, A. T. (1999). *Federal law prohibits student-on-student sexual harassment: The Supreme Court rules that Title IX reaches hostile acts between students.* Retrieved from http://www.apa.org/monitor

Ysseldyke, J., Burns, M., Dawson, P., Kelley, B., Morrison, D., Ortiz, S., . . . Telzrow, C. (2006). *School psychology: A blueprint for training and practice III.* Washington, DC: National Association of School Psychologists.

CHAPTER 3

Portfolios and Competency-Based Evaluation

LEARNING OBJECTIVES

At the conclusion of this chapter, readers should be able to:

1. Acquire familiarity with a variety of practica evaluation components
2. Acquire knowledge of the portfolio approach to demonstrating competencies
3. Learn strategies for developing professional case presentations

DEMONSTRATING ACQUISITION OF KNOWLEDGE AND SKILLS

School psychology programs are typically approved and/or accredited by state departments of education, the National Association of School Psychologists (NASP), and the American Psychological Association (APA) depending on the scope of the training and the degree track. The approval and accrediting processes established by these agencies provide accountability for the rigor of programs, track the program's success in producing graduates, and safeguard the public well-being by ensuring that highly qualified personnel are practicing in this field (see Appendix A, Exhibits A.1 and A.2).

Each agency requires that programs demonstrate effective training outcomes through multilevel evaluation, often including descriptive information, as well as both distal and proximal data sources. Descriptive information would delineate the curricula, sequence, and depth/breadth of the programming; as well as possible demographic factors (e.g., program success in recruiting diverse students). Proximal data focus on changes that occur in the acquisition of graduate students' skills, knowledge, and professional behaviors. Examples might include measuring the acquisition of competencies across domains in student performance through practica. Distal data focus on long-term

39

outcome information that reflects program-level results in producing effective professionals. Examples of distal data might include graduation rates, employment statistics, and percentage of graduates acquiring professional credentials. As a part of the approval and accreditation process, programs may utilize a variety of evaluation measures as outcome data (e.g., grades, performance rating scales, product portfolios, publications, and professional presentations) to measure student progress toward acquiring competencies and ultimately graduation, job procurement, and credentialing. For programs with multiple approval and accrediting bodies, their evaluation systems can be complex and include a variety of broad program standards (Table 3.1).

Although practica requirements have been a requirement of training programs for years, there is little national guidance on the specific components. Throughout the past decade these criteria are continuing to develop. As an example, the APA provides the Practicum Competencies Outline, which delineates skills that should be demonstrated prior to entering a practica setting to ensure students have the foundational professional demeanor to serve in practica roles (Hatcher & Lassiter, 2007). The document also specifies ten areas of professional competencies that should be monitored across practica experiences for development (Table 3.2). In 2009 the Council of Directors of School Psychology Programs (CDSPP) Practicum Taskforce reviewed the

TABLE 3.1 Comparing NASP and APA Domains

NASP www.nasponline.org/standards	APA www.apa.org/ed/accreditation
Data-Based Decision Making and Accountability	Domain A: Eligibility
Consultation and Collaboration	Domain B: Program Philosophy, Objectives, and Curriculum Plan
Interventions and Instructional Support to Develop Academic Skills	Domain C: Program Resources
Interventions and Mental Health Services to Develop Social and Life Skills	Domain D: Cultural and Individual Differences and Diversity
School-Wide Practices to Promote Learning	Domain E: Student–Faculty Relations
Preventive and Responsive Services	Domain F: Program Self-Assessment and Quality Enhancement
Family–School Collaboration Services	Domain G: Public Disclosure
Diversity in Development and Learning	Domain H: Relationship With Accrediting Body
Research and Program Evaluation	
Legal, Ethical, and Professional Practice	

Source: American Psychological Association (APA), 2013; National Association of School Psychologists (NASP), 2010b.

TABLE 3.2 APA Practica Competency Domains

A. Baseline Competency—Prior to Entering the Practica Experience	
1. Personality Characteristics, Intellectual and Personal Skills	Empathy, respect for other cultures, listening skills, verbal skills, organization, hygiene, and tolerance
2. Knowledge from classroom experience	Scientific theory, evidence-based knowledge, empirical constructs of assessment (reliability, validity etc.), diagnoses, case conceptualization, intervention/treatment, individual differences, and ethical behavior
B. Skills Developing During Practica	
1. Relationship and Interpersonal Skills	Ability to work with colleagues, peers, clients; respect for others and collaboration skills
2. Application of Research	Seek out and apply research-supported diagnosis criteria, intervention, and treatment options
3. Assessment	Knowledge of psychometric properties, astute selection of appropriate measures, integration of data to inform diagnoses, and treatment/intervention
4. Intervention	Knowledge of empirically supported methods, skilled and effective application to ameliorate specific needs
5. Consultation and Collaboration	Knowledge of consultant role, communication skills, effective implementation of systematic data collection
6. Diversity	Multicultural competency and sensitivity
7. Ethics	Knowledge of standards, guidelines, codes; demonstrate ethical practice, assertiveness in defending ethical principles
8. Leadership	Understanding multiple facets of leadership (e.g., financial responsibility, systems management, and evaluating)
9. Supervision	Understanding supervisory roles and literature base, knowledge of individual differences, adaptive supervision skills, and evaluation of others' performance
10. Professional Development	Self-management, organizational skills, self-awareness, and self-monitoring

APA, American Psychological Association.

APA outline and noted ways in which the language of the APA guidelines could be better adapted to reflect the practice of school psychology (Caterino, Li, Hanse, Forman, Harris, & Miller, 2012). An extension of the APA competency framework, the Competency Benchmarks in Professional Psychology, structures the acquisition of skills across a three-pronged time frame; readiness for practica skills, readiness for internship skills, and readiness for entry into practice competencies (APA, 2011, 2012).

Competency Ratings

The practica setting often contributes to these data through site supervisor ratings of graduate students' acquisition of core skill competencies (e.g., assessment, intervention, consultation, and program evaluation). Rating scales may employ a Likert scale that notes skill development designed on the models of Benner (1984) and Dreyfus (1986) that range from novice level to expert level. Based on the fact that students will be exposed to more complex concepts throughout their course work and increasingly multifaceted applications will be expected, it is understood that ratings should increase over time. Faculty also understand that students can be at different levels of skill acquisition across domains depending on the sequence of curricula and the length of practice with specific skills (see Appendix B, Exhibit B.2, Sample Site Supervisor Evaluation of Practica Student Form). For programs that also must document the caliber of program resources, practica measures may evaluate students' ratings of the practica site facilities and the quality of site supervisor services as well (see www.springerpub.com/school-psychology-practicum for additional examples, Exhibits 3.3 through 3.6). Review of practica competencies often occurs each semester to afford an opportunity to document accomplishments and skills learned. It also is an excellent opportunity to review the types of experiences provided and to make adjustments in the level of supervision as well as depth and breadth of responsibilities. Reviewing the competency ratings with the supervisor can serve to facilitate this discussion.

Through the evaluation process, graduate students may be asked to sign a consent for release of information form acknowledging the exchange of performance data between the practica site supervisor and the school psychology program (see Appendix B, Exhibit B.3). It is important to note that information requested from students and/or shared between practica supervisors and program faculty also has very clear limitations. These restrictions apply for in-class discussions, any program activity such as practica, and program assignments. The APA (2002) ethics standards prohibit requests for or disclosure of personal student information specifically related to a student's own history of abuse, neglect, psychological treatment, and relationships with parents/peers/spouses.

Professional Work Products Review—Portfolio

In addition to competency rating scales, programs also have the option of measuring skill acquisition through the review of a portfolio. This process provides information on the student's development, knowledge, and applied skills through a collection of accomplishments and work products (Johnson, Mims-Cox, & Doyle-Nichols, 2010). Portfolios typically include two types of products: formative and summative. A formative work product demonstrates a developmental process, whereas a summative work product is typically a final product. Items in the portfolio may include a vita, statements of professional goals, psychological reports, intervention summaries, conference presentations, publications, and literature reviews. These products are often accompanied by reflection papers that have guiding questions to consider in reference to the product. Questions might require explaining the orientation that guided the assessment or noting the strengths and limitations of the report. The portfolio is reviewed by faculty and scored qualitatively through the use of rubrics that delineate the components that products must demonstrate to be considered satisfactory or exemplary. The specific descriptors and details will vary by the product and faculty design of the rubric. Although the portfolio is a collection of important demonstrations of specific skills, there generally are one or more comprehensive cases included to reflect cumulative skills. These are called capstone cases.

Capstone Cases

Capstone cases can be structured by programs in several different ways. The *multimethod capstone case format* requires demonstrating proficiency in several psychoeducational methods to serve an individual student's needs. An example might include providing a student's initial assessment, deriving an intervention plan from the assessment data, implementing the intervention, and then progress monitoring outcomes. Some programs also require that the final intervention data must reflect a successful intervention to qualify as a capstone case.

A *multidomain capstone case format* focuses on a case study that integrates academic, behavioral, social-emotional and/or mental health domains. An example of this type of assignment might be a multifaceted assessment for a child with a specific learning disability in math that also demonstrates classroom behavioral concerns related to task avoidance and withdrawal as well as a mental health diagnosis of generalized anxiety. This multidomain assessment case will require demonstrating evaluation skills in identifying discrete math deficits, behavioral assessment to determine the functions of classroom task avoidance and withdrawal, as well as proficiency in utilizing diagnostic mental health instruments for anxiety to document symptom severity. The multidomain capstone case format also can be applied to intervention competencies. As an example, using the case just noted, requirements might include providing and progress monitoring a multifaceted intervention for math skills, coupled with a classroom behavior plan that addresses task avoidance and withdrawal while supplementing these interventions with a cognitive behavioral therapy protocol for anxiety.

The *multiprovider capstone case format* incorporates many of the principles of consultation. An example of this type of capstone case might be collaborating with school personnel and outside mental health service providers to successfully coordinate reentry of a student from hospitalization or homebound schooling with scaffolded supports for the child.

The capstone practica case report is often utilized by programs as an outcome measure of obtaining overall program goals. The comprehensive nature of capstone cases makes them good showcase products to include in internship or career application materials as well. The scope of any practicum or internship assignments, including capstone cases, will vary by institution and program accreditation requirements. Report formats also can be variable based on faculty or site and field placement supervisor preferences. In addition, assessment and intervention course work will generally provide instruction on report writing as well as sample templates. If your program utilizes a portfolio assessment, a detailed description will most likely be available through the student handbook.

CONFLICT BETWEEN SUPERVISOR EVALUATION AND STUDENTS

For students who disagree with competency ratings or product reviews a discussion with the site supervisor and, if need be, the practica coordinator or faculty advisor may be warranted. Differences and conflicts can emerge for a variety of reasons. Some common sources include differing understandings of the expectations or requirements based on assumptions or a lack of clarity in instruction. In these types of cases, differences may be easily resolved through discussion. Sometimes creating explicit written expectations will be helpful and a plan can be agreed on that will ameliorate the circumstance. Another source of misunderstanding can be the level of self-initiation expected by the site supervisor and the student. The practicum is a preliminary professional experience and unlike many job or work experiences that student have encountered prior to graduate school, the level of expectation for critical thinking skills and personal problem solving can be high. Often early undergraduate jobs are the only work experience that practica students have encountered prior to practica. Those types of jobs may be prescriptive and repetitious, thus expectations for being proactive in finding solutions or seeking out supervisor assistance may not prepare individuals for the higher self-directed expectations of practica. An additional category of conflict can arise from failure to meet foundational competency requirements; this type of circumstance may require more than a clarifying conversation as a structured sequence of remediation activities may be warranted.

Harvey and Struzziero (2008) further differentiate conflicts in light of *goal* and *method* types. *Goal* conflicts may occur when supervisors or their training program perspectives have differing perceptions. For example, a student's priority may be timely completion of an academic report encompassing all the test elements required by the program. A supervisor's goal, however, may be to focus on extended intervention prior to evaluation or to broaden the evaluation to include other preferred academic diagnostic measures. A solution to this dilemma may include closer communication and perhaps more flexibility between the program and field supervisors in setting report or case parameters. *Method* conflicts involve differing opinions and expectations regarding the delivery of supervision. For example, some supervisors may prefer private individual review of cases with supervisees, whereas others may endorse a group discussion model for reviewing cases. Group review is often the model used in clinical settings and for inpatient treatment practica, this may occur as a discussion with the patient in the room in addition to graduate student peers and the supervising psychologist (i.e., often called *rounds*). This level of open critique among peers can be difficult for those new to graduate school, especially for those who are introverted. There is a body of research on trainee shame-proneness that indicates the higher a supervisee's propensity to feel intimidated by group of public supervision approaches, the more likely the graduate student is to keep secrets from the supervisor and to also rate their perceptions of alliance with the supervisor as low (Bilodeau, Savard, & Lecomte, 2012).

In situations where performance is determined to be less than adequate, programs will generally have procedures delineated that offer a series of steps for identifying the skills deficit components and for readdressing skills development. This may entail repeating a specific assignment once or several times to build proficiency. If multiple skills are weak, repeating a practica unit may be the solution. In some rare circumstances the conflicts between a student and supervisor are so disparate that mediation by an objective third party may be required. It is important to note that students are entitled to a fair hearing of their concerns and perspectives as well as due process. Programs will generally have a formal grievance appeals procedure established for students and this is often found in the program or practica handbook.

Student Strategies for Fostering Supervision Alliance

Throughout an individual's career there will invariably be a series of supervisors with differing communication and training styles; therefore, the best solution for avoiding supervisor conflicts may be prevention. Thus, a number of authors as well as NASP/APA ethical standards have provided strategies for best practices in supervision as well as ways to avoid and ameliorate disagreements (APA, 2002; Dittman, 2005; NASP, 2010a, 2010b, 2010c). Student strategies include:

- Clarifying expectations from the first day (e.g., providing a written set of goals and a time frame for accomplishing those goals)
- Periodically self-initiated check-ins with the supervisor to ensure you are on track
- Being prepared for practica work as you would for a college class. Strategies may include reviewing literature for particular cases in advance (e.g., if a child has ADHD, review the *Diagnostic and Statistical Manual of Mental Disorders* (5th ed.; *DSM-5*; American Psychiatric Association, 2013) symptoms and interventions literature, and NASP/APA resources prior to beginning the case), come to supervision with notes, a plan, organized case folders, and a list of questions.
- Discussing theoretical orientations and approaches to assessment or intervention services. Inquiring regarding your supervisor's understanding of best practices and how those align with your own program training may help bridge any misunderstandings. For examples, supervisors with a strong behavioral orientation may expect to utilize behavioral modification strategies first in addressing behavioral concerns, whereas those with a more cognitive behavioral approach may consider a blend of behavioral modification and cognitive restructuring methods as the best practice approach. If the practice orientation of the supervisor is highly disparate from the program philosophy, it is important to discuss this with a faculty advisor or the practica coordinator for guidance.
- Resolving conflicts in a professional, collegial manner. Although there are times when a mediator for conflicts is beneficial, ethical guidelines do recommend first trying to resolve conflicts with the individual.
- Striving to discuss and diffuse conflicts or misunderstandings quickly. At times, there will be inevitable miscommunications between individuals and early efforts to resolve them can eliminate larger problems later. Sometimes the use of humor, clarifying questions, or just acknowledging a need to talk through a problem can resolve issues, especially if the misunderstandings do not linger.
- Accepting responsibility for your own work and monitoring personal effectiveness. Supervisors will respect and appreciate early self-disclosure of skill limitations or confusion regarding expectations. Part of their role as mentors is to be encouraging and supportive, and to foster professional growth in their supervisees. Just as school psychologists are ethically obligated to monitor their own work effectiveness and conduct as well as accept responsibility for their work, this principle can be extended to practica students as well.
- Avoid discussing conflicts during high stress moments. Discussions of conflicts are best approached when both parties are relaxed, open to

discussion, and nondefensive. Therefore, selecting a specific time to review differing opinions when all individuals are rested, calm, and have had time to collect their thoughts may facilitate better solutions.

- Staying within the hierarchical sequence when addressing disagreements. Most disagreements can be resolved with open communication. However, when the natural "chain of command" or hierarchical procession for addressing disagreements is circumvented, individuals may feel betrayed or defensive, a circumstance that can compound negative outcomes. For example, a student who bypasses discussing a disagreement on a practica rating with the supervisor or program faculty and goes to the school principal is likely to set up a highly negative set of events for all parties involved. Thus, as ethical guidelines recommend, first addressing issues with the site supervisor, then faculty or department administrators as outlined in the program handbook is a sequence that can help.

Supervisor Strategies for Fostering Trainee Alliance

Most of the literature and formal national guidelines on supervision have been related to the internship experience or early career supervision. However, over the last decade standards and guidelines are emerging that address best practices in the caliber and structure of practica supervision as well (APA, 2011, 2012, 2013; NASP, 2010a, 2010b, 2010c). These principles can serve to structure practica experiences that are sensitive to the needs of students, offer comprehensive oversight of practica work, and may eliminate potential sources of conflict or underperformance. Supervisor strategies include:

- Ensure that evaluation is consistent with ethical codes of conduct and expected skill levels. When supervisors model ethical behaviors and high levels of professional competency, students have a better understanding of expectations for their own evolving practices. In addition, it is recommended that evaluation fairly reflect the level of practice expected for the individual's current level of training.
- Provide greater levels of supervision for lesser experienced individuals. Supervision for beginning practitioners in school psychology by NASP is recommended at 1 hour weekly and, for interns, 2 hours weekly. The APA recommends 4-hour weekly internship supervision. An exact recommendation for practica does not exist at this time; however, it is presumed that lesser experienced students would require greater oversight and mentoring than interns or beginning practitioners.
- Supervisors are responsible for the work of their supervisees. With responsibility for the reports and interactions of their trainees, supervisors need

48 • SECTION I: PRACTICUM

to stay informed of the students' work, only assign tasks consistent with the trainees' competency level, and provided continuing feedback on performance that fosters professional growth.

- Supervisors should be appropriately credentialed. Best practices and ethical standards require that professional supervisors possess appropriate credentials based on the setting in which the supervision occurs (e.g., credentialed or licensed school psychologist or psychologist in schools; licensed psychologist or other appropriate professional in clinical settings). In addition, 3 years of practice experience is considered a qualification for supervision.
- Supervisors receive training in supervision skills. It is highly recommended that supervisors have training in the roles, responsibilities, and techniques of best practices in supervision.
- Supervisors possess metacognitive abilities for self-appraisal. It is the responsibility of supervisors to be aware of their own competencies and limitations in practice skills as well as supervisory effectiveness. Thus, self-monitoring their ability to successfully foster professional development in trainees is an ongoing process.

PERFORMANCE COMPETENCY VIGNETTES

Vignette 3.1

Walter, although not shy or reticent, has a quiet demeanor and prefers to problem solve new things he is learning in a private manner. In class, he will often wait till others have spoken before entering the conversation as this gives him the opportunity to carefully consider his answers and sometimes adjust his comments based on other ideas he has learned from the class discussion. He is having difficulty adjusting to his practica supervisor's style of group case discussions and direct questioning on cases, especially since there are other, more advanced practica students at the site who know more about assessment and intervention at this point than he does. His instinct, at this time, is to stay in the back of the group, try to not be seen, and avoid answering questions. His supervisor ratings for assertiveness, critical-thinking skills, and self-initiation are low.

Discussion Questions:

1. What phenomena in supervision might Walter be experiencing?
2. What options does he have to improve his performance?

Walter may be experiencing a shame-proneness reaction given his concern that others know more. He could be worried that he will answer incorrectly or feel inadequate. Thus, self-reflection on his own performance may be an important first step. Options might include prior preparation for case discussions by reviewing the data ahead of the case discussions, discussing his personal style of answering questions with his supervisor, and also seeking his or her advice on ways to feel more confident. In addition, acknowledging that this process is new and uncomfortable, and by not withdrawing, he is likely to acclimate to the group discussion format better. It is inherently the responsibility of the supervisor to ensure that group discussion is a respectful, productive, and safe format for sharing ideas.

Vignette 3.2

Alicia is currently a second-year practica student with course work in IQ testing and assignments to administer a Wechsler Intelligence Scale for Children (WISC) to an elementary child. The supervisor arranged this experience after Alicia had conducted a number of practice administrations through her course homework, had observed the supervisor administer the WISC, and then was observed by her supervisor administering the WISC. Thus, the supervisor was confident in Alicia's ability to provide a valid administration. However, at the last minute, the supervisor found a prior psychological report for the child that utilized the WISC. Therefore, the supervisor asked Alicia to administered a different IQ test, the Kaufman Assessment Battery for Children (K-ABC) noting that all IQ tests are similar so it should be no problem to proceed. Alicia feels this is not ethical since she is new to IQ testing and has no training yet in the K-ABC.

Discussion Questions:

1. Do you think that asking Alicia to administer the K-ABC is inappropriate?
2. What are Alicia's options?

Best practice guidelines, standards, and principles require that supervisors take responsibility for the work of trainees, know their competency levels, and only assign work that is appropriate. In this case Alicia is new to the process of IQ testing and does not have basic training in the administration rules or procedures for the K-ABC. She also has not had the benefit of observing a K-ABC administration or receiving feedback on her own ability to administer the test. Therefore, the request is inappropriate. Alicia's options are to directly express her concerns with the supervisor, request additional support prior to administering a K-ABC, and reschedule the test administration. It is incumbent upon the supervisor to exercise sound judgment as to when trainees have the prerequisite skills to be assigned particular responsibilities in practica regardless of assignment deadlines.

CHAPTER REVIEW

This chapter has provided a discussion of the types of evaluation approaches that may be utilized in monitoring competency building through practica experiences. Competency ratings offer Likert scale data that can delineate novice to expert or independent-level skill achievement, whereas portfolios of assignment product evaluations typically utilize rubrics to qualitatively analyze the quality of work. Both methods can yield important information in determining when skills are adequately demonstrated. At times, supervisors and trainees may disagree on performance evaluation scores and a discussion of differing perspectives is warranted. When agreement cannot be reached through review, programs will have additional processes to resolve conflicts including formal grievance procedures. The chapter also delineated a number of ways graduate students and supervisors alike can facilitate practica structures that will prevent many potential conflicts. Generally, the evaluation processes within the practica structure will be informative to both the student and supervisor and can foster continued collaboration in designing meaningful goals for this part of training.

REFERENCES

American Psychiatric Association. (2013). *Diagnostic and statistical manual of mental disorders* (5th ed.). Washington, DC: American Psychiatric Publishing.

American Psychological Association. (2002). Ethical principles of psychologists and code of conduct. *American Psychologist, 57,* 1060–1073.

American Psychological Association. (2011). *Revised competency benchmarks for professional psychology.* Washington, DC: Author.

American Psychological Association. (2012). *A practica guidebook for the competency benchmarks.* Washington, DC: Author.

American Psychological Association. (2013). *Guidelines and principles for accreditation of programs in professional psychology.* Washington, DC: Author.

Benner, P. (1984). *From novice to expert: Excellence and power in clinical nursing practice.* Menlo Park, CA: Addison Wesley.

Bilodeau, C., Savard, R., & Lecomte, C. (2012). Trainee shame-proneness and the supervisory process. *Journal of Counselor Preparation and Supervision, 4,* 37–49.

Caterino, L., Li, C., Hansen, A., Forman, S. G., Harris, A., & Miller, G. (2012). A reference for school psychology doctoral programs. *The School Psychologist.* Retrieved from http://www.apadivisions.org/division-16/publications/newsletters/school-psychologist

Dittmann, M. (2005). Facing your new supervisor: Experts and students share advice on preparing and adjusting to a new supervisor on practicum and internship. *Monitor on Psychology, 36*(7), 66.

Dreyfus, H. L., & Dreyfus, S. E. (1986). *Mind over machine: The power of human intuition and expertise in the era of the computer*. New York, NY: The Free Press.

Harvey, V. S., & Struzziero, J. A. (2008). *Professional development and supervision of school psychologists: From intern to expert*. Thousand Oaks, CA: Corwin Press.

Hatcher, R. L., & Lassiter, K. D. (2007). Initial training in professional psychology: The practicum competencies outline. *Training and Education in Professional Psychology, 1*, 49–63.

Johnson, R., Mims-Cox, J. S., & Doyle-Nichols, A. (2010). *Developing portfolios in education: A guide to reflection, inquiry, and assessment* (2nd ed.). Los Angeles, CA: Sage.

National Association of School Psychologists. (2010a). *Model for comprehensive and integrated school psychological services*. Bethesda, MD: Author.

National Association of School Psychologists. (2010b). *Principles for professional ethics*. Bethesda, MD: Author.

National Association of School Psychologists. (2010c). *Standards for graduate preparation of school psychologists*. Bethesda, MD: Author.

National Association of School Psychologists. (2011). *Supervision in school psychology* (Position statement). Bethesda, MD: Author.

CHAPTER 4

Peer Mentoring and Peer Supervision

LEARNING OBJECTIVES

At the conclusion of this chapter, readers should be able to:

1. Demonstrate an understanding of the benefits of peer supervision
2. Understand strategies for fostering development of test administration, scoring, and report writing
3. Gain knowledge of supervision models

Peer mentoring and peer supervision are vital components of the postsecondary educational experience for all degree tracks that can promote retention, acclimation to graduate studies, and a sense of community within programs (Budge, 2006; Fleck & Mullins, 2012; Grant-Vallone & Ensher, 2000). When the mentoring process includes junior faculty and graduate students in research teams, outcomes are even more positive for longer term career success (Waitzkin, Yager, Parker, & Duran, 2006). Additionally, the positive effects of peer mentoring are of particular importance in retaining minority students.

The terms "peer mentor" and "peer supervisor" are often used interchangeably as they share many overlapping components and responsibilities. Generally, both peer supervisors and peer mentors provide encouragement, socialization to the graduate school program, networking connections, and informal advice. There also are some important differences between the two roles: Peer supervision refers to a multifaceted and more formalized process of scaffolded activities than peer mentoring. The peer supervision elements may include teaching by modeling skills and preliminary review of assignments. Additionally, some evaluative elements such as critique of work may be expected. Peer supervision often exists between cohorts (e.g., third-year students may supervise first- and second-year students) and can vary in format. The process generally occurs in person via one-on-one meetings between mentors and mentees; however, supplemental phone and e-mail communication are also often useful for pressing questions and for maintaining contact between face-to-face meetings.

Some programs may formally match advanced students with incoming students across the program based on common specialization interests or degree tracks, whereas other programs may consider matching based on the logistics of practica placement or joint participation in a research team project. Both peer supervision and peer mentor responsibilities are often defined in program handbooks and/or contracts offering clear delineation of duties, timelines, any feedback components, and limitations. (Examples of a peer supervision contract and a peer supervisee end-of-semester feedback rating form can be found at www.springerpub.com/school-psychology-practicum, Exhibits 4.1 and 4.2.)

ROLES AND RESPONSIBILITIES

The primary role of the peer supervisor is to serve as a guide and support system for the mentee. The peer supervisor has the opportunity to share his or her knowledge, experience, and skill sets learned during the program with the supervisee. Peer supervisors may discuss numerous aspects of the supervisee's experience in the school psychology program including course work, practicum, internship (and internship applications), and research. Peer supervisors also may discuss opportunities related to graduate school more broadly, particularly for first-year students who are transitioning to graduate school for the first time or who have recently moved to the area. This could include information about funding opportunities, knowledge of the local area, university campus and graduate school environment, and tips or advice that the student has learned over the course of his or her program that would be valuable to an incoming student. Additionally, peer supervision affords an opportunity for supervisees to ask various questions of their peer supervisors. Creating a safe and accepting context in which mentees can share ideas with a colleague or ask clarifying questions is vital to the success of the peer supervision relationship.

Peer supervision is an excellent opportunity for graduate students to adopt new roles within the school psychology program. Peer supervision allows the mentor to better develop his or her own communication skills and to share knowledge and experiences with a new generation of future school psychologists. As part of this process, peer supervisors have an opportunity to teach their mentees and also to learn from their experience teaching others. Additionally, peer supervision affords experienced graduate students the opportunity to assume a leadership role while in graduate school. This supervisory experience can provide the mentor with important experience that may be helpful in the development of further leadership skills and professional development.

On a social level, the mentorship process helps build a support system and sense of community for mentees that can be carried with them throughout their time in graduate school. In addition, mentorship allows more experienced students to share much of the informal information they have learned during their program experiences with the mentee. Mentors have likely learned a great deal about what works (and what doesn't work!) in graduate school during their time in the program. The mentorship relationship gives the mentor a chance to impart knowledge to improve the overall programmatic experience. Many incoming students will have limited knowledge of school psychology vocabulary, and some may still be discovering what being a school psychologist entails. Peer supervisors can help orient their supervisees to the profession and acquaint them with useful terminology or other tips. Additionally, peer supervisors and supervisees often share a continued collegial relationship even after graduate school ends. Thus, peer supervision allows students to become engaged in building a network of professional relationships and colleagues who can be referenced throughout their careers.

LEVELS OF SUPPORT

Peer mentorship does not take the place of the mentee's relationship with his or her practicum supervisor and university-based program adviser. Rather, it provides an opportunity for scaffolded support in which mentees receive multiple levels of supervision (e.g., peer supervisors, practicum site supervisors, university-based supervisors) so that there are more easily accessible opportunities to discuss professional development factors. As part of a larger scaffolded system, additional supports and guidance are often provided at the beginning of the mentorship relationship (e.g., when the mentee is first becoming acquainted with the program). These supports may become less directive or proscriptive as the mentee matriculates through the program.

Effective peer supervisors (and supervisees) will be able to distinguish issues and concerns that merit further attention from faculty or field supervisors from those that can be addressed within the peer mentorship context. When in doubt, it is recommended that peer supervisors refer their supervisees to the program adviser for additional guidance and support, especially regarding any topic or issue that is outside their own competency. Ideally, the peer supervisor will work in conjunction with the university-based adviser or practicum supervisor to coordinate a multipronged approach to addressing supervisee issues. Should significant stress beyond what typically results from graduate school demands become evident, faculty may refer students for more formalized emotional support. Most universities have student counseling and mental health centers that will provide structured support for graduate students experiencing significant life stressors.

FACILITATING POSITIVE INTERACTIONS

While peer supervision styles will vary depending on the individual and the context, general guidelines for positive interactions should be considered when meeting with the mentee or mentor. Peer supervisors should strive to be an encouraging and positive presence in the supervisee's graduate school experience. In keeping with a common phrase, *graduate school is more of a marathon than a sprint.* With any such feat of endurance, there will likely be challenging moments to overcome. The mentor should seek to be as affirmative and supportive as possible, especially if the mentee faces challenges or difficulties during his or her graduate school experience. The role of the school psychologist as a problem solver can also be applied to the school psychology graduate student in a mentoring relationship. Peer supervisors may find it useful to help their supervisees find answers for their issues or concerns by brainstorming possible solutions, thinking creatively, and affirming the mentee's good efforts and successes.

When providing feedback to peer supervisees, it is often helpful for peer supervisors to begin with the highlights of the event (be it a paper, report, testing protocol, observation, or any other assignment). Leading with what the supervisee did well can help build confidence and demonstrate acknowledgment of the mentee's strengths. For example, when reviewing a mentee's report, a mentor could open a feedback discussion with an explanation of what the mentee did particularly well. This could include comments about the overall project, such as the mentee's writing style or the structure of the report. It also could include comments about specific details of the project that were noteworthy, such as the mentee explaining a particular test result well or providing comprehensive recommendations in a report.

In addition to opening the conversation with positive feedback, it is also beneficial for mentors to be able to offer positive alternatives for any limitations noted. If a mentee needs additional guidance or support in a particular area, it is within the role of the mentor to provide that guidance as applicable. Constructive feedback should be focused on the specific shortcoming noted and should provide an alternative solution to consider. Creating positive alternatives will help the mentee assess the range of options available to him or her in a given situation and can provide an opportunity for the mentee to make appropriate changes as necessary. For example, if a peer supervisor is reviewing a report written by a supervisee that contains inappropriate phrasing (e.g., use of slang or jargon), the supervisor could provide feedback that is constructive and that provides an alternative to the potential issue. In this situation, the supervisor could let the supervisee know in their face-to-face discussion that professional language is preferred because of the educational (and often legal) importance of such reports. The mentor could then provide the mentee with a few examples of specific phrases that could be used instead. This suggested framework for mentor–mentee interactions (being encouraging and supportive, emphasizing the positives, and providing constructive feedback by proposing viable alternatives) should help facilitate the collegial relationship that the mentorship process seeks to create.

MODELS OF SUPERVISION

As stated previously, styles of supervision may differ depending on a number of factors including the type of work to be supervised, the characteristics of the organization within which supervision is occurring, and the characteristics of the individual supervisor and supervisee. Peer supervisors may wish to consider what type of leader they would like to be for their supervisees and how they expect to manage the mentor–mentee relationship. Struzziero and Harvey (2008) review four of the basic styles of workplace supervision, which include transactional, laissez-faire, transformative, and contingency-based or contextual leadership.

Supervisors who take a transactional approach to the mentor–mentee relationship would view mentees as requiring constant reinforcement or incentives to meet goals. They would view their relationship with mentees as being highly proscriptive and would likely assume an authoritative stance over the mentee, focusing on efficiency and outcomes (Struzziero & Harvey, 2008). Leaders who assume a laissez-faire approach would be just the opposite of transactional leaders—instead of being overly controlling, laissez-faire leaders would be very flexible and nondirective with their mentees. They would be unlikely to set hard deadlines or goals and would be hesitant to engage in discussions that may lead to disagreement or conflict (Struzziero & Harvey, 2008).

A transformative approach to leadership diverges from the dualistic nature of the transactional and laissez-faire approaches. Transformative leaders construct a clear vision for the goals of their leadership, place value on individual strengths, and seek to achieve systemic change where warranted (Struzziero & Harvey, 2008). These supervisors view their supervisees as competent individuals who are capable of success, and they strive to provide guidance and implement structures that will help their supervisees succeed. Transformative leaders will likely be inspiring, innovative, and able to adjust their behaviors and outlooks to fit numerous situations (Struzziero & Harvey, 2008). Supervisors who have a contingency-based

CRITIQUING TEST ADMINISTRATION

One way that peer supervisors can be particularly helpful to supervisees is by ensuring that supervisees are administering tests and scoring any assessment protocols correctly, particularly for supervisees who are new to the field. Ways to facilitate the correct administration of tests may include first modeling the administration. Modeling may be especially helpful for assessments with numerous manipulatives or for those with many large components to juggle (e.g., multiple easels, manuals, protocol forms, CD audio/visual diskettes). Modeling can assist with pronunciation of uncommon words or sounds, such as those with a high emphasis on individual phonemes or nonsense words.

After modeling the correct administration, the peer supervisor may observe the graduate student's practice administration. To those who are new to school psychology, the idea of being observed completing an important task for evaluation purposes can be intimidating. Peer supervisors may help alleviate any anxiety around assessment administrations by acknowledging that many people will be nervous during their first assessment administration but that assessment administration will likely grow easier with time. Making errors is part of the natural learning process that such practice administrations are designed to encourage. Peer supervisors may wish to share their own experiences with new assessment administrations to normalize the experience. Being available for questions about the administration is also helpful to supervisees. This gives mentees the opportunity to ask questions that they may be most comfortable asking a peer or requesting feedback on their performance that will not be linked to their evaluation.

Another method for initially learning test administration is to videotape the process. This allows for multiple practice sessions and self-improvements before submitting a videotape for peer supervisor or faculty critique. It is important to note that if the practice test administration is with a child, parental consent to videotape is required. Many test publishers also offer videos of their assessments being administered that can be used for instructional purposes. If these resources are available through the program's test library, the mentee and peer supervisor may wish to watch and discuss these together, particularly for areas that the mentee has difficulty administering. Workshops, conventions, and conferences are another excellent resource for learning assessment or having a chance to practice with guidance and materials present.

Starting with simple measures, such as curriculum-based measures, screening instruments, or progress monitoring probes, is an easy way to help supervisees become familiar with the basics of test administration such as rapport-building, starting points, basals, and ceilings. For new peer supervisors, the use of an administration review guide may be particularly helpful in directing the discussion (Table 4.1). When coupled with a self-review of the administration (Table 4.2), the discussion can compare insights the student already has about his or her own performance with the observations of the peer supervisee.

TABLE 4.1 DIBELS Administration Peer Review Form

Graduate Student Name: _____	Date(s): _____
Supervisor/Observer: _____	Class/Grade/Teacher: _____

Scale: 1 = needs improvement, 2 = satisfactory, 3 = good

1. Established rapport before beginning to test	1	2	3	9. Read all directions verbatim	1	2	3
2. Prepared student for the tests	1	2	3	10. Used accurate timing procedures	1	2	3
3. Appeared at ease/ comfortable with the student	1	2	3	11. Recorded responses accurately on protocol or in the test booklet	1	2	3
4. Avoided distracting mannerisms	1	2	3	12. Praised the student appropriately (e.g., for effort rather than for correct responses)	1	2	3
5. Wore appropriate attire	1	2	3	13. Handled disruptions adequately	1	2	3
6. Had the necessary materials present and organized	1	2	3	14. Adhered to standardized procedures	1	2	3
7. Arranged materials so students could not review test items other than those in use	1	2	3	15. Ended the session appropriately	1	2	3
8. Manipulated the materials with ease and confidence	1	2	3	16. Followed accurate scoring procedures	1	2	3

Additional Comments/Feedback:

DIBELS, Dynamic Indicators of Basic Early Literacy Skills.

60 • SECTION I: PRACTICUM

TABLE 4.2 DIBELS Administration Self-Review Form

Graduate Student Name: _____		Date(s): _____
Supervisor/Observer: _____		Class/Grade/Teacher: _____

Scale: 1 = needs improvement, 2 = satisfactory, 3 = outstanding

1. Established rapport before beginning to test	1 2 3		9. Read all directions verbatim	1 2 3
2. Prepared student for the tests	1 2 3		10. Used accurate timing procedures	1 2 3
3. Appeared at ease/ comfortable with the student	1 2 3		11. Recorded responses accurately on protocol or in the test booklet	1 2 3
4. Avoided distracting mannerisms	1 2 3		12. Praised the student appropriately (e.g., for effort rather than for correct responses)	1 2 3
5. Wore appropriate attire	1 2 3		13. Handled disruptions adequately	1 2 3
6. Had the necessary materials present and organized	1 2 3		14. Adhered to standardized procedures	1 2 3
7. Arranged materials so students could not review test items other than those in use	1 2 3		15. Ended the session appropriately	1 2 3
8. Manipulated the materials with ease and confidence	1 2 3		16. Followed accurate scoring procedures	1 2 3

Additional Comments/Feedback:

DIBELS, Dynamic Indicators of Basic Early Literacy Skills.

Reviewing protocols for assessments that require elevated attention to detail and thorough knowledge of the assessment's rules and changes, such as measures of cognitive ability or academic achievement, may be the next logical step to help supervisees. For example, the Wechsler Intelligence Scale for Children (WISC), the Wechsler Individual Achievement Test (WIAT), the Woodcock–Johnson Tests of Cognitive Abilities (WJ-Cog), and the Woodcock–Johnson Tests of Achievement (WJ-Ach) all have detailed scoring and administration procedures. Such assessments would be highly appropriate for additional feedback on scoring procedures for mentees and will require more detailed review guides (see sample WIAT guides, Tables 4.3 and 4.4).

As with any mentor–mentee interaction, peer supervisors should strive to be positive and affirmative of the mentee's strengths when delivering

4: PEER MENTORING AND PEER SUPERVISION • 61

TABLE 4.3 WIAT-III Administration Self-Review Form

Graduate Student Name: _____ Date(s): _____
Student Age/Grade: _____

Scale: 1 = needs improvement, 2 = satisfactory, 3 = outstanding

1. Established rapport before beginning to test and prepared student for the tests	1	2	3		9. Transitioned smoothly between subtests	1	2	3
2. Appeared at ease/ comfortable with the student	1	2	3		10. Used accurate timing procedures (when required)	1	2	3
3. Avoided distracting mannerisms	1	2	3		11. Recorded responses accurately in the protocol	1	2	3
4. Had the necessary materials present and organized	1	2	3		12. Praised the student appropriately (e.g., for effort rather than for correct responses)	1	2	3
5. Administered appropriate subtests given student's age/grade, and began subtests at appropriate start points	1	2	3		13. Handled any disruptions adequately	1	2	3
6. Arranged materials so the student could not review test items other than those in use	1	2	3		14. Adhered to standardized procedures (e.g., queried responses when necessary)	1	2	3
7. Manipulated the materials with ease and confidence	1	2	3		15. Followed appropriate discontinue and reversal rules	1	2	3
8. Read all directions verbatim	1	2	3		16. Followed accurate scoring procedures	1	2	3

Please provide feedback regarding your administration and scoring for each subtest:

SUBTESTS	ADMINISTERED? (CHECK IF YES)	FEEDBACK (DIFFICULTIES? ISSUES? CONCERNS?)
Oral Language		
Listening Comprehension		
Oral Expression		
Reading		
Early Reading Skills		

(continued)

62 • SECTION I: PRACTICUM

TABLE 4.3 WIAT-III Administration Self-Review Form (*continued*)

SUBTESTS	ADMINISTERED? (CHECK IF YES)	FEEDBACK (DIFFICULTIES? ISSUES? CONCERNS?)
Reading Comprehension		
Word Reading		
Pseudoword Decoding		
Oral Reading Fluency		
Written Expression		
Alphabet Writing Fluency		
Sentence Composition		
Essay Composition		
Spelling		
Mathematics		
Math Problem Solving		
Numerical Operations		
Math Fluency		
Administration Strengths:		
Area(s) in Need of Improvement:		

WIAT-III, Wechsler Individual Achievement Test, Third Edition.

feedback. Supervisors should also provide clear, concise suggestions for improvements or changes when warranted. It is important for peer supervisors to be aware of common mistakes made by inexperienced examiners so that they are alert to potential errors and can provide appropriate corrective feedback as necessary. Specific rules for establishing a basal or ceiling

4: PEER MENTORING AND PEER SUPERVISION • 63

TABLE 4.4 WIAT-III Practice Test Administration Peer Review Form

Student Name: _____ Administration Date: _____
Peer Reviewer's Name: _____

1. Used appropriate starting points

2. Established basal correctly (reversed if necessary)

3. Established ceiling correctly (followed discontinue rules)

4. Administered appropriate item sets (reading comprehension, oral reading fluency)

5. Recorded correct and incorrect answers clearly

6. Scored individual items correctly

7. Computed subtest raw scores correctly

8. Recorded time correctly (on fluency subtests)

9. Entered scores correctly into computer scoring program

WIAT-III, Wechsler Individual Achievement Test, Third Edition.

on a subtest will vary by assessment but are critical to the correct interpretation of assessment results. Supervisors can help their supervisees by ensuring that all basal and ceiling cut-points have been met appropriately by reviewing the protocol and by asking the supervisee how he or she performed the assessment. This can also be a good opportunity for the supervisor to provide the supervisee with any tips or hints he or she has learned from doing assessments to make the process easier (e.g., highlight the original basal/ceiling cut-points based on age before the assessment, keep track of how many incorrect answers the child has given as the assessment progresses).

SCORING PROTOCOLS

Feedback of the scoring of assessments that require the child to give verbal examples (such as the Similarities or Vocabulary subtests on the WISC) or written responses (such as the writing samples portions of the WJ-Ach and WIAT) may also be especially helpful. While such subtests do have scoring guides, children may give responses that do not fit neatly into one category or another. Peer supervisors can provide their supervisees with their rationale for why a particular answer would merit a certain score. Guiding the mentee through the mentor's decision-making process and reasoning for scoring an ambiguous item in a certain way can help build the mentee's ability to score difficult items on his or her own. Supervisors may also wish to discuss some of the scoring examples provided in assessment manuals with the supervisee for a more direct training experience.

Peer supervisors can assist their mentees with assessment scoring by reviewing other aspects of the protocol as well, such as double-checking the protocols for calculation errors. A quick evaluation of the scores obtained in each subtest and how they contribute to the overall score can save the mentee the trouble of having to rewrite findings due to a calculation mistake. Mentors also may share tips with the mentee on how to perform common tasks, such as calculating a child's age. Many mobile applications are available for smartphones to make such tasks easier. For example, Psychological Assessment Resources (PAR) Inc., which publishes a number of psychological assessments, provides a complimentary phone app for handheld devices that contains an age calculator, score conversions for certain assessments, and a normal curve for reference (PAR Inc., n.d., toolkit.parinc.com). To guide discussions about protocol scoring, it is helpful to use a protocol review template to ensure that all of the important points are covered.

PROOFING COMMON WRITING ERRORS

A final area in which peer mentors can be of assistance to their peer mentees is report writing. Having the ability to write a well-constructed, logical, and comprehensive psychoeducational report is a skill that all graduate students are continuously developing. To aid mentees in this process, peer mentors may wish to give their mentees copies of prior reports that the mentors have completed. Sample reports can give the mentees ideas on how to structure a psychoeducational report, what kinds of information to include (or not include), and references for the type of language that is appropriate in such documents. In addition, mentors can offer to edit and provide suggestions on early drafts of mentees' reports. These early comments can help the mentee shape the report in the most appropriate way for a given case.

When reviewing reports for mentees, mentors should look for common writing errors (Table 4.5). These could include spelling, grammatical, or punctuation errors, which may or may not be identified by a word processing program. Stylistic issues, such as the consistency of the report's formatting, the use of first person, and potential redundancy, are important to look for since the computer program will not identify them automatically. Supervisors may also review the different sections of the report to ensure that pertinent information is included in the appropriate places. For example, the final summary should not introduce new information that was previously unstated in the report, and recommendations should be germane to the child's specific condition (as opposed to repeated from a preset list or report-writing template).

4: PEER MENTORING AND PEER SUPERVISION • 65

TABLE 4.5 Report Writing, Proofreading, and Peer Editing

General Writing Ability Review
Spelling
Punctuation (e.g., possessive plurals such as children's, students')
Format Consistency (e.g., subtest titles use same format [bold, initial caps, etc.])
Colloquialisms—may include slang, informal speech, regional phrases (e.g., "The teacher
    is <u>gonna</u> follow up with...."; "He solved the puzzle in a <u>cool</u> way," "In figuring this out....";
    "I saw the student for 15 minutes in his playing time") or complete aphorisms (e.g., "As
    frightened as a kitten up a tree")
Spell out acronyms first time used (e.g., ESE, IEP, SLD, WJ-III, FCAT)
Avoid first-person references to the examiner (e.g., "I saw the child on....")
Grammar
    Subject/verb agreement (e.g., he is, we are, data are)
    Verb modifiers (always are)
    Mixing tense in a sentence/paragraph (e.g., His IQ was 91 and he is off-task 10% of
        the time.)
    Redundancy in how sentences begin or redundancy in use of key phrases (e.g., Charlie's IQ
        is.... Charlie was off-task.... Charlie is....)

Integrated Report-Writing and Hypothesis Support
    How thorough is the background information? Birth issues, early health issues, diagnoses,
        grades, standardized assessment scores, attendance, early educational interventions,
        prior psychoeducational assessment summaries, vision and hearing screenings
        documented?
    Behavioral Observations/Descriptions
        For testing situation and classroom observations
    Test Interpretation
        Describe the child NOT the tests (percentile, category, with behavior, etc.)
        Describe tasks/skills NOT subtests
        Pinpoint skills needed
        Personalize
        Add positives as well
        Put scores in back with standard error of measurement (SEM) for total IQ
        Is there a validity statement?
        Are critical items on protocols addressed? (e.g., hearing voices)
    Summary and Recommendations
        Do intervention recommendations fit the data result?
        Is the summary concise (i.e., 1–2 paragraphs)?
        Does summary include ALL of the important themes?
        Is any new information introduced in the summary?

PEER SUPERVISION VIGNETTES

Vignette 4.1

Maria is providing peer supervision in practica to an entering school psychology student. She has reviewed and modeled administration rules for the DIBELS with her mentee twice and answered all the mentee's questions. The student also has received instruction on the administration in her academic assessment class and passed her multiple-choice classroom quizzes on administration rules. However, when Maria endeavors to schedule an appointment to observe the student administering the DIBELS probes, she receives a number of excuses and postponements. What are Maria's options?

Discussion Questions:

1. Should Maria notify her practica supervisor of this issue first before discussing it with her peer supervisee?
2. What might the possible reasons be for the mentee's avoidance of scheduling an observation?

A number of hypothesis come to mind as to why this student is not scheduling the test administration observation, thus Maria will need to explore each of these. It could be the student does not understand the test, is nervous about being observed, or is unorganized in her scheduling. First, the student appears to know the rules as demonstrated on her class quizzes, thus it is unlikely that she does not understand how to administer. However, it still would be good for Maria to discuss this with the student and inquire if she is unsure of any aspect of administration. Maria may also offer to review any components again. Second, Maria may need to explore whether the student is anxious about being observed. If so, she can reassure the student that everyone is a bit nervous at first but this will subside and can also share her own personal recollections of her first administration. Third, if the student is not apprehensive it may be important to discuss expectations for timely completion of assignments in order to move her progress in skill acquisition forward. Lastly, it is generally recommended that mentors first try to resolve issues with mentees directly; however, if these strategies are not successful, Maria will want to discuss the peer supervision dilemma with her practica supervisor.

Vignette 4.2

Walter, an advanced education specialist student, is providing peer supervision for Alan, a first-year practica student. Over time they have developed a strong supportive rapport and collegial friendship, whereby Alan has come to appreciate and respect Walter's advice. Walter's responsibilities include providing a preliminary review of the first draft of reports, which are then also reviewed by the practica site supervisor before turning the reports in as a class assignment. Alan has just finished his first functional behavioral analysis (FBA) case, an assignment for his current FBA assessment class. Alan followed the report template format provided by the class instructor; however, his report is riddled with misspelled words, errors in the accuracy of reporting FBA data, and is missing some basic punctuation. Additionally, he gave the report to Walter for review on short notice prior to the due date. To help out his mentee, Walter stayed up late into the evening reviewing Alan's report despite pressing deadlines for his own work. When Alan receives Walter's broad feedback on the types of errors and need to more carefully proofread his work, he enthusiastically thanks Walter for his guidance but asks for an additional favor. Alan notes he is really backed up with course work, the report deadline is the next morning, and he would like to send an electronic copy of the report to Walter and have Walter make the final changes. He thanks Walter for his friendship and understanding and assures Walter he'll be more careful next time.

Discussion Questions:

1. What are the appropriate boundaries or expectations for peer supervision in this scenario?
2. How can Walter best respond to Alan's request while maintaining rapport?

The scenario of Walter and Alan's dilemma is not unusual in that peer supervision and mentoring relationships often evolve into collegial friendships and, given the multiple demands of a rigorous graduate training program, students will at times feel significant pressure to complete a number of converging requirements. However, acknowledging these factors does not change the appropriate boundaries and expectations for a peer supervision relationship. Walter will need to remind Alan of the parameters of his role. Walter's responsibilities are to provide a preliminary proofreading of the report with suggestions, not to complete another student's work, as completing someone else's work also raises issues of ethical behavior. Walter may also want to acknowledge that he understands the pressure of cascading graduate school assignment deadlines while sharing some strategies he has found helpful in organizing assignments and managing time. Additionally, it would be good for Walter to establish a boundary regarding how much advance notice he requires to provide the preliminary edits, as he also needs to protect his own time so he can meet his own graduate requirements as well.

CHAPTER REVIEW

This chapter addressed key points to consider for peer supervisors and students in mentor–mentee relationships. Peer supervisors serve as guides for their supervisees. Mentors create an important support system for the mentee that can be continued throughout graduate school and often into the future. The peer mentorship process is only one level of a scaffolded, multifaceted supervision system that will include faculty members and site-based supervisors. Peer supervisors should strive to create positive, encouraging relationships with their supervisees through their interactions. There are multiple styles of leadership that may be employed in supervisory relationships, and the style used may vary depending on the context of the relationship. Mentors may assist mentees by providing feedback on mentees' scoring of assessment protocols, providing feedback on assessment administration techniques, and reviewing drafts of psychoeducational reports. When giving any feedback, supervisors should strive to highlight what the supervisee did well and provide a viable alternative for potential problems. Evaluation tools and checklists for reviewing test administrations were also included in this chapter to guide feedback discussions and promote effective mentor–mentee relationships.

REFERENCES

Budge, S. (2006). Peer mentoring in postsecondary education: Implications for research and practice. *Journal of College Reading Learning*, *37*(1), 71–85. doi:10.3102/00346543061004505

Fleck, C., & Mullins, M. (2012). Evaluating a psychology graduate student peer mentoring program. *Mentoring and Tutoring: Partnership in Learning*, *20*(2), 271–290.

Grant-Vallone, E. J., & Ensher, E. A. (2000). Effects of peer mentoring on types of mentor support, program satisfaction and graduate student stress. *Journal of College Student Development*, *41*(6), 637–642.

Psychological Assessment Resources. (n.d.). *PAR Assessment Toolkit v3.0*. Retrieved from http://toolkit.parinc.com/

Struzziero, J. A., & Harvey, V. S. (2008). *Professional development and supervision of school psychologists: From intern to expert*. Thousand Oaks, CA: Corwin Press.

Waitzkin, H., Yager, J., Parker, T., & Duran, B. (2006). Mentoring partnerships for minority faculty and graduate students in mental health services research. *Academic Psychiatry*, *30*(3), 205–217.

CHAPTER 5

Advanced Practica

LEARNING OBJECTIVES

At the conclusion of this chapter, readers should be able to:

1. Be familiar with the concept of an advanced specialization practicum

2. Differentiate transition, postsecondary, forensic, and clinical/medical model site practica experiences

3. Have knowledge of the considerations for conducting research through a practicum site

As noted in Chapter 1, core practica sites for school psychology programs typically offer a variety of opportunities to work with varying grade levels and student needs within local school districts. The overarching goal is to learn core competencies for assessment, intervention, consultation, and systems-level pedagogical supports. Programs also may offer *specialization* or *advanced* practica experiences. A *specialization* practicum emphasizes a specific area of practice expertise with an in-depth focus beyond the foundational competencies of general practice. School-based specialization examples might include bilingual assessment specialist, crisis intervention team specialist, applied behavioral analyst certification experience, systems-level administrative consultation, or program evaluation.

Additionally, there is an increasing need for school psychologists with expertize in high school transition and postsecondary evaluations as well as dual enrollment collaborative evaluations. The need for expertise in postsecondary and dual enrollment evaluations has been precipitated by several factors: (a) an increasing national trend in younger students matriculating into college, (b) an increase to 71% of high schools now offering college dual enrollment for students, and (c) the need to understand the differing laws and policies for accessing services across secondary and postsecondary educational settings (Joyce & Grapin, 2012; Joyce-Beaulieu & Grapin, 2014; Karp, Calcagno, Hughes, Jeong, & Bailey, 2007). Dual enrollment presents

69

several complex issues because of (a) differing disability qualifying criteria, (b) which institution is responsible for disability accommodations, and how those accommodations may change across settings (e.g., online college course accommodations for reading disabilities, university entrance exam testing), and (c) individual state guidelines for mandated career transition plans.

Clinic-based examples of specialized practica might include forensics evaluation through a law clinic or adjudicated youth programs, inpatient or outpatient hospital units, community mental health agencies, and private practice. These additional experiences may later help facilitate acquisition of specialized internship opportunities and sometimes additional certifications (e.g., Applied Behavior Analyst Certification). Some programs offer specialization practica opportunities near the middle of the training sequence after a year or two of school-based competencies are secured. Other programs offer these opportunities as a rotation within the core practica training or to students entering the program who already have advanced degrees (e.g., master's, specialist). For many programs, the specialization or advanced practica may occur in the later part of the doctoral training sequence.

Students beginning advanced practica are expected to possess basic competencies in assessment and intervention and to be ready to demonstrate increased independence in their service delivery (while continuing to receive high-quality supervision). To ensure that your advanced practicum meets your specific training needs, you should work closely with your university practicum coordinator early on to discuss your professional goals and interests. The following describes important considerations for pursuing a variety of advanced practicum experiences, including coordinating postsecondary transition services, conducting forensic evaluations, and working within settings that utilize a medical model. Although this chapter cannot review all the possible types of advanced practica placements, it does discuss a few additional training and research opportunities as illustrations of what advanced practica options might include.

TRANSITION AND COLLEGE STUDENT EVALUATIONS

Specialized practica opportunities to learn about college transition evaluations will most likely occur within the public school system and are conducted by school psychologists assigned to high schools. Postsecondary or college-level evaluations are often provided through either private practice clinics or college and university disability offices. Some postsecondary institutions hire school psychologists as part of their full-time professional staff to provide the evaluations and coordinate student support services. If this type of career setting is of interest, acquiring advanced practica experience in this capacity can enhance one's vita for applying to these positions later.

A list of local licensed school psychologists and psychologists also may be maintained by the postsecondary institution and these professionals are contracted to provide specific evaluation or support services. Additionally, the school psychology program or clinic may be contracted to conduct the on-campus postsecondary student evaluations and/or provide support services (e.g., mentoring, tutoring program) for the general college student population at the respective institutions. This type of arrangement is mutually beneficial to the program and institution as school psychology faculty have expertise that bridges academic, mental health, and the young adult age span and also can involve their advanced graduate students in assessment services as a training opportunity.

College-level transition evaluations differ from traditional K–12 special education evaluations in several ways. First, the focus of disability documentation at the college level is on securing appropriate educational *accommodations* rather than *modifications*. Accommodations refer to services that allow the individual to access an institution's standard curriculum, whereas modifications involve changes to the content of the curriculum itself. In some instances, certain types of curriculum modifications are available to college students (e.g., a language course substitution for a student with a speech disability); however, more often, disability services at the postsecondary level center on providing appropriate academic accommodations (e.g., extended time on tests, access to a scribe or note-taker, and access to a calculator for assessments and class activities). Moreover, different standards and federal legislation dictate requirements for disability documentation and services at the college level. These laws and regulations are applied to the diagnostic model outlined in the *Diagnostic and Statistical Manual of Mental Disorders* (5th ed.; *DSM-5*; American Psychiatric Association [APA], 2013) rather than the special education classification model specified under the Individuals with Disabilities Education Improvement Act (IDEIA, 2004). As a result, an individualized education program (IEP) or other document that specifies the individual's IDEIA disability classification only is not sufficient to meet college-level eligibility requirements. Therefore, participation in a practica setting that offers transition evaluations will require a keen knowledge of the *DSM* and college accommodation criteria.

Assessing College Accommodations

To secure disability services at the college level, eligible students are required to submit acceptable documentation. Typically, this documentation assumes the form of a psychoeducational report that is developed by a qualified professional. These reports are designed to describe the individual's disability status and functional limitations. Moreover, they are intended to provide recommendations for supports that would facilitate the student's full participation in university activities.

Currently, three primary organizations specify standards for disability documentation at the postsecondary level: the Association on Higher Education and Disability (AHEAD), the Educational Testing Service (ETS), and the National Joint Committee on Learning Disabilities (NJCLD). The documentation standards developed by individual colleges and universities often are based largely on the recommendations provided by these three organizations. Collectively, AHEAD (2012, 2015a, 2015b), ETS (2007, 2012, 2015), and NJCLD (2007) recommend that college-level reports adhere to the following standards:

- Evaluations must be conducted by an appropriately qualified professional, such as a certified school psychologist, licensed psychologist, psychiatrist, or licensed clinical social worker. The evaluator should clearly specify his or her credentials (e.g., degree, certification number, or license number) in the report and have sufficient experience in conducting assessments with the appropriate populations (adolescents and adults, individuals with learning disabilities, etc.).
- Evaluations should be conducted no more than 3 years prior to their submission to the college or university so that scores reflect recent abilities. For individuals with emotional or psychiatric disabilities, institutions may require more recent documentation (i.e., within the past 6 months or year). The reason for requiring more recent verification of diagnoses is based on the inherent instability of some mental health symptoms (e.g., depression) and a desire to document the current level of functioning.
- Evaluations must include adult rather than child instruments. This is important to note, as some instruments commonly used in K–12 settings (e.g., Wechsler Intelligence Scale for Children, Fifth Edition [WISC-V]) are limited in age. If students were last evaluated before the age of 16, their most recent psychoeducational evaluation may include child measures of cognitive ability, achievement, and social/emotional functioning. College-level reports must include adult measures only, such as the Wechsler Adult Intelligence Scale, Fourth Edition (WAIS-IV), the Woodcock–Johnson, Fourth Edition—Tests of Cognitive Ability (WJ-IV-Cog), and the Wechsler Individual Achievement Test, Third Edition (WIAT-III).
- Evaluations should be comprehensive in nature and should incorporate a variety of assessment techniques. These techniques may include a record review, behavioral observations, a student interview, and standardized test administrations. For standardized assessments, all standard scores and percentile ranks should be indicated clearly in the report. Ultimately, the assessment methods chosen should accurately capture the nature and breadth of the student's strengths and needs.
- Evaluations should include detailed and specific recommendations for accommodations and services. Each recommendation should be

accompanied by a clear rationale that is based on the needs and functional limitations of the individual. This section is among the most important in the report, as institutions often base decisions for accommodations on the recommendations provided by evaluators (Gormley, Hughes, Block, & Lendmann, 2005). It is important to note that the level of rationale and specificity of recommendations needed may differ dramatically from those typically found in school psychology special education eligibility reports. For example, a typical school-based report may recommend "extended time on tests" due to attention deficit hyperactivity disorder (ADHD). However, some national college test accommodation applications will requirement documentation of the exact amount of extra time needed (e.g., 50% or 100% more time) and the rationale as to why based on specific assessment score measures that compare tasks under time-limited and without time limit conditions. As an example, the ETS guide on college-level entrance exams (i.e., Test Takers With Disabilities or Health-Related Needs) documentation and eligibility certification forms can be viewed at www.ets.org/s/disabilities.

College Accommodations

Disability services available in postsecondary settings also differ from services typically offered in K–12 settings. As noted, these services center on providing accommodations rather than curriculum modifications. Examples of accommodations commonly offered through university settings include: (a) extended time to complete assignments and tests; (b) permission to use a tape recorder in class; (c) private feedback on assignments from instructors; and (d) permission to use a calculator on tests and other assignments. Additional accommodations that evaluators may include in their report recommendations are listed in Table 5.1. School psychologists may wish to encourage high school students to contact specific institutions regarding available services. This information is helpful to the student in targeting potential colleges and to the school psychologist in developing

TABLE 5.1 Examples of College-Level Accommodations by Domain[a]

Reading
• Reader (for test questions, assignments, etc.) • Textbooks on tape • Verbal summarization or clarification of directions or course readings • Outlines or study guides to support comprehension of course readings • Assistance from learning/tutoring centers in practicing reading comprehension strategies (e.g., periodic self-monitoring of comprehension, summarizing key ideas during or at the end of reading a passage, posing and responding to questions about passage content, using graphic organizers)

(continued)

74 • SECTION I: PRACTICUM

TABLE 5.1 Examples of College-Level Accommodations by Domain[a] (*continued*)

Math

- Use of a calculator for assessments, assignments, and in-class activities
- Access to formula sheets, scripts, and other prompts for solving problems
- Access to peer tutor for additional review and support
- Shorter, more frequent assessments rather than longer, cumulative assessments
- Increased access to instructor or teaching assistant for more frequent and immediate feedback
- Access to additional study resources (e.g., study guides and practice problems) for more intensive review of concepts

Written Expression

- Assistive writing software (e.g., text-to-speech, speech synthesizers, and phonetic spell checker)
- Access to note-taker and/or copies of PowerPoint and other types of class presentations
- Scribe for assignments and exams
- Permission to submit handwritten or typed assignments

Oral Language

- Flexibility with assignment formats (e.g., oral presentations, written work, portfolio, role play)
- Visual aids to assist with comprehension of lecture material
- Tape recording lectures to listen multiple times
- Paraphrasing and summarizing directions and concepts

Attention/Hyperactivity

- Preferential seating (near front of class or an exit)
- Minimize distractions in classroom or student's immediate environment
- Frequent breaks
- Assignments segmented into shorter, manageable pieces

Social/Emotional

- Access to university counseling center and peer support groups
- Beverages or food permitted in class
- Flexibility in attendance to allow for counseling or medical treatment
- Assignment assistance during hospitalization
- Private feedback/evaluation from instructor

Vision

- Materials with clear headings and high color contrast between text and background
- Access to assistive technology (e.g., Brailler, closed captioning, speech-to-text)
- Preferential seating to allow access to best lighting and/or appropriate distance from instructor
- Tape recorder/player to record lectures and discussions
- Allow use of desktop lamp in class to improve lighting at workspace
- Large print texts
- Allow for tactile handling of objects presented in class
- Access to appropriate writing materials (bold lined paper, raised lined paper, etc.)

Hearing

- Sign language interpreter
- Peer note-taker
- Provide written directions, resources, and materials in class

(*continued*)

TABLE 5.1 Examples of College-Level Accommodations by Domain[a] *(continued)*

- Transcripts of lectures and oral presentations
- Access to assistive technology, such as Telecommunications Device for the Deaf (TDD), assisted listening devices (e.g., Frequency Modulation [FM] system)
- Allow for longer response times in class (to allow student to watch interpreter or reference written materials)

Physical/Motor
- Accessible classrooms
- Alternatives to assignments that involve walking, standing, and/or other physical activity
- Preferential seating to ease access to exits and classroom resources
- Note-taker

Studying/Organization/Executive Functions
- Advance notice of assignments to allow for planning
- Assignments completed in smaller pieces
- Peer mentor to support organization, scheduling, and planning
- Access to learning centers to support acquisition of learning and study strategies
- Peer support networks for reminders, encouragement

[a] Accommodations listed in one domain often are applicable and/or adaptable for students with a range of needs.

Adapted from Joyce and Grapin (2012), Joyce-Beaulieu and Grapin (2014), and Joyce and Rossen (2006).

report recommendations that are likely to be well received by disability support staff.

Americans with Disabilities Act

Disability services for college students are regulated largely by the Americans with Disabilities Act (ADA, 1990), among other legislation (e.g., Rehabilitation Act of 1973). Specifically, Title II of the ADA prohibits institutions that receive federal funding from discriminating against or denying access to individuals with disabilities. As a result, colleges and universities are required to provide reasonable accommodations and services to individuals with disabilities to facilitate their full participation in university life. Reasonable accommodations are defined as support services that do not bring undue hardship, including significant financial difficulty, to the institution. Most postsecondary institutions (both public and private) receive some degree of federal financial assistance and therefore are required to comply with Title II of the ADA. For institutions that do not receive any federal funding, protections for individuals with disabilities are stipulated under Title III of the ADA. As compared with Title II statutes, Title III statutes impose less demanding requirements for qualifying institutions (which presumably have fewer resources than federally funded institutions) but still require colleges and universities to accommodate students with disabilities in a similar manner.

Under the ADA, the term *disability* refers to a "physical or mental impairment that substantially limits one or more major life activities" (ADA, 1990, 42 U.S.C. #12102(2)(A)). Since its initial codification, the ADA has defined *major life activities* as including eating, sleeping, walking, speaking, and standing. More recently, the 2008 amendments to this legislation expanded the definition of *major life activities* to include reading, concentrating, thinking, communicating, and working as well as major bodily functions (e.g., normal cell growth and digestive, circulatory, endocrine, and reproductive functions). Knowledge of these changes to federal legislation is critical for evaluating the comprehensive impact of a student's disability on a range of life activities that may directly or indirectly affect educational performance.

Working With College Administration

Once the student has secured appropriate disability documentation, this documentation must be submitted for formal review by the institution. The ADA requires all covered institutions to designate a point of contact for individuals who are interested in pursuing disability services. Most colleges and universities have a centralized support center available to students with disabilities that is commonly referred to as a Disability Resource Center (DRC) or Disability Supports Services (DSS). The DRC (or DSS) is responsible for reviewing students' disability documentation in order to determine their eligibility for college-level services. Once an individual's eligibility for services has been established, the DRC is responsible for determining the specific supports that she or he is entitled to access. These determinations are made based on the nature of the student's needs, the recommendations for accommodations provided in the psychological report, and the availability and/ or feasibility of various supports offered through the institution. Students may be encouraged to utilize services that are available to all individuals enrolled in the college (e.g., student counseling centers, writing labs, and tutoring centers) or informed of special services offered only through the disability center (e.g., separate quiet testing rooms, assistive technology for physical disabilities).

Generally, it is incumbent on matriculating students to submit all necessary documentation and to self-disclose their disability status to the institution. Additionally, when a student becomes 18 years of age, he or she garners privacy rights that prohibit colleges from discussing or disclosing information with others including parents or caregivers without the student's consent. Students should be reminded that registering with the DRC alone does not ensure that individual course instructors will receive the information necessary to implement accommodations. Rather, on a case-by-case basis, students may choose to approach their instructors about receiving accommodations in the classroom. In requesting these accommodations, a student typically submits secondary documentation prepared by the DRC that verifies the individual's disability status and lists the accommodations to which he or she is entitled. Because the task of securing accommodations in the classroom requires students to advocate for their educational needs, school psychologists should work with high school students to practice self-disclosure and self-advocacy skills in preparation for the college transition. These skills may include selecting an appropriate time to approach instructors, choosing which information to disclose, and following up regarding the subsequent implementation of accommodations.

ADVANCED PRACTICA VIGNETTES

Vignette 5.1

Aaron is a 16-year-old student in his senior year at Model High School. In fifth grade, he was identified as having a specific learning disorder (SLD) in the area of reading comprehension and has continued to receive special education services throughout middle school and high school. Aaron also has difficulty regulating his attention and level of activity in the classroom. As his senior year approaches, he has expressed interest in attending college. Upon graduating, Aaron would like to pursue a career in music, specifically as a vocalist and guitarist. As a school psychologist at Model High School, Haruka has been asked to work with the other members of the high school Child Study Team (CST), including the guidance counselor and school social worker, to provide a reevaluation with a transition plan for Aaron.

Discussion Questions:

1. What additional information does Haruka need to write both short- and long-term goals for Aaron's transition plan?
2. What type of evaluation information needs to be in the report to document that Aaron meets postsecondary criteria for a specific learning disorder?

The response to this scenario should include acquiring an interview with Aaron that discusses his personal career goals and aspirations so that the transition plan can provide logical educational steps he needs to take to facilitate his ambitions. In order for the evaluation data to be useful in establishing college accommodation criteria, they must include adult-age instruments and document the *DSM-5* criteria for Specific Learning Disorder rather than just the IDEIA criteria.

Vignette 5.2

Haruka, Aaron, his parents, and the CST meet to discuss both his short-term and long-term goals following graduation. First, they encourage Aaron to consider the many ways in which a college education would facilitate his success as a musician. Through this conversation, Aaron acknowledges the importance of taking courses in music theory, composition, marketing, and other areas relevant to the industry. Bearing in mind these considerations, the team encourages Aaron to consider some short-term goals that would allow him to move forward with his long-term career plans. Collectively, Aaron and the CST agree that he will need to complete high school requirements, obtain good scores on college entrance exams (e.g., SAT or ACT), build his résumé, further develop critical academic and musical skills, identify appropriate postsecondary institutions, and eventually, submit college applications. These short- and long-term goals are noted in the evaluation report and subsequently are incorporated in his IEP.

Following the CST meeting, Aaron works with his guidance counselor to identify appropriate colleges and universities and to select the necessary college preparatory and music course work for his senior year. The counselor also assists him in revising his résumé and identifying potential internship opportunities in various local music studios. Meanwhile, Haruka and Aaron also meet to discuss procedures for accessing disability services in postsecondary settings. She explains that disability documentation and supports are handled differently at the college level. After Haruka describes the process of connecting with disability support staff and securing accommodations, she encourages Aaron to contact several institutions in order to inquire about available learning assistance services. To facilitate this process, Haruka assists Aaron in formulating questions he may wish to ask when speaking with a disability services coordinator.

Next, Haruka plans a comprehensive reevaluation of Aaron's current educational functioning. In line with college-level documentation requirements, she documents prior interventions and includes adult measures of intellectual functioning (WAIS-IV) and academic achievement (WJ-IV). She also includes behavioral observations and a student interview to ascertain Aaron's perspective on his individual strengths and needs. Test results indicate significantly low reading comprehension and reading fluency scores despite multiple years of quality instruction and supplemental interventions. He was noted to take considerable time to finish reading even short passages and was subject to fatigue on longer passages. Additionally, Aaron is occasionally off-task whenever there are distracting noises in the room but otherwise exhibits good work habits.

Discussion Questions:

1. Based on the evaluation results, what recommendations for accommodations might Haruka include in her final report?
2. How should Haruka coach or prepare Aaron for self-advocacy in college?

The response to this scenario could including the following recommendations: (a) extended time on tests; (b) opportunities to complete all tests and quizzes in a quiet environment with minimal distractions; (c) access to tutoring centers to support his continued development in reading comprehension; and (d) opportunities to take periodic breaks during class assignments. Haruka could assist Aaron to build his skills in the areas of self-advocacy, goal setting, and planning, as these skills are critical for accessing supports at the postsecondary level. In particular, role play and discussion regarding how to disclose his disability status, approaching instructors to request accommodations, and accessing various resources on campus may be helpful.

FORENSIC PSYCHOLOGY

Forensic psychology is a blended specialization that applies the frameworks of psychological principles and law. A practica setting in forensics might include working at a university's law clinic that specializes in child/adolescent or special educational cases. Another avenue for forensic school psychology is working with government agencies or private law practices that protect and advocate for children (e.g., trauma or abuse clinics, child protective services, truancy hearings). These types of practica are less common than school-based and clinic-based practica; however, opportunities often can be fostered within larger communities and universities. In fact, many school psychology faculties are called upon to provide expert witness testimony based on their prolific research in a particular area and their in-depth knowledge of specific syndromes. For individuals interested in careers that include forensic evaluations or expert witness testimony, a practica experience in this area is an excellent way to begin acquiring these specialized skills. Additionally, seeking mentorship from a faculty member who engages in forensic services is beneficial in understanding the nuances of establishing one's reputation and credentials for this field of expertise. Lastly, familiarity with the literature for forensics is important to acquiring expertise in this discipline and there are a number of journals that specialize in forensics (e.g., *American Journal of Forensic Psychology, Journal of Clinical Child and Adolescent Psychology, Open Access Journal of Forensic Psychology*).

Forensic Evaluation

Forensic school psychologists are called upon to provide psychoeducational evaluations that can inform courts regarding the negative impacts of trauma or abuse and neglect, psychopathology for adjudicated youth, and home environment stability factors in custody hearings. At times, the cases involve civil law regarding educational issues. For example, a parent may challenge a school's decision for special education placement. Forensic evaluations are also provided in criminal cases and the school psychologist may be asked to provide guiding information for either a victim or a perpetrator. Examples of forensics in criminal cases include advocating for a child who has been abused or traumatized and providing evaluations for an adjudicated youth charged with a crime.

Practitioners who engage in offering forensic psychoeducational evaluations will need a thorough knowledge of multiple areas of psychology depending on the type of case and the decisions sought from the expert testimony. In instances of individuals with intellectual disabilities, the forensic evaluation may be utilized to establish IQ, adaptive skills, and to make decisions regarding culpability given diminished higher order reasoning and critical thinking skills. For evaluations involving abuse, an understanding of child forensic interview techniques, police physical evidence standards, resiliency measures, and instruments that measure negative stress impact (e.g., depression, anxiety, withdrawal) are often required (Annon, 1994). For criminal activity cases, expertise in pathology instruments, an understanding of malingering and false confessions, as well as considerations for one's own safety while conducting the evaluation are important considerations (Cutler & Zapf, 2015). Additionally, illicit drug use and addictions often accompany chronic pathology, thus individuals providing forensic consultations must be knowledgeable regarding these factors. In criminal cases that involve psychosis, the forensic psychologist may be asked to determine if the individual's actions are a manifestation of the symptomology of their disorder (e.g., schizophrenia, hallucinations, delusions, paranoia).

For forensic psychologists with training as a school psychologist, the developmental trajectory of the child/adolescent and consideration for educational and social adjustment factors will be important factors. Unlike most school-based referrals where parents and teachers are seeking an evaluation and the child is generally agreeable, forensic evaluations for adjudicated youth are a special consideration. These evaluations may be court mandated with clients who are disagreeable. The examiner will need an understanding of several concepts not typically considered in school-based evaluations. Those factors include malingering, how to measure at-risk indicators for lethality, recidivism risk, and false confessions (DeClue, 2013; Fries, Rossegger, Endrass, & Singh, 2013). Additionally, any professionals including practica students working with this population will need training in personal safety guidelines when conducting evaluations (Foster et al., 2013).

Forensic Expert Testimony

In addition to evaluations, the other major role of forensic psychology is to provide expert testimony related to diagnosis and recommendations. This testimony is based on analysis of report findings, a comprehensive understanding of the short- and long-term outcomes for victimized or perpetrating individuals, and an adept knowledge of treatment or intervention needs. The types of decisions made from expert testimony may include long-term Social Security benefits for students with disabilities; parental custody placement; court hearings on mandatory school attendance (often called educational neglect or truancy hearings), which can result in removing children from parental custody; or emotional impact of injury and abuse, which may result in criminal damages payment and prosecution of the perpetrator. Adjudicated youth cases will generally result in prosecution or acquittal of a crime and decisions regarding consequences if convicted. There often is more latitude for courts when sentencing minors and the forensic psychologist can be influential in providing a rationale for treatment programs (e.g., adjudicated youth programs, addiction treatment, release with mandated counseling parameters, etc.) instead of jail. Any of these recommendations would of course be based on the psychologist's understanding of human behavior and interpretation of psychological evaluation results.

Forensic Professional Credentials

Hiring of forensic expert testimony is generally facilitated by defense lawyers and prosecuting attorneys based on a school psychologist's or psychologist's established record of expertise in a particular area of practice and appropriate credentials. Requirements may vary by state; however, the APA guidelines for a forensic psychologist recommend a PhD or PsyD degree that was issued by an accredited program (Ward, 2013). In addition, 2 years of supervised experience is required and one of those years can be an internship with a structured forensic focus. States may require a written and/or oral exam for certification in this area. As a last note on forensic evaluation and expert testimony, it is important to consider one's own personality variables when pursuing this type of experience. By nature of the civil and criminal case trial dynamics, this process can be adversarial, lawyers can and will challenge credentials and opinions of the psychologists providing evaluations or testimony in addition to opposing parties who may disagree with the findings. Therefore, a strong, confident personality, good public speaking skills with the ability to articulate succinct rationales for recommendations and an in-depth knowledge of presenting issues are crucial.

RESEARCH CONSIDERATIONS THROUGH PRACTICUM

In addition to providing clinical experience, advanced practica also may present valuable opportunities to conduct research. Often a variety of existing data are readily available through practica sites, including archival records of students' academic achievements and behavioral, social, and emotional functionings (e.g., past behavioral screening data, progress monitoring data, course grades, and standardized test scores). Moreover, there may be opportunities to conduct original data collection. Original data collection involves the use of new measures (i.e., assessment procedures that are not part of the site's routine or existing practices) to collect student or systems-level information. These techniques may include quantitative and qualitative methods, such as conducting focus groups, interviewing students and faculty, and administering surveys or standardized tests. Both archival and original data collection can be useful for investigating a variety of research hypotheses, including questions about the efficacy of interventions, the implementation of evidence-based practices, and the adoption of systems-level programs. When there is an interest in conducting research through your practicum site, it is important to first consult with a faculty advisor regarding options and to also cultivate strong collegial relationships with administrators and personnel at the practica site who can facilitate access to these data. Within some school psychology programs, faculty will have funded research grant projects where data collection is facilitated through local schools and these studies can become a combined practica and research experience. The structure often involves a team project approach with a designated supervising project leader. These types of arrangements can serve to enhance graduate school learning as the service delivery and data monitoring processes succinctly encompass a scientist–practitioner model.

As with all other university-based research projects, it is necessary to secure approval for research from the Institutional Research Board (IRB) at your respective university (see sample IRB application, Table 5.2). A separate IRB review also may be needed from the school district office or clinic where the research will be conducted. In cases where a school district or clinic does not have their own internal IRB process, the university may require a letter of approval from the site noting they are aware of and agree to the study (see sample school approval letter, www.springerpub.com/school-psychology-practicum, Exhibit 5.1). Depending on the nature of your research and the anticipated risks to participants, your project may fall in one of three review categories: *exempt*, *expedited*, or *full board*. If you are pursuing original data collection with children/minors, who constitute a protected population according the Department of Health and Human Services (2009), your project may require more intensive review.

TABLE 5.2 Sample University Institutional Review Board Study Application

Title of Study	Dynamics in Reading and Math Instruction Effects for Kindergarten Students	
Principal Investigator	Marlin	Marisa
Degree/Title	PhD, Professor	Campus Address: PO Box 87654
Department	School Psychology	Telephone #: 123-456-7890
Research Assistant	Walters	Tony
Degree/Title	BA, Graduate Research Assistant	Campus Address: PO Box 87654
Department	School Psychology	Telephone #: 123-456-7890
Dates of Research	October 2014–August 2015	

Purpose: The purpose of this study is to investigate the possible learning effects of the Dynamics in Reading and Math supplemental instructional curricula and learning activities on academic outcomes for kindergarten students.

Research Methodology: For all kindergarteners with parental consent to participate, the regular classroom progress monitoring data for core reading and math will be reviewed. One half of the students with parent/guardian consent for participation will be invited to participate in supplemental Dynamics in Reading and Math afterschool instruction modules (20 minutes per day for one semester). This quantitative research design will compare curriculum-based measure (CBM) scores on brief (i.e., typically 1 minute) discrete academic skill probes at preintervention and postintervention. All personally identifiable information will be removed from CBM data and replaced with a code number as either intervention group or control group. All data will be housed on a password protected computer with encryption security at the school psychology office. This is a locked office and only authorized school personnel have access.

Potential Benefits: Benefits to the treatment group participants include possible positive academic achievement effects on the discrete skills measured.

Potential Risks: No known potential risks are indicated. Through informed consent, parents/guardians of participants will be made aware of their right to withdraw from the study at any time.

Recruitment: A parent consent letter (see attached letter) will be sent to parents/guardians of all enrolled students in kindergarten at ABC Elementary (see attached approval letter from school principal).

Principal Investigator(s) Signature	Date:
Graduate Research Assistant(s) Signature	Date:
College Assistant Dean of Research Signature	Date:

Specifically, for the IRB, you will need to complete an application describing your research methodology, anticipated number of participants, and potential risks and benefits to participants. When estimating the number of participants you will need for your study, it is important to account for unforeseen circumstances, such as missing data points and participant attrition (due to students changing districts, schedules, etc.). These are fairly common occurrences in school-based research. Applications for the IRB at some institutions also may require completion of online courses or modules on ethical guidelines for human subjects in research. If the data for the study are not archival, you most likely will be required to describe in detail your procedures for obtaining parental consent for working with children, participant consent for adults and/or assent for children, when appropriate. Samples of acceptable consent and assent procedures may be available through your college or university's IRB website (also see sample consent letter, www.springerpub.com/school-psychology-practicum, Exhibit 5.2). Requirements may vary by institution; however, it is recommended that IRB applications and letters of approval for research at sites include the following elements:

• Name of the principal investigator (your name)
• Title of the research project
• Anticipated time frame of data collection
• Basic research methodology (type of data that will be collected, anticipated number of participants, etc.)
• Name, title, signature, and site affiliation (i.e., institution and department) of the administrator authorizing the project
• Statement indicating that the research methodology has been described to the satisfaction of the administrator and that he or she approves of the project

In projecting a timeline for the project, it will be important to ensure enough time for both the clinical service aspects of the practica obligations as well as time for the research responsibilities. Although a valuable learning experience, research cannot substitute for the applied experience necessary to develop and demonstrate core skill competencies in the practice of school psychology.

As both a supervisee and researcher at your practicum site, it is important that you uphold the highest ethical standards in your professional roles. Both the National Association of School Psychologists (NASP, 2010) and the American Psychological Association (2010) delineate ethical standards for engaging in research in the field of psychology. The standards provide an excellent framework for evaluating your conduct and for ethical decision making. Specifically, both sets of ethical codes caution against the formation of dual or multiple relationships (i.e., APA Standard 3.05 of the Ethics Code; NASP Principles of Professional Ethics Principle III.2, Principle III.4), or relationships that require a clinician to assume multiple roles in interacting with clients (e.g., interacting with students or faculty who are both your clients and study participants). These situations should be avoided, as they can compromise the integrity of your service delivery and your research.

For example, if a practica student is providing counseling services to a school-age student while also collecting dissertation data on the effectiveness of the counseling protocol, the needs of the student receiving services must be considered first. It would be important to ensure that the counseling protocol is the best match for the student's needs and not just a convenience given the research study data needs. Strong consideration that the therapeutic relationship with the child during counseling is not compromised by the desire for data or a lack of objectivity regarding the protocol also would be important. Dual or multiple relationships can and do exist in the work of school psychologists; however, they must not be exploitative, they must protect the welfare of the individual receiving services, and they must not interfere with the psychologist's ability to competently deliver the services (Behnke, 2004).

As noted in Chapter 8, NASP's ethical standards also describe expectations for handling confidential client and participant information. These standards are further supported by federal legislation such as the Family Educational Rights and Privacy Act (FERPA, 2000), which limits access to confidential educational records to parents and guardians (or, alternatively, to students aged 18 and older) and to school personnel who have a "legitimate educational interest." Additionally, in clinical sites and some school situations, the security of personable identifiable medical information will need to remain within the confidentiality boundaries of the Health Insurance Portability and Accountability Act (HIPAA) mandates if services are provided by health care providers (U.S. Department of Health and Human Services, 2015). As a general rule, all data sets removed from practicum sites must be de-identified (i.e., they must not contain any information that indicates the participants' identities, such as student identification numbers, names, and dates of birth), transported in an encrypted format, and then secured. Potential university-based collaborators who have not received permission from the district and/or the IRB to access identified data should not be given access to such information. Ultimately, it is critical that student research assistants be well informed of the ethical and legal standards that govern research conduct and the handling of protected educational and health information. As described, these standards are vital for ensuring that the appropriate protections for participants are in place.

MENTAL HEALTH SETTINGS

Acquiring a clinical site practica rotation can offer a number of benefits including opportunities to collaborate with a wide range of other mental health professionals (e.g., psychiatrists, clinical social workers), experience working with severe and chronic needs, as well as opportunities to better understand a wide range of diagnoses and the role of inpatient and outpatient treatment regimens. For individuals interested in later working with students transitioning from inpatient to homebound schooling and then back to school, these types of practica settings especially may offer new insight. Another possible benefit of clinical experience is the opportunity to work in specialized practices that are tailored to meet the needs of specific populations (e.g., spectrum center, trauma unit, anxiety clinic). These types of clinics will provide greater repeated exposure to individuals with specific disorders and needs, thus increasing the opportunities to gain expertise in providing direct targeted services in a particular area. For graduate students who plan to pursue internships in children's hospitals or clinics, and consortia that bridge school and hospital units, clinical practica experiences will greatly enhance the application.

School psychologists that serve K–12 populations generally rely on disability classification criteria outlined in the IDEIA, evaluation documentation for services as specified by their state Departments of Education statutes, intervention service models based on pedagogical literature, and programs specific to their school district. In contrast, practitioners who are employed in other settings (e.g., private practice, hospitals, outpatient clinics) utilize a medical model based on the *DSM* for disability criteria, evaluation documentation for services that aligns with insurance mandates, inpatient or outpatient treatment models, and programs specific to local community agencies. At times, practica students placed in school settings also may receive psychological reports from outside evaluators who use diagnostic language from these systems.

Because the two domains utilize differing classification systems, terminology, and service delivery taxonomies, moving from a school to a clinical practica site can be confusing at first. The easiest way to overcome this obstacle is to set aside time to memorize new terminology, review the respective new classification systems, meet with personnel at the new site to discuss their differing roles, and ask lots of questions of site supervisors. A supervisor's strong mentorship can help graduate students transition easier to new paradigms.

Practica students also may find that (a) clinical sites are more formal in their interactions, (b) billing and coding for services become an important aspect of helping children and families access services, and (c) collaboration with medical personnel regarding psychopharmacology is more common. Additionally, clinical sites present some barriers and challenges that are less prevalent in schools such as fewer opportunities for naturalistic behavioral observations, input from teachers, access to educational history and current school interventions, as well as time for direct intervention with progress monitoring data.

CLASSIFICATION MODELS BEYOND THE *DSM*

In addition to the *DSM*, several other classification systems exist and are worth mentioning for practica settings that may reference these structures. The *International Classification of Diseases* (*ICD*) is a taxonomy that can be used by mental health service providers (especially by those who work outside of school settings) for insurance billing purposes and statistical data collection (Joyce-Beaulieu & Sulkowski, in press). The *ICD* also is utilized worldwide, thus if the practica setting is in an internationally recognized hospital or treatment center, patients from other counties may have medical history documentation that references the *ICD* rather than the U.S. *DSM* system.

World Health Organization

The World Health Organization (WHO) is the United Nations' designated clearinghouse and authority on health issues worldwide. The agency has nearly 194 member countries, and provides a range of important functions. The mission of the WHO (2015a) is to offer guidance on international matters concerning health, to direct research on health problems and treatments, and to serve as a clearinghouse resource for countries striving to enhance the overall wellness of their citizens. In addition to providing information on communicable diseases and health issues, the WHO also offers intervention support guidance for disabilities and health problems.

The WHO has also developed the Family of International Classifications (WHO-FIC). The purpose of this network is to design culturally appropriate classification systems that are internationally relevant and represent multidimensional aspects of health. Two complementary international taxonomies are embedded within the WHO-FIC: the *International Classification of Functioning, Disability, and Health* (*ICF*; WHO, 2001) and the *ICD* (WHO, 2003). Together, these document prevalence, diagnostic features, and context of mental health conditions and disabilities.

International Classification of Diseases

The *ICD* is an international classification resource utilized in reporting prevalence rates and other features of diseases. It offers a common system of categories for comparing the incidence and impact of health conditions internationally. The *ICD* is used widely by practitioners and researchers for diagnosis. The most recent version, the *ICD-10–Clinical Modification* (*ICD-10-CM*), was published in 2015 (World Health Organization, 2015b) and the *ICD-11* version is expected to release in 2017. The current *DSM-5* appendix includes corresponding *ICD-10-CM* codes to assist in collaborating across the two classification systems (American Psychiatric Association, 2013).

International Classification of Functioning, Disability, and Health

In contrast to the *ICD*, the *ICF* delineates functioning and disability. The WHO (2010) describes disability as an overarching term that refers to impairments (i.e., body function or structure), activity limitations (i.e., difficulty performing tasks), and participation restrictions (i.e., problems with group activities). In this guide, disability is acknowledged to be a complex phenomenon that reflects the ways individuals' physical abilities and/or capacities interact with the environment (e.g., social institutions and physical surroundings).

The *ICF* classifies health in two parts: (1) functioning and disability; and (2) environmental and personal contextual factors (WHO, 2010). Functioning and disability are noted in the context of body functions and structures as well as activities and participation. Body functions include several psychological functions (e.g., intellect, personality, and memory). They can also refer to physical abilities demonstrated in sensory and neuromuscular functions (Joyce & Dempsey, 2009). The second part of this system discusses environmental and personal contextual factors (WHO, 2010). These include a range of external elements that either impede or facilitate functioning (e.g., assistive technology, human support, community agency services, and general policies [Joyce & Dempsey, 2009]).

A strength of the *ICF* model is that it prompts professionals to assess ecological factors in evaluating individuals' strengths and limitations. The classification format acknowledges that physical impairments demonstrate differently depending on the context of the various environmental and personal factors that either impede or enhance an individual's daily routines.

CHAPTER REVIEW

This chapter has provided several examples of advanced practica training opportunities that may be available through your graduate program. These practica may involve coordinating transition services for college-age students with disabilities, conducting forensic evaluations, developing research projects, and providing services in hospitals, among other experiences. As you prepare for practicum experiences outside of the schools, it is important to be aware of the range of diagnostic tools (e.g., *DSM*, *ICD*, and *ICF*) and interventions used by practitioners in other types of settings. To ensure that you are on track to pursue an advanced practicum in your chosen area of specialization, it is helpful to discuss professional interests with an advisor and practicum coordinator early on in your graduate studies. Overall, advanced practica can provide valuable opportunities for developing in-depth, specialized knowledge, and for making a smooth transition to the internship experience.

REFERENCES

American Psychiatric Association. (2013). *Diagnostic and statistical manual of mental disorders* (5th ed.). Washington, DC: American Psychiatric Publishing.

American Psychological Association. (2010). *Ethical principles of psychologists and code of conduct (2002, Amended June 1, 2010)*. Retrieved from http://www.apa.org.ezproxy.montclair.edu:2048/ethics/code/index.aspx

Americans with Disabilities Act of 1990. 42 U.S.C.A. § 12101.

Americans with Disabilities Amendments Act of 2008, Pub. L. No. 110–325, 42, U.S.C.A. § 12101–12102.

Annon, J. S. (1994). Recommended guidelines for interviewing children in cases of alleged sexual abuse. *American Journal of Forensic Psychology, 1*(6), 17–21.

Association on Higher Education and Disability. (2012). *Supporting accommodation requests: Guidance on documentation practices*. Retrieved from https://www.ahead.org/uploads/docs/resources/Final_AHEAD_Supporting%20Accommodation%20Requests%20with%20Q&A%2009_12.pdf

Association on Higher Education and Disability. (2015a). *Foundational principles for the review of documentation and the determination of accommodations*. Retrieved from http://www.ahead.org/resources/best-practices-resources/principles

Association on Higher Education and Disability. (2015b). *Seven elements of quality disability documentation*. Retrieved from http://www.ahead.org/resources/best-practices-resources/elements

Behnke, S. (2004). Multiple relationships and APA's new Ethics Code: Values and applications. *Monitor on Psychology: Ethics Rounds, 35*(1), 66.

Cutler, B. L., & Zapf, P. A. (2015). *APA handbook of forensic psychology, Vol. 2: Criminal investigation, adjudication, and sentencing outcomes*. Washington, DC: American Psychological Association.

DeClue, G. (2013). Years of predicting dangerously. *Open Access Journal of Forensic Psychology, 5*, 16–28.

Department of Health and Human Services. (2009). *Code of federal regulations. Title 45, Public Welfare; Part 46, Protection of human subjects*. Retrieved from http://www.hhs.gov/ohrp/policy/ohrpregulations.pdf

Educational Testing Service. (2007). *Documenting learning disabilities: Policy statement for documentation of learning disability in adolescents and adults* (2nd ed.). Retrieved from https://www.ets.org/s/disabilities/pdf/documenting_learning_disabilities.pdf

Educational Testing Service. (2012). *Guidelines for documentation of psychiatric disabilities in adolescents and adults* (2nd ed.). Retrieved from https://www.ets.org/s/disabilities/pdf/documenting_psychiatric_disabilities.pdf

Educational Testing Service. (2015). *Disability documentation policies*. Retrieved from https://www.ets.org/disabilities/documentation/

Family Educational Rights and Privacy Act of 2000. 20 U.S. C. A. § 1232g et seq.

Foster, E. E., Strohmaier, H., Filone, S., Murphy, M., Galloway, M., & DeMatteo, D. (2013). The importance of safety training in forensic psychology graduate programs. *Open Access Journal of Forensic Psychology, 5*, 1–15.

Fries, D., Rossegger, A., Endrass, J., & Singh, J. P. (2013). Utility of a violence screening tool to predict recidivism in offenders with schizophrenia: A total forensic cohort study. *Open Access Journal of Forensic Psychology, 5*, 40–52.

Gormley, S., Hughes, C., Block, L., & Lendmann, C. (2005). Eligibility assessment requirements at the postsecondary level for students with learning disabilities: A disconnect with secondary schools? *Journal of Postsecondary Education and Disability, 18*, 63–70.

Individuals with Disabilities Education Improvement Act of 2004. 20 U.S.C. § 1400 et seq.

Joyce, D., & Dempsey, A. (2009). The *DSM* model of impairment. In S. Goldstein & J. Naglieri (Eds.), *Assessment of impairment: From theory to practice*. New York, NY: Springer Publishing Company.

Joyce, D., & Grapin, S. L. (2012). School psychologists' role in facilitating successful postsecondary transitions for students with disabilities. *Communiqué, 41*(1), 20–24.

Joyce-Beaulieu, D., & Grapin, S. L. (2014). Support beyond high school for those with mental illness. *Phi Delta Kappan, 96*, 29–33.

Joyce-Beaulieu, D. K., & Sulkowski, M. L. (in press). The *DSM* model of impairment. In S. Goldstein & J. A. Naglieri (Eds.), *Assessing impairment: From theory to practice*. New York, NY: Springer Publishing Company.

Karp, M. M., Calcagno, J. C., Hughes, K. L., Jeong, D. W., & Bailey, T. R. (2007). *The postsecondary achievement of participants in dual enrollment: An analysis of student outcomes in two states*. St. Paul, MN: National Research Center for Career and Technical Education.

National Association of School Psychologists. (2010). *Principles for professional ethics*. Bethesda, MD: Author. Retrieved from http://www.nasponline.org/standards/2010standards/1_%20Ethical%20Principles.pdf

National Joint Committee on Learning Disabilities. (2007). *The documentation disconnect for students with learning disabilities: Improving access to postsecondary disability services*. Retrieved from http://www.ahead.org/uploads/docs/resources/njld_paper.pdf

U.S. Department of Health and Human Services. (2015). *Health information privacy*. Retrieved from http://www.hhs.gov/ocr/privacy/hipaa/understanding/consumers/index.html

U.S. Department of Labor. (2014). *The why, when, what, and how of disclosure in an academic setting after high school*. Retrieved from http://www.dol.gov/odep/pubs/fact/wwwh.htm

Ward, J. T. (2013). What is forensic psychology? *American Psychological Association: Psychology Student Network*. Retrieved from http://www.apa.org/ed/precollege/psn/2013/09/forensic-psychology.aspx

World Health Organization. (2001). *International classification of functioning, disability, and health*. Geneva, Switzerland: Author.

World Health Organization. (2010). *International statistical classification of diseases and related health problems: Instruction manual* (10th ed.). Retrieved from http://www.who.int/classifications/icd/ICD10Volume2_en_2010.pdf?ua=1

World Health Organization. (2015a). *About WHO*. Retrieved from http://www.who.int/about/en/

World Health Organization. (2015b). *International classification of diseases* (10th ed.). Retrieved from http://www.cdc.gov/nchs/icd/icd10cm.htm#icd2014

SECTION II

Internship

CHAPTER 6

Preparing for Internship

LEARNING OBJECTIVES

At the conclusion of this chapter, readers should be able to:

1. Develop a professional internship curriculum vita (CV)

2. Identify appropriate internship sites to meet program requirements and professional goals

3. Successfully navigate the internship application process

As course work and practica experiences draw to a close, graduate students in school psychology must now begin to consider their applications for internship. Given the role of internship in graduate preparation and finding employment after graduation, internship is among the most important decisions in graduate school. Regardless of the anticipated internship setting, all school psychology graduate students should prepare an effective and updated CV.[1]

WRITING A WINNING CURRICULUM VITA

A CV differs from a résumé—a CV is longer and more detailed, whereas a résumé typically is no longer than two pages. Both are designed to outline your education and professional experiences. The purpose of your CV is to focus on your selling points rather than provide a bulleted list. No standard format or structure exists for a CV, as it can be tailored to best highlight your

---

[1] There is regular confusion around whether to use "vita" or "vitae" when referring to your CV. Technically, "curriculum vitae" is a more accurate spelling based on its Latin origins, although "curriculum vita" has become more commonly used, as has the acronym CV. The plural of CV is "curriculum vitae."

skills relevant to the context. For example, applicants for more clinically based internship sites might prefer to highlight involvement in clinical settings or research opportunities, whereas those applying for school placements may prefer to list their varied school experiences first. Despite this flexibility, some basic components should always be included (see Exhibits 6.3 to 6.5 at www.springerpub.com/school-psychology-practicum).

Header and Contact Information

Place your contact information at the top of the CV, including your name and any graduate degrees or credentials you already hold (e.g., Brian Smith, MEd), mailing address, phone number, and e-mail address. This information is typically centered at the very top of the CV, with the name having the largest font of the entire CV. Be mindful of the outgoing message on the phone number provided on your professional CV. Additionally, ensure that the e-mail address is professionally appropriate; avoid nicknames, pet names, slang, or hobbies as part of your e-mail address.

Education

Identify the institutions attended along with the degree obtained (e.g., BA, MEd) and major area of study. Do not include information about high school, even if you graduated with honors. Graduate students should include dates, including an expected date of graduation from the current program. Upon graduation, many professionals choose not to include graduation dates on their CV. Depending on the intended setting, this section also can include any distinctions (e.g., magna cum laude), thesis or dissertation titles, declared specialties, or an advisor's name. Including grade point average (GPA) is not necessary, particularly for graduate-level education (Peña, 2008). Generally, education experiences should be ordered with the most recent (i.e., current program) first in descending chronological order. This general principle should be applied across all sections of the CV.

Experience

Any noteworthy professional experiences can be listed here. This can include practica or internship experiences, volunteer experiences, graduate assistantships, leadership experiences, editorial work, or other related work experiences. For example, a school psychology graduate student may include his or her practica site(s), a teaching assistantship, a day-care center where he or she volunteered, and previous experiences at a local crisis center, as a teacher's aide, or even acting as a group director at a summer camp. Graduate students that served leadership roles on campus or in state, regional, or national professional associations should also highlight those experiences.

When identifying each experience, graduate students should include the dates and names of the supervisor(s), and may also wish to include some of the specific activities and roles of that position. For example, a graduate student may wish to highlight his or her role in helping implement a school-wide violence prevention program in a high school as part of a practicum experience. A listing of research assistantships can highlight any relevant activities you participated in such as study design, data collection and analysis, and dissemination. In some instances, it may be helpful to specifically identify your work (e.g., completed over 80 hours of direct observation as part of the data collection process), although you should avoid having overly lengthy descriptions of your role or responsibilities.

Graduate students that hope to establish a research agenda and to highlight research experiences may wish to include those experiences (e.g., research assistantships, fellowships) at the top of this section. Another option is to develop different headers for each category of experience, such as "professional experiences," "graduate assistantships," "research experiences," "leadership experiences," and "volunteer experiences." Again, each individual can tailor the CV to fit his or her professional needs and best highlight personal strengths.

Professional Publications and Presentations

Presenting and publishing professionally suggests that you have the skills to write and effectively communicate information for a professional audience. Even if you do not plan to pursue an academic career, highlighting any of these experiences demonstrates your commitment to research-based practice and involvement within the professional school psychology community. Presentations can also include delivery of parent workshops or presentations to a local parent teacher association (PTA). Publications and presentations should each have their own section heading, with all listings cited using American Psychological Association (APA) style formatting. Some elect to have separate headings for different types of presentations (e.g., "conference presentations" and "workshops or in-services") as well as different types of publications (e.g., peer-reviewed in academic journals and non–peer-reviewed such as newsletters or book chapters) to highlight the differences in audiences and outlets.

Specific Skills or Areas of Proficiency

Some individuals may wish to include a section on specific skills, if applicable, such as familiarity with certain interventions (e.g., cognitive behavioral intervention for trauma in schools, Picture Exchange Communication System), language fluency, grant writing, or familiarity with particular statistical programs. Having a dedicated section should be considered based on the individual as well as the audience. An alternative to a separate heading could be mentioning these skills when describing duties and roles within the "Experiences" section. For example, within a description of your role in a practicum setting, you might mention that you administered bilingual assessments or provided a specific intervention. Those with research experience may highlight some of the statistical programs used as part of their roles on research projects or assistantships.

Professional Association Membership

Similar to professional presentations and publications, professional membership demonstrates a commitment to active engagement within the school psychology community. It is important to qualify the type of membership (e.g., National Association of School Psychologists [NASP], Student Member).

Credentials and Awards

Awards and current credentials obtained should each be listed under a separate heading. Listing credentials would be relevant for graduate students that have obtained related credentials prior to enrolling in the program, such as a teaching credential or even a state school psychology credential. This could also include any specialized trainings completed, such as NASP's PREPaRE: School Crisis Prevention and Intervention Training Curriculum (www.nasponline.org/prepare/index.aspx). You can also note if you have applied or expect to become eligible for a particular credential.

Other Considerations

The sections already discussed highlight what we consider necessary components of any CV. Other optional components that may be considered include:

- Conference attendance
- Courses completed
- Assessment measures administered
- References and contact information (be sure to notify those individuals if they are identified). Another option is to state at the bottom of your CV: "References available upon request"

The CV should be well-written. Review your CV numerous times for consistent fonts and spacing, accurate spelling and grammar, and elimination of distracting fonts or heavy bolding or underlining. Maintain consistency in descriptions throughout as well; for example, avoid describing your role in one section in the first person (e.g., I attended team meetings), and then describing your role elsewhere in the third person (e.g., research assistants maintained responsibility for obtaining child assent prior to the study). Additionally, be consistent in tense when describing roles and responsibilities; a common error is to use present tense in one section and past tense in another. Avoid overstating any skills or experiences, as that will often do more harm than good. Even if those embellishments help get you an internship, discovery of inaccuracies during the internship may make it difficult to get a job at that site or retain a quality reference letter when applying for other jobs. Finally, have others review the CV for input, or consider bringing your CV to faculty or even the writing center at your institution.

Remember that a CV is a living document. Throughout one's career, the CV will change as new accomplishments are added and experiences removed that at one point seemed relevant but are no longer important to mention. Update your CV regularly.

SELECTING INTERNSHIP SITES

Selecting an internship site presents an exciting yet potentially stressful opportunity. Despite the excitement of nearing the end of the program, graduate students must now consider lots of variables including geography; supervision; availability of a stipend; program requirements and national standards; credentialing opportunities; potential for future employment; and for doctoral candidates, setting (school, clinic, hospital, and consortium) and whether to pursue an APA-accredited or an Association of Psychology Postdoctoral and Internship Centers (APPIC) internship.

Internship Standards and Guidelines

NASP sets internship standards for both specialist- and doctoral-level students. Additionally, the APA, the Council for Directors of School Psychology Programs (CDSPP, 2012), and APPIC (2011) set their own standards, although with an exclusive focus on doctoral-level internships (Appendix A, Exhibits A.1 and A.2).

Not all preparation programs require their interns to meet all of these standards (i.e., NASP, APA, CDSPP, and APPIC). However, all prospective interns who plan to pursue credentialing and/or licensure should familiarize themselves with the various internship standards and guidelines of the state they wish to ultimately practice in, as that state's licensing requirements may have more stringent requirements than graduate programs, especially for doctoral-level students seeking psychologist licenses.

Program Requirements

Graduate students should identify their program's internship requirements and discuss them with program faculty. Some programs may identify more rigorous expectations or requirements than those listed in Table 6.1. Students in newly developed programs, or those currently seeking NASP or APA program accreditation, should start conversations early with faculty about anticipated changes in expectations and any special considerations involving internship planning in order to be eligible to meet licensure or certification requirements. Ideally, students form strong relationships with faculty and arrange for regular opportunities to discuss internship options and opportunities in the years leading up to internship.

School Settings

Specialist-level school psychology students typically pursue a full-time internship in a school setting. Many doctoral-level students also

TABLE 6.1 Internship Standards and Guidelines

	NASP (2010)		APA (2013a)	CDSPP (2012)	APPIC (2011)
	SPECIALIST LEVEL	**DOCTORAL LEVEL**	**DOCTORAL LEVEL**	**DOCTORAL LEVEL**	**DOCTORAL LEVEL**
Hours	≥1,200	≥1,500	No fewer than 10 months for school psychology internships (12 months for others)	≥1,500	≥1,500
Setting	≥600 in school setting[a,b]		Not specified	Not specified	Not specified
Supervision	An average of at least 2 hours of field-based supervision per week		At least 4 hours per week, with at least 2 from individual supervision from doctoral-level licensed psychologist	At least 2 hours individual supervision per week and at least 2 more hours in either group or individual supervision per week	No less than 1 hour for every 20 internship hours Expected that interns receive supervision from at least 2 different supervisors

(continued)

6: PREPARING FOR INTERNSHIP • 101

TABLE 6.1 Internship Standards and Guidelines (*continued*)

	NASP (2010)		APA (2013a)	CDSPP (2012)	APPIC (2011)
	SPECIALIST LEVEL	DOCTORAL LEVEL	DOCTORAL LEVEL	DOCTORAL LEVEL	DOCTORAL LEVEL
Supervisor	Appropriately credentialed school psychologist; if outside school setting, must be appropriately credentialed for that setting		Doctoral-level psychologist with appropriate credential for that setting	Doctoral-level psychologist with independent practice credential	Doctoral-level; clearly designated as clinically responsible for the cases supervised
Specific service requirement			≥25% providing direct services	≥25% providing direct face-to-face services	At least 2 hours per week in didactic activities such as case conference or seminars

[a] NASP defines a "school setting" as "one in which the primary goal is the education of students of diverse backgrounds, characteristics, abilities, disabilities, and needs. Generally, a school setting includes students who are enrolled in Grades pre-K–12 and has both general education and special education services. The school setting has available an internal or external pupil services unit that includes at least one state-credentialed school psychologist and provides a full range of school psychology services" (NASP, 2010, p. 8).

[b] "Programs may allow doctoral candidates who have met the internship requirement of at least 600 hours in a school setting through a prior, appropriately supervised, specialist-level internship or equivalent experience in school psychology to complete the entire 1,500+ hour doctoral school psychology internship in another internship setting that includes appropriately supervised and relevant school psychology activities in other educational contexts, as consistent with the school psychology program's goals and policies" (NASP, 2010, p. 8).

APA, American Psychological Association; APPIC, Association of Psychology Postdoctoral and Internship Centers; CDSPP, Council of Directors of School Psychology Programs; NASP, National Association of School Psychologists.

pursue internships in a school setting. The type of school setting for an internship can vary significantly, however. Consider whether the district can offer a range of experiences related to both the population and the services provided. Some districts allow interns the opportunity to participate in brief "rotations" in specialized centers or settings within the district to help create a broad and diverse learning experience. Other districts may be willing to customize an experience of that nature if the infrastructure is not already built in. Importantly, a full-time internship placement in a school that only serves a specific age group or population may not meet the definition of "school setting" within NASP standards (see Table 6.1). Private schools may be an appropriate internship site, although similarly may have difficulty meeting the definition of a school setting, or perhaps may not be viewed as sufficient for meeting the requirements of the graduate program.

Prospective interns should also consider whether the district has had interns in the past, has an organized and structured internship program (e.g., including history of sample contracts, university agreements), and whether it plans to have more than one intern. A district that does not have an established internship program or opportunities for more than one intern may be cause for concern about the quality of the internship.

Doctoral students pursuing a school-based internship should also be sure the internship will meet the 1,500 hours requirement and that appropriate supervision is available. For example, doctoral students looking to follow APA and CDSPP guidelines may wish to inquire about the availability of doctoral-level supervisors that maintain a credential with the board of psychology, which may be helpful if there is any intention to pursue licensure for independent practice. Despite views to the contrary, only a handful of states explicitly require an APA/Canadian Psychological Association (CPA) accredited or APPIC internship to be eligible for an independent practice license. All other states allow for an experience viewed as equivalent or meeting the standards and regulations of the state board; in many states the school setting with proper supervision and experiences can meet eligibility requirements. Various state requirements can be viewed by visiting the Association of State and Provincial Psychology Boards (ASPPB) website (www.asppb.net).

Doctoral students may consider applying to internships with school placements that also maintain APA accreditation or listing in the APPIC directory, although the availability of positions is quite limited. Based on a search conducted in fall 2014 on the APPIC website (www.appic.org), only 10 sites were listed on the APPIC directory as school districts, with only 5 of those maintaining APA accreditation. While other school placements exist through approximately 38 consortia that include school sites or rotations as part of the internship (Harris, in press), the general availability of internship sites through this process may seem limited for the majority of school psychology students that plan to meet the NASP standard of having at least 600 hours in a school setting.

Clinical Settings

Some doctoral school psychology students may plan to pursue internship settings that either blend school and clinical settings, or are almost exclusively clinical in nature. In fact, over one quarter of predoctoral school psychology interns in APA-accredited sites were based in nonschool settings (Harris, in press). Generally, clinical settings refer to those outside of a traditional school including hospitals, clinics, consortia, or even private practice. Some doctoral-level programs, particularly those with APA accreditation, may strongly encourage students to pursue some type of internship experience that includes at least some time in a clinical setting. Ask program faculty, your advisor, or the internship coordinator about expectations for doctoral-level internships as early as possible.

When referring to Table 6.1, one may notice the requirement for at least 600 hours in a school setting, which may preclude participation in a purely clinical setting. However, NASP standards allow for programs to determine whether previous internship or equivalent experiences may satisfy that particular requirement, which would then allow for such a placement (see footnote b in Table 6.1). The total required hours for internship does not change, however.

APA-Accredited and APPIC Internships

Advanced doctoral students have likely heard of or considered pursuing APA-accredited and APPIC internships. First, it's important to point out that they are not synonymous terms. APPIC internships refer to those listed as part of the APPIC process. APPIC was formed in 1968 with the intention to help provide a central database of internship programs and to facilitate the application and selection process. APPIC works with the National Matching Services Incorporated, an independent company that facilitates the process of matching interns with sites. The APPIC website (www.appic.org) provides a host of information including directories and statistics about the internship sites, such as number of applicants, expected slots, and preferred degree programs. Although APPIC does not accredit internships, agencies or sites must meet a set of membership criteria in order to be listed (www.appic.org/About-APPIC/Joining-APPIC/Members/Internship-Membership-Criteria).

APA-accredited internships are specific internship sites that participate in a periodic peer-reviewed process to ensure that they meet existing internship standards. All APA-accredited internships meet the membership requirements for APPIC, although not all APPIC listed internships are APA-accredited. Access to APA-accredited internships generally occurs through the APPIC process or through programs that have a direct affiliation with an internship site. Doctoral students should recognize that state boards of psychology or specific employers in clinical settings may prefer or even require an APA-accredited internship over those listed on the APPIC directory, so those choosing to go through the process should consider whether they only wish to apply to APA-accredited internship sites listed in the APPIC directory. Notably, beginning with the 2017 to 2018 APPIC match process for 2018 to 2019 internships, only doctoral students from APA-accredited programs or programs approved for a site visit can enter the match.

In fall 2014, with over 700 available internship sites listed in the APPIC directory, only 229 sites accepted applications from school psychology graduate students. Among those, only 139 maintained APA accreditation. Most concerning is that among those sites accepting school psychology applicants, approximately two thirds expressed a preference for applicants from clinical or counseling programs (Harris, in press).

Of note is the competitive nature and long recognized "internship imbalance," which refers to the consistently high number of prospective interns applying for an insufficient number of APPIC or APA-accredited internship positions. Overall, the match rate in 2014 for all doctoral-level psychology students (clinical, counseling, and school) was 79.8%, with approximately 75% of those matching at an APA-accredited site (Keilin, 2014). However, match rates for applicants from school psychology programs was only 69.5%.

On an individual basis, 593 doctoral-level school psychology interns were reported in 2013 to 2014 (Rossen & von der Embse, 2014), yet in that same year only 163 positions were available in APA-accredited internships that stated a preference for applicants from either school or combined programs (Harris, in press). Not all 593 interns applied through the match, though, with a reported 233 applicants from school psychology programs and another 103 from combined programs (Keilin, 2014). Match rates were notably higher for applicants in PhD programs compared to those in PsyD programs (Harris, in press).

Stipends

Among all agencies that review and accredit programs, internship stipends are either strongly encouraged or required. NASP (2014) notes "sites are strongly encouraged to provide interns a stipend that recognizes their graduate level of training and the value of services they provide." APA and APPIC note that unfunded internship positions are strongly discouraged and only allowable in rare, unusual, and infrequent circumstances. Both APA and APPIC further state the expectation for stipend equity across each site. CDSPP describes a standard for each intern to receive a written statement or contract that includes information related to salary and other benefits.

Approximately 61% of specialist-level students and 79% of doctoral-level students in school psychology receive internship stipends of any amount (Prus, Colvard, & Swerdlik, 2014). The figures varied significantly by region, with the lowest percentages of stipends available in the Northeast (32% and 67% for specialist level and doctoral level, respectively) and the highest in the Central region (76% and 90% for specialist level and doctoral level, respectively). Prus et al. (2014) note additional variability within each region, with some states reporting a 0% stipend rate and others close to 100%.

Average stipend amounts also ranged substantially, with average stipends of over $25,000 in the Central region, and less than $15,000 in the Northeast. Overall, doctoral-level stipends were higher than those for specialist-level students ($21,409 and $19,238), although differences based on degree level in the Central and Southeast regions were negligible. To help compare, APPIC (2014) and APA (2013b) noted an average median stipend for all doctoral students (including those from counseling, clinical, and combined programs) of $24,000.

Other Considerations

All interns must balance many factors when selecting sites, including geography and impact on family. All prospective interns should also consider the implications for credentialing in any of the states they expect to work in. Interns should avoid simply selecting sites based on perceived prestige and give more attention to factors related to fit, quality of training, alignment with the program, and career goals. Finally, for interns attending sites far from the program's institution, a plan should be determined for how university supervision will be provided (see Chapter 8 for more on telesupervision). To be safe, graduate students should always discuss their ideas and options with appropriate program faculty before completing any application or making final internship decisions.

APPLICATION PROCESS

Applying for internships may bring back all the fond memories of applying for graduate programs, and to some degree, the process is quite similar. First, a decision should be made on how many sites to apply to. Those engaging in a more competitive application process, such as those going through the APPIC process, may prefer to apply to up to 15 internship sites (Sulkowski, 2011). Those applying through the APPIC process may also want to consider submitting applications to both highly competitive and less competitive sites, which can be determined by looking at the available data for each site on the APPIC website (www.appic.org). Others may only need to apply to four or five sites.

Timeline

Ideally, graduate students should start considering internship plans and options approximately 1 year before application deadlines (Sulkowski, 2011), setting reasonable and manageable goals along the way. Notably, application deadlines vary substantially. APPIC internship applications typically require far more time to complete and are due in November, whereas school-based internships not listed in the APPIC directory are often due anytime from December through March or April to start the following July or August. Some school-based internship sites may start accepting applications as early as November or December and consider candidates on a rolling basis until available slots are filled, so ideally expect to have your materials ready for submission no later than November or December (including reference letters). See Sulkowski (2011) for a more detailed timeline and description of the APPIC application process for doctoral students, including information about the various essays required.

For those applying directly to school districts, consider contacting each site separately via e-mail or a phone call to state an interest in applying and asking whether they anticipate having any available internship openings. Avoid simply sending in your application materials, as each site may have specific requests or requirements to apply. Ask your faculty or previous graduates of your program if there are any connections in the sites you may have interest in; they can help connect you, put in a good word, offer a letter of reference, or in some cases steer you in a different direction.

STATEMENT OF INTEREST

Most internship applications will include a statement of interest, which can serve as your cover letter (see Exhibits B.4 and B.5 in Appendix B, and Exhibit 6.6 at www.springerpub.com/school-psychology-practicum). This statement allows you to articulate your professional interests and ambitions, describe your enthusiasm and interest in the internship site, and demonstrate your professional writing skills. Similar to the CV, there are multiple methods and styles to writing a successful statement of interest, although some key points are important to consider (Hodges, 2011).

Style and Length

Maintain a professional appearance, including an appropriate greeting (e.g., Dear Dr. Smith or Dear Internship Committee). If applicable, place on letterhead with a date and address. Use standard fonts, such as Times New Roman. Use first person to discuss experiences and interests. The letter should be succinct and generally no more than two pages.

Opening Paragraph(s)

The opening paragraph should immediately identify your interest or goals (i.e., pursuing a predoctoral school psychology internship with _____).

Explain why this particular site is of interest to you in the context of knowing about the site. This shows that you aren't simply copying and pasting your statement or submitting a standard statement to dozens of sites, and that you have done appropriate background research to make the case for a good fit. As an example, you might highlight that the school district has a diverse student population with a high number of children of immigrants, which would allow you to pursue experiences working with varying cultures. Another example could be that the district's school psychologists actively participate and lead district-level crisis response or positive behavior supports, which align with your professional interests.

Highlight Your Experiences

The statement of interest offers a great opportunity to showcase your unique experiences and skills while acknowledging your interest in developing and growing as a future practitioner. Sell yourself as a competent professional while also demonstrating that you recognize your role as an incoming supervisee that is ready to learn. Cite your professional experiences thus far and how they can help contribute to the current work of the internship site; how you believe the site is a great fit with your strengths and interests; and can support your professional growth. Importantly, clearly identify your personal goals related to training experiences and career aspirations.

End Strong

Conclude with a statement about why you believe the structure of the internship site is ideally suited for your needs. Offer thanks for considering your application and that you look forward to meeting and discussing this opportunity further. Provide your contact information again even though the information is available on the CV.

INTERVIEW

Most internship sites will request an interview. Similar to your interview experience when applying to school psychology graduate programs, the interview offers an opportunity for both the student and the internship site to determine goodness of fit. In fact, many internship directors note that many of the final decisions or offers come down to the fit related to personalities, goals, and expectations (Chamberlin, 2006).

Format

Graduate students should be prepared to possibly engage in a variety of different interview formats, particularly for those applying to numerous internship sites. Formats may include:

- Single, face-to-face interview with one or two people
- Group or panel interview
- Rotations or individual interviews with different staff and/or current interns
- Telephone interview
- Online interview using web technology and webcams

Additionally, some interview sites may ask you to participate in an on-site activity. For example, you may be asked to review some information about a case and share what process you would follow to address the concern. Other sites may give you an allotted time to develop a writing sample on the spot, such as writing the introduction to a report or an analysis based on a case study given to you. Upon receiving an invitation for an interview, feel free to ask about the format prior to arriving.

The Basics

Some basic interview suggestions, while seemingly intuitive, may make for an easier and less stressful experience:

- Bring water with you—there may not always be water available to you
- Bring gum—particularly for the full day interviews
- If flying, avoid checking your bag, as you don't want to get stuck without your interview outfit if your bag is misplaced or lost
- Bring copies of your CV
- Bring your own notepad and pens
- Be early
- Dress professionally
- Do your best to remember everyone's name. Write down their name, ask for a card, or ask them how they spell it—whatever technique is needed. Knowing names is helpful in making a connection and for identifying those individuals when you send a follow-up thank you note after the interview
- Thoroughly research the internship site ahead of time. Know about the location, the history, the staff and the population served, and use that to ask informed questions during the interview. If possible, learn about the interviewers and their professional interests
- Expect to spend some money. Nearly all internship sites will expect you to pay your own way to the interview, which may include the flight, hotel,

ground transportation, and food. For those applying to multiple locations out of town, be sure to budget for those expenses ahead of time

Interviewing the Interviewer

As stated earlier, the interview offers the potential intern an opportunity to learn more about the internship site and determine the quality of fit. Coming prepared with a set of questions to ask demonstrates preparedness, interest, and commitment to finding a good internship placement. In fact, some interviewers will expect interviewees to ask some questions. Questions should demonstrate some basic understanding of the internship site already. If you only have an opportunity to ask a few questions, avoid the general questions that would apply to any internship site, and consider questions specific to that placement. And while the best questions are often those that flow from the current conversation, having prepared questions offers a good backup plan.

Some potential questions to the staff or internship director may include:

- How much time is typically devoted to assessment, direct and indirect student-level services, or systems-level services for interns?
- Are there specific expectations for interns related to number of cases or specific activities?
- Please describe the method of supervision throughout the year. Does this method change as the interns develop more skills?
- What do you hope your interns achieve during their internship year?
- Are there opportunities to participate in professional development activities?
- Are there opportunities to participate in district-led initiatives, leadership, or research?
- What are the typical travel expectations for interns (e.g., between schools)?
- Do you ever hire interns for full-time positions after completion of the internship?
- What do you look for most in an intern?
- What are some of the greatest strengths of this district/internship site?
- What is the ratio of school psychologists to students? How many schools are typically assigned to the school psychologists?
- How do you handle conflicts that may emerge?
- Is there a workspace for the interns?
- How many internship hours do interns receive by the end of the year?
- What are some future directions for the district/internship site?

Internship sites will often give applicants an opportunity to talk with current interns. This is a great opportunity to hear from fellow graduate students fully enmeshed in the process. Note that while they are your peers, you want to maintain a professional demeanor, as the staff may ask the current interns about their impressions before making any final offers.

Some potential questions to current interns may include:

- What are the best components of the internship?
- Why did you choose this internship placement?
- What are some components you wish would change or be different? What is most frustrating to you?
- Do you plan to apply for a position here next year?
- Describe the district or students/families served.
- Do you feel supported?
- How often do you get to work or communicate with each other as interns (if there are multiple interns)?
- Please describe a typical week.
- How often do you get to engage with other school psychologists on staff aside from your supervisors?
- What is it like to live in the area?

Finally, avoid questions that demonstrate you know little about the internship site or did no research leading up to the interview. Questions that can be easily answered from the website should not be asked.

Questions to Anticipate

It's helpful to anticipate some commonly asked questions for school psychology internship interviews. As noted, the best interviews become conversations, with the preset questions facilitating in-depth discussion. It would be difficult to include every possible question, although the following will give you a sense of what to expect and an opportunity to practice:

- Please describe a conflict and how you handled it. (Note: It's acceptable to describe the conflict, even if you assume some fault. Importantly, don't speak overly critically of other people, and instead focus on what you learned and how you grew from the experience.)
- Discuss your practicum experiences.
- Describe a difficult case and how you handled it.
- Have you ever experienced a conflict with a student's parent or family? Describe what happened?
- Do you have experiences working with diverse populations? Are there populations you hope to work with during your internship?
- What are your strengths (professional and personal)?
- What are your weaknesses?
- What areas do you hope to develop during your internship year?
- What is your career plan? Where do you see yourself in 5 years?

- Why do you want this internship? (Avoid saying things such as "It's close to home," or "You offer the best stipend." Even if that is true, focus instead on the merits of the educational experience you expect to have.)
- What do you know about our district/site?
- Why did you choose a career in school psychology?
- What tests are you comfortable with? What interventions are you comfortable with? (You may receive more specific questions regarding techniques depending on the internship site.)
- Tell us about yourself. What do you like to do in your personal time?
- When do you plan on completing your thesis/dissertation?
- Are you interviewing elsewhere? (Be honest, noting that you did an exhaustive search prior to selecting the internship sites to apply to.)
- Do you have preferences for setting (e.g., pre-K, elementary school, middle school, or high school)?
- How would you describe the role of a school psychologist?
- What are your views on multitiered systems of support (MTSS) or response to intervention (RtI) approaches?
- What approach do you use for identifying specific learning disabilities?

Practice these questions with your peers, or perhaps with faculty, an internship coordinator, or even a practicum supervisor who can give you input from different perspectives. Responding to the questions aloud will help you deliver a more polished response during the actual interview.

It's common to get frazzled by a question during an interview. It's completely acceptable to apply some "stall tactics" to give you a moment to relax and respond to the question as calmly and thoughtfully as possible. Sulkowski (2011) notes some potential scripts to use:

- That is an interesting question. May I take a moment to think about it?
- Can you please rephrase the question so I'm sure I know what you are asking?
- It sounds like you want to know more about _____, is that correct?
- Would you like me to discuss _____?

After the Interview

At the conclusion of the interview and prior to leaving, thank everyone that you met, including the person who offered you water when you walked in or showed you where to find the restroom. Do your best to thank everyone by name, and highlight some of the components that excite you the most about the internship. For example, you might say, "I'm so appreciative of the opportunity to meet you all today and hear more about what this internship has to offer. I'm particularly excited about the opportunity to learn more about the Early Childhood Center for Students with Autism and Developmental

Delays, as that's an area of interest for me." Being specific demonstrates that you have been listening. Additionally, internship sites want to make offers to those they think will likely accept an offer; showing interest conveys that likelihood.

Within the week after the interview, consider sending a thank you note to all those you had interviewed with. A single card in the mail intended for the entire interview team, or even an e-mail, demonstrates professionalism and respect and the skills to develop positive relationships—qualities any supervisor would look for in an intern or employee. In the letter, recite again some specific components of the internship that piqued your interest, ending that you look forward to hearing from them and hopefully working and learning from them in the future.

LETTERS OF RECOMMENDATION

Letters of recommendation represent an important component of the application process. Be sure to ask for recommendations from individuals that can speak to your attributes in a positive way, and reflect your range of experiences. Some basic tips include:

- Ask up to four individuals on their willingness to write a positive letter of recommendation. Consider asking individuals representing your range of experiences, if possible. For example, you may ask your faculty advisor, a practicum field supervisor, a supervisor during your graduate/research assistantship, and the principal of a school you have worked in.
- Give them ample time to write a letter—at least 3 to 4 weeks.
- Be specific about what you're applying for and what to highlight. Those willing to write a letter of recommendation often appreciate the specific guidance.
- Offer to send your CV, work samples, or other documents that may help the writer.
- In some cases, you may wish to offer to write a draft of your own recommendation letter, giving the writer the opportunity to edit as he or she sees fit. While this may feel awkward, it becomes a good exercise and can help tailor the letter to your liking.
- Some internship sites may have a standard recommendation form with checkboxes, giving an option to attach a letter. If possible, always attach a letter.

For those applying to multiple sites, your references will likely prefer to create a generic letter of recommendation rather than creating a specific letter for each site. If possible, offer writers the opportunity to send you the draft of the letter so you can personalize each of them for each site, and print them out for their signature later on. While generic letters of recommendation are often sufficient, tailoring them to each site is a nice touch.

NO OFFERS—NOW WHAT?

In some cases, despite best efforts, prospective interns emerge through the application cycle without an offer. Understandably, this could be frustrating, demoralizing, and humbling. First, recognize that this does not necessarily reflect on your personal or professional skills; rather, it could suggest strong competition, an imperfect "fit," or perhaps you had viewpoints that differed in some way from the perspectives of those making final offers. Second, not all hope is lost.

Just as some students do not get an initial offer, many internship sites do not fill all of their available internship slots at first. Some may not receive funding or support for an internship position until sometime in the spring, or others may have made offers that were not accepted, leaving available vacancies. Continue contacting districts and looking at different postings on websites (e.g., NASP Career Center, state school psychology associations that offer their own match systems) to inquire about the availability of an internship for the upcoming school year. In some cases, internship sites that pay a stipend for selected spots may be willing to provide a high-quality internship without pay, as a last resort.

APPIC offers a Phase II matching process for those that did not match in Phase I. This offers benefit to the unmatched interns as well as the internship sites that do not fill all available positions. Further, APPIC offers a postmatch vacancy service to inform applicants of vacant positions.

FINAL CONSIDERATIONS

Remaining calm and minimizing stress (perhaps easier said than done) will make a difference mentally and physically. Absorbing continuous pressure and chronic stress can truly hinder performance and personal health. Some temporary stress and anxiety are natural, and in fact can lead to improved performance during your interview process and final stages of graduate preparation. However, high levels of stress and pulling multiple all-nighters without life balance can lead to diminishing returns.

Avoid Asking "What If?"

Stressing over hypotheticals such as "What if I get sick the day before my interview?" or "What if I don't get an internship and have to wait a year?" only leads to stress. There is a difference between having a contingency plan and worrying for the sake of worrying.

Use Your Support System

Make time to stay connected with others close to you, and do not fear seeking support with the application process from your faculty, family, or friends. Asking for help demonstrates confidence and maturity, and typically leads to both improved materials and improved relationships. Consider participating on listservs with other students going through the same experiences, including the NASP Communities, the APPIC Intern-Network E-Mail List, or forums through psychcentral.com. Lean on your support system for insight, perspective, input, or even better, an escape.

Sleep

Avoid underestimating the value of sleep or taking the mind-set that you can sleep when various tasks have been completed. Lack of sleep reduces efficiency, memory, alertness, and work quality. Rather than pull an all-nighter, consider stopping, saving your document, and getting a good night's rest. You may find that your approach the next morning is quite different.

Focus on the Positives

Mired in full-time course work, completing program requirements, and preparing for internships can cloud recognition of previous accomplishments. Recognize and have faith that the program has prepared you well. Focus on having made it to the final stage of the program. Look forward to the opportunity to have a full year to hone skills and learn from other professionals. Think back to when you applied for the program or started during your first year, and think about how far you've come personally and professionally.

Recognize and Counter the Imposter Phenomenon

The well-known yet often rarely spoken about "imposter phenomenon" refers to the feelings of inadequacy among otherwise capable and intelligent individuals, or the fear that others will find them out for the frauds they are if given the opportunity. Such feelings can lead to anxiety, self-doubt, difficulties internalizing success, or even reluctance to pursue ambitious goals (Craddock, Birnbaum, Rodriguez, Cobb, & Zeeh, 2011). The imposter phenomenon, to varying degrees, is "a normal part of graduate study" (Craddock et al., 2011, p. 439).

Perspective

While difficult to recognize during the application process, your internship decision alone will not completely shape your career. Certainly, the experience is a capstone to your graduate preparation, but each site will likely offer unique learning experiences. Additional opportunities for field-based supervision will also be there if needed or desired in the future.

Give Yourself a Break

In the literal sense, take a break. Go get lunch with a friend or read a magazine instead of eating at your desk. Go see a movie or some live music. Figuratively, allow yourself to not be perfect. Successfully obtaining an internship is less about perfection and more about simply relying on the skills you already have.

CHAPTER REVIEW

This chapter provided details and information to help graduate students successfully acquire a school psychology internship that meets both program and personal goals. Specifically, the anatomy of effective internship CVs and statements of interest were provided, along with methods to prepare for internship interviews. This chapter also addressed the various considerations to take into account when selecting an internship site.

REFERENCES

American Psychological Association. (2013a). *Guidelines and principles for accreditation of programs in professional psychology.* Retrieved from http://www.apa.org/ed/accreditation/about/policies/guiding-principles.pdf

American Psychological Association. (2013b). *Commission on accreditation (CoA) 2013 annual report online: Summary data: Internship programs.* Retrieved from http://www.apa.org/ed/accreditation/about/research/2013-internship-summary.pdf

Association of Psychology Postdoctoral and Internship Centers. (2011). *APPIC membership criteria: Doctoral psychology internship programs.* Retrieved from http://www.appic.org/About-APPIC/Joining-APPIC/Members/Internship-Membership-Criteria

Association of Psychology Postdoctoral and Internship Centers. (2014). *2012 APPIC match: Survey of internship applicants.* Retrieved from http://www.appic.org/Match/MatchStatistics/ApplicantSurvey2012Part1.aspx

Chamberlin, J. (2006). Primed to shine. *Monitor on Psychology, 37*(7), 50.

Council for Directors of School Psychology Programs. (2012). *Doctoral level internship guidelines.* Retrieved from https://sites.google.com/site/cdspphome/2012guidelines

Craddock, S., Birnbaum, M., Rodriguez, K., Cobb, C., & Zeeh, S. (2011). Doctoral students and the impostor phenomenon: Am I smart enough to be here? *Journal of Student Affairs Research and Practice, 48*(4), 429–442. doi:10.2202/1949-6605.6321

Harris, A. M. (in press). Assuring the availability and quality of school psychology doctoral internships. *Psychology in the Schools*.

Hodges, S. (2011). *The counseling practicum and internship manual: A resource for graduate counseling students*. New York, NY: Springer Publishing Company.

Keilin, G. (2014, March). *Association of Psychology Postdoctoral and Internship Centers (APPIC) match statistics: Combined results phase I and II*. Retrieved from http://www.appic.org/Match/MatchStatistics/MatchStatistics2014Combined.aspx

National Association of School Psychologists. (2010). *Standards for graduate preparation of school psychologists*. Bethesda, MD: Author. Retrieved from http://www.nasponline.org/standards/2010standards/1_Graduate_Preparation.pdf

National Association of School Psychologists. (2014). *Best-practice guidelines for school psychology internships*. Retrieved from http://www.nasponline.org/trainers/documents/2014_Best_Practice_Guidelines_for_SP_Internships.pdf

Peña, A. M. (2008). *Bringing your vita to life: Preparing for internship and early career positions*. Retrieved from http://www.nasponline.org/students/Curriculum%20Vitae.pdf

Prus, J. S., Colvard, H., & Swerdlik, M. E. (2014). The prevalence of paid school psychology internships in the United States. *Communiqué, 43*(3), 1, 28–30.

Rossen, E., & von der Embse, N. (2014). The status of school psychology graduate education in the United States. In A. Thomas & P. Harrison (Eds.), *Best practices in school psychology: Foundations* (pp. 503–512). Bethesda, MD: National Association of School Psychologists.

Sulkowski, M. (2011). *Doctoral training in school psychology: Navigating the internship and application process*. Retrieved from http://www.nasponline.org/students/documents/Doctoral_Internships.pdf

CHAPTER 7

Internship 101

LEARNING OBJECTIVES

At the conclusion of this chapter, readers should be able to:

1. Effectively apply record-keeping and time-management strategies during internship
2. Identify strategies in building a professional image
3. Understand the role of competency ratings in evaluating internship performance

Arriving to a point of considering or entering the internship experience is cause for celebration. Internship is an important benchmark toward professional practice and the experiences acquired will greatly influence later career opportunities.

DOCUMENTATION, LOGS, AND RECORD KEEPING

An essential part of making the most of your internship experience is keeping accurate records of the activities you complete during your service. Your graduate program as well as your site and site supervisor will most likely require you to maintain a log of your hours spent on internship. Some clinically based internship sites and school systems may also require documentation for billable hours of services provided by interns, which could be accompanied by a variety of billing software logging systems. Accurate record-keeping skills are not only vital at the internship phase, they were likely important in your practicum experiences and will continue to be crucial as you move into your future career. Maintaining accurate records of the range of services you provide during your internship will help keep you accountable to your site, supervisor, program, and to your own goals for what you hope to learn from your internship experience. Additionally, appropriate documentation will allow you to keep track of the range of students, clients, or patients you

117

see during your experience and the different capacities in which you provide services for them (e.g., assessment, consultation, and therapy).

Documentation and School Psychologist Credentialing

Documentation of internship hours is vital in establishing eligibility for eventual licensure and credentialing. While licensure and credentialing requirements for school psychologists vary among states, some states have an option that requires a 1-year (1,200 clock hours or 2,000 clock hours) internship experience to receive the state's school psychology credential. The National Association of School Psychologists (NASP, 2010b, 2014a, 2014b) website maintains a list of credentialing requirements for school psychologists by state (www.nasponline.org/certification/state_info_list .aspx). Additionally, NASP's Standards for the Credentialing of School Psychologists (2010a, www.nasponline.org/standards) offers a model for state educational agencies regarding requirements for the school psychologist credential.

NASP also offers the Nationally Certified School Psychologist (NCSP) credential. Many states recognize the NCSP as meeting some or all of the requirements to earn the state's school psychologist credential. An essential component of the NCSP is the completion of a 1,200 clock hour–internship in school psychology with at least 600 of those hours being completed in a school setting. Further information about the NCSP is available through NASP (www.nasponline.org/certification/becomeNCSP.aspx). The precise and accurate documentation of internship hours is thus essential for demonstrating the depth and breadth of students' applied experiences, information that will be important to note in future job applications as well.

Documentation and Psychologist Licensure

Accurate documentation of internship hours is also highly recommended by the American Psychological Association (APA, 2007, 2010b) for doctoral-level graduates seeking to obtain licensure as a general psychologist. The Model Act for State Licensure of Psychologists, adopted in 2010, is currently in its fifth iteration. This document provides guidelines for states seeking to develop legislation regulating psychological practice. As part of the Model Act, it is recommended that states require "the equivalent of two full-time years of sequential, organized, supervised professional experience" (p. 7) for those who seek to become licensed psychologists. Of those 2 years, one may be "an APA or [Canadian Psychological Association] accredited (or equivalent) predoctoral internship" (p. 7, www.apa.org/about/policy/ model-act-2010.pdf).

To meet state requirements for licensure as a general psychologist, a predoctoral internship spanning between 1,500 and 2,000 clock hours

(1 year full-time or 2 years half-time) is generally required. However, these requirements differ by state, and additional hours of supervised postdoctoral experience may be required (Dittmann, 2004; www.apa.org/gradpsych/2004/01/get-licensed.aspx). NASP (2010b) requires that at least 600 of these hours be completed in a school setting. The Association of State and Provincial Psychology Boards (ASPPB, n.d.) oversees psychology licensure boards in the United States and Canada. The ASPPB also maintains a record of licensure requirements for different states that includes the number of hours of supervised experience required from internship and/or postdoctoral experiences. Additionally, contact information for each jurisdiction's local psychology board for additional questions is provided (www.asppb .org/HandbookPublic/before.aspx).

It is recommended that you investigate the specific licensure and credentialing requirements for the state in which you intend to practice as guidelines vary considerably among states. For example, the state of Florida generally allows 2,000 predoctoral internship hours to be applied toward the 4,000 hours of supervised experience necessary for licensure, whereas California allows 1,500 hours from the predoctoral internship to be applied toward an overall requirement of 3,000 supervised clock hours. Additional requirements from internships that may "count" toward licensure also vary by state (e.g., if the internship must be accredited by another organization such as the APA, or if the approval of the doctoral program is sufficient). As with the school psychologist credential, it is important that individuals pursuing licensure as psychologists maintain accurate, up-to-date, and detailed records of their activities during the internship year. This documentation will ensure that you are equipped with the information necessary to demonstrate evidence of your new experiences and competencies to your doctoral program as well as to apply for licensure in your given state.

Personal and Professional Benefits of Internship Documentation

In addition to the benefits of maintaining a comprehensive log of internship hours for licensure and credentialing, there are numerous personal and professional advantages that result from keeping such documentation. Documenting your internship experiences can serve as a reflection of the breadth and depth of experiences you've accumulated over your internship year (APA, 2007). Regularly documenting your activities as you complete your internship will give you the opportunity to reflect on what you have accomplished and what skills you would still like to gain. Internship should ideally allow you to develop expertise in areas in which you were initially comfortable as well as gain proficiency in new areas that you might not have had the opportunity to explore in your program. Consistent logging of your hours spent in various activities (e.g., consultation, individual therapy, group therapy, school-based counseling, intervention implementation, intervention planning, systems-level organization, program evaluation, professional training, supervision, research, report writing) can ensure that your activities reflect a range of skill development opportunities that move beyond the traditional assessment and report-writing responsibilities often associated with school psychology.

The use of logs can also serve to document more specific information about the nature of the services you have provided over your internship. This can include the demographic information of the clients you have worked with. Any demographic information should not allow the client to be identified but can include factors such as age, gender, race, primary language, and diagnoses or special education classification. Also, it may be helpful to include the types of assessment instruments utilized, intervention strategies or programs employed, and the counseling techniques or therapeutic approaches employed. This information can be useful in preparing applications for postdoctoral positions or future employment opportunities as employers are often interested in the specific nature of professional services rendered. These records also verify to your doctoral or specialist-level program that you have completed their graduate requirements for internship (and for your degree). Keeping track of the types of services you provide during internship and to whom you have provide the services is vital to maintaining a comprehensive log of internship hours that will be useful to you in the future and that will keep you accountable to your site and program.

Setting Internship Goals

To further this accountability effort, consider making an outline of goals at the onset of your internship. Goals may include specific assessment instruments that you wish to gain greater proficiency in administering, learning new intervention curricula, or working with specific diagnoses or populations to gain more in-depth expertise. The listed goals can be periodically compared to what is recorded in your log throughout the duration of your internship to ensure you are holding yourself accountable to your own high expectations and goals.

- What would you like to accomplish during internship?
- What kinds of populations would you like to work with?
- Which populations are you most comfortable with, and which populations do you have the least experience with?
- In what capacity would you like to work with such populations?
- What skills would you like to learn for the first time?
- What preexisting skill sets would you like to further develop?

All of these questions can help lead you toward maximizing your time spent on internship and focusing on the skills that will be important for your future practice.

Periodically reviewing your internship log with your site supervisor can be an excellent opportunity to ensure that your goals for your internship experience are being met as much as possible. Initiating such a discussion with your site supervisor (if you are not already prompted to do so) may allow for a productive dialogue about the ways in which the internship is fulfilling your preparation needs as an emerging professional. Such discussions can also serve as an opportunity to adjust the ratio of hours that you are engaged in certain types of activities to better serve your training and skill development needs. For example, if one of your primary goals upon entering internship was to gain more individual counseling experience and your log demonstrates that you have been primarily engaged in assessment, bringing this discrepancy between your log and goals to your supervisor's attention can be a helpful starting place for a discussion about gaining new and different experiences within the context of your site.

Sample Logs

There are numerous log resources available online and through different organizations for internship (Association of Psychology Postdoctoral and Internship Centers, n.d.). For example, the APA offers sample logs for monthly internship activities under its "Trainee Resources" section (www .appic.org/Training-Resources/For-Training-Directors). Additionally, a sample internship log can also be found in Appendix B for your use and reference (Appendix B, Exhibit B.6); see also www.springerpub.com/school-psychology-practicum for additional samples, Exhibits 7.5 and 7.6. You may also wish to create your own log in a word processing or spreadsheet program to tailor your log to your individual needs. One advantage of using a spreadsheet program is that the spreadsheet can be designed to automatically sum your hours across different specified dimensions (e.g., assessment, therapy, intervention, and consultation) and to automatically create color-coded bar graphs, tables, or pie charts of your hours to help visualize the proportion of activities (see Appendix B, Exhibit B.7).

Records Retention

As noted in the section on record keeping for practica, internship logs are equally important. It is vital to be aware of records retention guidelines and legal implications for any documentation you produce related to your internship (e.g., evaluations, reports, and progress notes). While specific guidelines may vary by site, the Family Educational Rights and Privacy Act

(FERPA, 2009) dictates that parents and guardians of all children in publicly funded schools (and some students as well) have a right to inspect and review the student's educational records. Written consent is generally necessary to release any information from a student's educational record to a third party, although this does not apply to school staff with a "legitimate educational interest." An additional law, the Health Insurance Portability and Accountability Act of 1996 (HIPAA), applies to children and adults in medical settings. HIPAA also may apply to some school settings when health care providers within the school are providing billable services for which electronic health care claims (e.g., Medicaid) are submitted (U.S. Department of Health and Human Services, 2014). Parents and guardians are generally allowed access to the medical records of minors through HIPAA, but stringent regulations are in place for sharing information with third parties. The APA has created a series of 14 guidelines detailing expected procedures for record keeping and retention (www.apa.org/practice/guidelines/record-keeping.pdf). These guidelines note the importance of keeping accurate, confidential, and secure records in both printed and electronic formats. The APA recommends keeping adults' records for 7 years, and children's records for at least 3 years after the child reaches adulthood.

TIME MANAGEMENT FOR INTERNS

Time management was not just important during your graduate studies—time management is also one of the keys to facilitating a successful internship experience. As you probably learned in graduate school, it is rare to check off everything on your to-do list and be completely free of responsibilities. It may seem as if there is always more work to be done, more cases to see, more reports to write, and more opportunities to access. If this is the case for you, then you have done well to find yourself in a position with an overabundance of opportunities for potential development and learning. The key to balancing all of these exciting yet competing prospects, responsibilities, and obligations is to be selective and purposeful in accepting opportunities to maximize the long-term benefits of your endeavors.

Prioritization

Effective time management begins with the recognition that all tasks may not be accomplished immediately, which calls for prioritization. This thought may seem frightening at first, especially if all of the tasks in front of you seem equally important and pressing. However, acknowledging that you may not be able to administer three test batteries, write four comprehensive evaluations, and attend a professional development seminar all in 1 week is critical to your long-term success as a school psychologist (and likely to your happiness as well). Prioritization will allow you to see which deadlines are "hard," inflexible, and meaningful deadlines that have actual effects on outcomes (such as state-mandated timelines for completing evaluations) and which are more flexible, self-imposed, or "soft" deadlines that have room for adjustment (such as making a follow-up phone call either this afternoon or tomorrow morning). Your needs and priorities also may change from day to day. For example, your priorities on a Monday might be to start an assessment battery, begin an extended comprehensive report, and review your week's cases to determine which are most pressing. Your priorities on a Friday, however, may be to finish progress notes from your week's counseling sessions and to send your final evaluation report to a multidisciplinary team for staffing.

Effective prioritization requires an understanding of the requirements of the tasks at hand, their urgency, how comprehensive they are in size and scope, and the resources needed to accomplish each task. While time is one of the most common resources needed to accomplish a task, there are many other components that may be vital to facilitating your task. For example, you may need to collect assessment results or a parent interview for a report, review your site's materials on cognitive behavioral therapy techniques for a counseling case, or facilitate teacher-collected classroom data for a consultation. Many of these components that will contribute to your final product (report, counseling session, consultation, etc.) cannot be procured overnight. Some will take substantial time to collect and analyze before you are able to start on your final product. Prioritization over an extended period of time will allow you to see which components of a task need to be started immediately so that you are able to meet your final outcome goals on time. To this end, prioritization is not to be confused with procrastination. Procrastination implies that you are not using your time wisely. Prioritization is just the opposite of that—it entails maximizing the use of your time to accomplish as much as you can in a given day by focusing on what tasks need immediate attention and which can be completed after the most urgent, pressing tasks have been attended to.

Tools for Time Management

In order for prioritization to be successful, it is helpful to have a way to keep track of all of your commitments. Many different types of planners, agendas, and calendars that are either hard-copy/print or electronic suit this purpose. Some web-based calendars may be linked to your e-mail account (e.g., Gmail, Outlook) and can be used to synchronize your appointments on your smartphone or tablet with your e-mail from your web-based e-mail service provider. It can be helpful to have a calendar that you keep up to date on a daily basis, such as an agenda in a weekly format, and a separate calendar containing several months or a semester for recording important deadlines or long-term due dates (e.g., dissertation deadlines, comprehensive evaluation due dates). Color-coding your appointments by certain criteria, using tabs/sticky notes, and setting up recurring appointments in electronic calendars are just a few of the strategies that may be useful in helping you stay organized. While electronic agendas and calendars are often helpful, some may find them to be over-stimulating and unproductive, especially if the devices are set to notify the receiver every time a new message appears. If this poses a problem, consider changing the settings on your device to help you be productive.

Self-Care

An important tool for making time management work is ensuring that you are including time for self-care. Self-care refers to activities and strategies that support the individual's overall well-being, tranquility, and happiness. It can be very challenging to make time for yourself in daily life, especially when task demands are high. When the workload is intense, however, self-care is even more important. As a school psychology intern, it is vital that you take time to keep yourself physically healthy and mentally refreshed so that you can perform your best in your job and avoid burnout (i.e., becoming overworked to the point that your performance suffers). Self-care strategies include activities related to physical health such as eating a well-balanced diet, exercising regularly, good sleep hygiene, and attending to medical concerns as needed. Self-care needs also extend into the social–emotional realm and can be addressed by cultivating strong support networks with friends, family, or partners; engaging in creative activities like journaling, playing music, or crafting art; and spending time in whichever activities are relaxing to you, such as meditation, taking a walk, or listening to music. Continued professional development through reading or attending workshops also can provide additional knowledge and inspiration that make some parts of our work less effortful. Self-care is an especially important component of time management on internship, because internship sets the stage for the habits and expectations an individual is likely to continue in future practice. Stephen Covey (2013), an international motivation speaker and the author of *The 7 Habits of Highly Effective People*, describes the need for self-care through a rendition of the story of a woodcutter who starts his job cutting down an impressive number of trees each day only to find that the harder he works overtime, the less trees he is successful in cutting down. In explaining his dilemma to his supervisor, the boss asks how long it has been since he sharpened his saw to which the woodcutter replies, "I have been too busy to stop and sharpen the saw." The moral of the story is obvious—time spent in rejuvenating our energy and refining our expertise can make the job easier.

Lastly, self-care that targets stress reduction may benefit from some of the same behavioral modification and cognitive restructuring techniques we apply to others. A schedule of small rewards (e.g., movie, new book, and dining out) for accomplishments during internship can help motivate perseverance. Self-talk that is positive, affirms success, and acknowledges effort as well as achievement also may be helpful. Remembering prior achievements and successes that overcame obstacles or the struggle of learning new paradigms can reassure us we are able to meet the challenges (e.g., I made it through grad school, I can make it here also). Visualizing ourselves as competent professionals and skilled practitioners also can serve as a bridge during transitioning roles. Another visualization tool is creating a graphic timeline of goals toward the completion of internship and tracking progress toward those accomplishments. In those unusual circumstances where internship responsibilities may become overwhelming, a discussion with supervisors both onsite and at the university level as well as accessing student mental health resources may be necessary.

SETTING BOUNDARIES AND EXPECTATIONS

Expectations for ethical practice are established by NASP (2010a) and APA (2010a), and both address the idea of setting boundaries for professional practice. NASP's ethical code revolves around four defining principles: (1) respecting the dignity and rights of all persons, (2) professional competence and responsibility, (3) honesty and integrity in professional relationships, and (4) responsibility to schools, families, communities, the profession, and society (p. i, www.nasponline.org/standards/2010standards/1_%20 Ethical%20Principles.pdf). The five general principles espoused by APA include (a) beneficence and nonmaleficence, (b) fidelity and responsibility, (c) integrity, (d) justice, and (e) respect for people's rights and dignity (www .apa.org/ethics/code). These standards indicate that school psychologists will not practice outside the bounds of their competency and that they will establish boundaries regarding confidentiality in relation to privacy laws. The American Counseling Association (ACA, 2014) provides its own code of ethics for counselors, which also is relevant to school psychologists engaged in counseling work (www.counseling.org/resources/aca-code-of-ethics.pdf).

In addition to aligning with the expectations for ethical practice held by national organizations, it is important for interns to begin to set their own personal boundaries as well. As mentioned previously, the habits one forms for practice in one's early career can set the tone for later years of professional work. It is perfectly acceptable (and even advisable) to have personal boundaries that you carry throughout your professional career. Where these boundaries are set will vary among individuals depending on their comfort level, the populations they work with, the requirements of their job, and many other factors. Many practitioners choose to maintain a strict divide between their personal and professional lives. This can be reflected in work-related decisions to not share a personal cell phone number with clients or their parents, or to "leave work at work" by only completing job-related tasks on site during office hours. Some may extend this divide to their personal lives by avoiding offering unsolicited advice in personal situations, not taking on more than can be handled, or resisting becoming a therapist for friends and family.

To facilitate meeting the goals of the internship and keeping preconceived boundaries in place, clear expectations can be built into the internship contract (see Chapter 8 for Internship Contract Samples). Written descriptions of what is expected of the student as well as what the student expects to gain from the internship can be included to show clear role designation from the onset of the experience. These roles can be clarified periodically through close communication with field and university-based supervisors. It is vital to be clear about the roles and expectations for the intern up front to avoid potential miscommunications or misperceptions. Equally critical is the intern's own recognition of boundaries for work within his or her professional practice. Interns should be aware of their workload and how they feel they are responding to the expectations that are placed on them. Are you being asked to do too much? Are you not being challenged enough? How does your experience align with what you expected? Do you need more supervision or guidance (from field or university supervisors) to assist in your professional development? Remember that having expectations and boundaries is a two-way street—just as there are expectations for what the student will do in his or her role as an intern, there also are expectations for what field- and university-based supervisors will do to help the intern meet his or her goals.

TRANSITIONING TO THE ROLE OF PROFESSIONAL

When you begin your internship, you will have just spent the past few years immersed in course work, practicum placements, and other activities, all largely in the role of a student. Internship reshapes your identity from student to the role of an emerging professional—someone who is still learning but who also has a wealth of experience, knowledge, and skills to contribute to the practice. As an emerging professional, you will be expected to demonstrate increasingly more autonomy and independence in your practice. This shift in your role and responsibilities in practice may correspond to an evolution of your self-image as you learn how to apply skills and problem solve new circumstances. Subtle changes will include greater self-initiation and self-monitoring of your own activities, less frequent need to ask questions, more automaticity in routine tasks (e.g., test administration, interviewing, consulting), and a growing internal knowledge base from which to draw solutions.

Seeing yourself as an emerging professional may be difficult at first—you may wonder what you have to contribute to the field, or whether or not you are adequately prepared to take on increasingly more responsibility. Chances are, though, that you are much more prepared than it may seem. Think about the cases you have assisted with during your practicum placement(s) and the experiences you have gained as part of your course work in your program. These experiences have given you a background of important skills and knowledge competencies that will greatly assist you in your internship and as you become an independent practitioner.

Building Your Professional Image

Part of transitioning to the role of an emerging professional involves building your image as a professional and beginning to perceive yourself in this manner. A key part of this change is acquiring confidence and certainty in your skills. Projecting confidence is important, especially when working with those who may not fully understand the role of a school psychologist (e.g., some parents, teachers, or administrators). The more successful experiences you have in the field, the more likely you are to feel comfortable in your skills and therefore competent.

Building your image as a professional also requires that you project an appropriate image to your clients and to the other stakeholders that you work with. To this end, your attitude and demeanor go a long way. Consider what kind of attitude you want to project to the people you work with. How would you like others to perceive you? Is this desire consistent with how you actually act or appear? One way to find out is to videotape common activities (e.g., mock introductions, presentations, or interviews) or to ask for feedback from a trusted peer or supervisor. Voice tone and modulation, speech cadence, use of colloquialisms, posture, eye contact, facial expressions, energy, and nonverbal gestures all contribute to the general impressions others perceive during interpersonal interactions. Therefore, self-awareness of these factors can be helpful in enhancing the image one strives to portray. Additionally, organization and appearance of materials also can effect image (e.g., using a briefcase or portfolio instead of a student backpack, keeping papers neatly clipped, presenting graphs that are concise with high-quality resolution).

It is important for school psychologists to be able to create and maintain an atmosphere of respect, dignity, and open-mindedness. Such environments can stem from your behavior, language, and manner of interacting with clients. Professional dress is another important component of the professional image you are cultivating. What you wear to internship can serve to align you with your profession and the colleagues you work with. The level of professional dress that is appropriate may vary dramatically depending on site and setting, but overdressing for the occasion is likely preferable to underdressing as you begin your placement. Often observing the dress of other administrators, supervisors, or professionals can offer insight into the agency's or institution's expectations for appropriate clothing choices. Consider that as an emerging professional, you are now shaping what others will perceive a school psychologist to be, how a school psychologist acts, and what a school psychologist's role entails. Making these distinctions for yourself is critical to deciding what kind of professional image you would like to portray in your own career.

Interpersonal Skills and Administrative Interactions

As you begin to envision yourself in the role of the emerging professional, you may also transition into a period of self-evaluation and refinement of your interpersonal skills when collaborating with other professionals. While your site- and university-based supervisors will still certainly be providing you with feedback, it will be increasingly important for you as an emerging professional to be able to evaluate your own strengths and areas for further improvements.

Audience and Purpose

This is particularly important in regard to your interpersonal skills. Much of the job of a school psychologist involves interacting with others in a variety of settings, whether it is collaborating with school staff members, consulting with teachers and administrators, interviewing parents, counseling students, presenting a paper at a conference, or delivering reports at staffing meetings. School psychologists need to be able to assess the sophistication and complexity of their own social skills so that they can adapt their interaction style to fit different audiences (e.g., administration, parents, students, peers) and purposes (e.g., achieving a goal, sharing information, teaching a lesson, answering a question, gathering data). Being aware of the audience and purpose of any interaction can help you tailor your style to be responsive to the needs of the situation. For example, students and parents will likely benefit from nontechnical descriptions of findings from a report, whereas administrators and teachers would benefit from additional focus on the educational aspects of the report, and consultation with mental health colleagues may require both pedagogical and medical nomenclature.

It is also important to consider the degree to which your different audiences will be familiar with specific terms in your report (Lichtenstein,

2013). If you present a report to a parent that is filled with unexplained jargon like response to intervention (RtI), specific learning disabilities (SLDs), attention deficit hyperactivity disorder (ADHD), and individualized education program (IEP), the parent will likely not have a clear understanding of what you were trying to convey. On the other hand, those same abbreviations may be commonplace for many educators. Parents and teachers often find graphic presentations of data most meaningful. It is thus critical to consider how fluent your audience is with educational terminology, programs, options, and even the process of the interaction (e.g., eligibility staffing meeting).

Time is often a valuable resource at interdisciplinary meetings such as placement meetings or reports of evaluation feedback. Recognizing the different time-related needs of all parties at a meeting can be helpful in ensuring a smooth and collaborative process. Administrators and teachers often have very limited time, so succinct and concise delivery of pertinent information can demonstrate respect for their presence. Parents and students may need more time for rapport building in conversations, especially at the beginning of an interview or counseling case. They also may need more time for questions at the end of a meeting or at a later time and it is the responsibility of the school psychologist to answer them as thoroughly and accurately as possible.

Resources for Communication With Parents

Many caregivers may benefit from handouts, resource lists, or diagrams of scores and concepts, particularly if a diagnosis or special education identification is given. NASP maintains a collection of almost 300 reproducible handouts on relevant conditions and exceptionalities for teachers and families in its electronic guide, "Helping Children at Home and School III: Handouts for Families and Educators" (Canter, Paige, & Shaw, 2010; www.nasponline.org). It may also be helpful for you to maintain your own database of relevant materials, organizations, resources, and websites for different conditions. There are numerous organizations that seek to provide awareness and education about different diagnosable conditions, and some may have local affiliates in your area. For example, if you are explaining a child's norm-reference reading scores, you may wish to show the parent a graph of a normal curve with the cutoffs for each standard deviation displayed as well as the child's scores on each important assessment (see Appendix B, Exhibit B.8). You could then explain to the parent what the child's scores mean in relation to the same-age peers who took the same assessment on the curve. After taking questions from the parent, you could provide him or her with NASP's handout on autism spectrum disorder (ASD) as well as websites and brochures from other relevant autism organizations

INTERNSHIP EVALUATION MEASURES AND COMPETENCIES

in your area. Including time both before and after school eligibility meetings to caregivers in order to answer questions is another strategy for enhancing family–school collaboration.

INTERNSHIP EVALUATION MEASURES AND COMPETENCIES

Internships should conform to the guidelines established by the Standards for Graduate Preparation of School Psychologists from the NASP (NASP, 2010b). In addition, doctoral-level internships accredited by the APA should conform to APA's Guidelines and Principles for Accreditation of Programs in Professional Psychology (2013). High-quality internships that are not accredited by the APA will likely still adhere to many of the guidelines and principles espoused by the APA as standards of good practice.

NASP guidelines for internship stipulate that the internship should serve as the "culminating experience" in the program with emphasis on providing a diverse range of experiences and achieving expertise in school psychology competency areas across domains (2010c, p. 8). The internship should provide opportunities for the intern to deliver services that produce quantifiable enhancements or improved outcomes in the lives of clients, including children, teachers, families, school systems, and other stakeholders. Internships should value diversity and include multiple performance-based assessments of interns with feedback throughout the internship and at the end of the internship. NASP (2010b, 2010c) guidelines also require that interns receive consistent and appropriate supervision from their field-based site supervisors, which includes weekly supervision with a credentialed or licensed (school) psychologist for at least 2 hours per week on average. To assist in meeting the goals of internship and attaining competencies in the required areas, evaluations of school psychology intern competencies and skills can be used throughout the internship and as its culminating assessment.

It is expected that interns will sequentially build upon their skills over the course of the internship while also gaining more independence as a practitioner, especially toward the end of the internship year. NASP (2010c) lists ten different competency domains necessary for practicing school psychologists, which include (a) data-based decision making and accountability, (b) consultation and collaboration, (c) interventions and instructional support to develop academic skills, (d) interventions and mental health services to develop social and life skills, (e) school-wide practices to promote learning, (f) preventive and responsive services, (g) family–school collaboration services, (h) diversity in development and learning, (i) research and program evaluation, and (j) legal, ethical, and professional practice (pp. 5–7). It is essential that emerging school psychologists develop competency in all of these areas, because each domain encompasses a distinct but interrelated component of the school psychologist's potential job duties. Inherent in the evaluation process is the idea that the public can trust someone who holds the designation of school psychologist because he or she will meet the requirements of the field; the integrity of school psychology therefore relies on some degree of consistency among its graduates. A successful evaluation implies that interns are ready for independent practice and credentialing at the end of their internship.

Sample internship evaluation forms are provided in Appendix B (see Exhibit B.9) and through the Springer online resources website (www.springerpub.com/school-psychology-practicum, Exhibit 7.7). The evaluation form in Appendix B is aligned with NASP's approval and competency domains. The second online evaluation addresses core competency and skill development areas in a more open-ended format. As the intern is considered an employee in many settings, additional evaluation forms from the human resources perspective that focus on work ethic and employee relations may also be required. All evaluations may be accompanied by or supplement additional information gathered by your program (e.g., letter of verification of internship completion, narrative review of progress).

CHAPTER REVIEW

This chapter provided a rationale for the importance of accurate record keeping during internship both as a mechanism to document graduate program requirements and also a method for substantiating possible licensure eligibility criteria. The topics of time-management strategies, transitioning to a professional self-image, and self-care offered practical tips to prepare young professionals for their new roles in the workplace. Additionally, a discussion of communication emphasized the importance of tailoring discussions and reports to meet the needs of specific audiences from parents to teachers and administrators. The chapter also reviewed the components often rated in internship evaluations and provided common sample forms. The internship is an exciting opportunity to self-select experiences that can open many professional opportunities in the future and with careful planning, it can launch a long and rewarding career.

REFERENCES

American Counseling Association. (2014). *ACA code of ethics*. Retrieved from http://www.counseling.org/resources/aca-code-of-ethics.pdf

American Psychological Association. (2007). Record keeping guidelines. *American Psychologist*, 62(9), 993–104.

American Psychological Association. (2010a). *Ethical principles of psychologists and code of conduct*. Retrieved from http://www.apa.org/ethics/code/

American Psychological Association. (2010b). *Model act for state licensure of psychologists*. Retrieved from http://www.apa.org/about/policy/model-act-2010.pdf

American Psychological Association, Office of Program Evaluation and Accreditation. (2013). *Guidelines and principles for accreditation of programs in professional psychology*. Retrieved from http://www.apa.org/ed/accreditation/about/policies/guiding-principles.pdf

Association of Psychology Postdoctoral and Internship Centers. (n.d.). *For training directors and programs*. Retrieved from http://www.appic.org/Training-Resources/For-Training-Directors

Association of State and Provincial Psychology Boards. (n.d.). *ASPPB handbook on licensing and certification requirements*. Retrieved from http://www.asppb.org/HandbookPublic/before.aspx

Canter, A. S., Paige, L. Z., & Shaw, S. (2010). *Helping children at home and school III: Handouts for families and educators*. Bethesda, MD: National Association of School Psychologists.

Covey, S. R. (2013). *The 7 habits of highly effective people*. New York, NY: RosettaBooks.

Dittmann, J. (2004). What you need to know to get licensed. *gradPSYCH Magazine, 2*(1). Retrieved from http://www.apa.org/gradpsych/2004/01/get-licensed.aspx

Family Educational Rights and Privacy Act. (2009). 20 U.S.C. § 1232g; 34 CFR Part 99.

Lichtenstein, R. (2013). *Writing psychoeducational reports that matter: A consumer-responsive approach*. Retrieved from http://www.nasponline.org/publications/cq/42/3/professional-practice.aspx

National Association of School Psychologists. (2010a). *Principles for professional ethics*. Retrieved from http://www.nasponline.org/standards/2010standards/1_%20Ethical%20Principles.pdf

National Association of School Psychologists. (2010b). *Standards for graduate preparation of school psychologists*. Retrieved from http://www.nasponline.org/standards/2010standards/1_Graduate_Preparation.pdf

National Association of School Psychologists. (2010c). *Standards for the credentialing of school psychologists*. Retrieved from http://www.nasponline.org/standards/2010standards/2_Credentialing_Standards.pdf

National Association of School Psychologists. (2014a). *Becoming a nationally certified school psychologist (NCSP)*. Retrieved from http://www.nasponline.org/certification/becomeNCSP.aspx

National Association of School Psychologists. (2014b). *State school psychology credentialing requirements*. Retrieved from http://www.nasponline.org/certification/state_info_list.aspx

U.S. Department of Health and Human Services. (2014). *Health information privacy*. Retrieved from www.hhs.gov/ocr/privacy/hipaa

CHAPTER 8

Ethical and Professional Practice: Potential Conflicts

LEARNING OBJECTIVES

At the conclusion of this chapter, readers should be able to:

1. Describe the ethical standards related to practicing within one's competencies
2. Identify and anticipate potential personal and clinical conflicts during internship
3. Describe the pros and cons of electronic supervision

The school psychology internship represents the culminating, comprehensive, supervised field experience prior to engaging in full-time employment. Internship offers an opportunity to integrate and apply the range of skills acquired through course work and practica while learning new skills as well. The internship ideally transitions the intern from supervisee to autonomous practitioner. However, this transition can create the potential for confusion or conflict as school psychology interns must navigate roles as a student *and* professional simultaneously. They must also be cognizant of the ethical principles, state and federal laws, and state and district policies that govern their practice as both a supervisee and provider of services to students.

SCHOOL PSYCHOLOGY INTERNS' OBLIGATIONS TO THE ETHICS CODE

Any professional engaged in serving student needs in public schools has an obligation to practice ethically and to safeguard the interests of children. Often, professional organizations and agencies for a variety of disciplines offer specific guidelines and standards related to ethical behavior. Within school psychology, the National Association of School Psychologists (NASP) as well as the American Psychological Association (APA) offer the primary guidelines for professional ethics.

133

Only members of NASP and those holding the Nationally Certified School Psychologist (NCSP) credential are bound to abide by the NASP Principles for Professional Ethics (NASP, 2010b). In other words, only NASP members or those holding the NCSP credential would be subject to review and possibly corrective action from NASP's Ethical and Professional Practices Committee following an ethical violation. However, all school psychologists should consider the ethical principles as a guideline for best practice. Similarly, the Best Practice Guidelines for School Psychology Internships (NASP, 2014) indicate that interns should adhere to NASP's ethical principles. The principles further note that "the principles in this code should be considered by school psychologists in their ethical decision making *regardless of employment setting*" (NASP, 2010a, p. 2).

The APA's Ethical Principles (APA, 2010) state that psychologists must "encourage ethical behavior by students [and] supervisees" (p. 3), suggesting an expectation that interns behave ethically with direct oversight by supervisors. Both NASP and the APA recommend that all school psychologists and interns familiarize themselves with the ethics codes so they are better prepared to make thoughtful choices when challenging situations arise. The ethical standards of both organizations can be accessed online through their respective websites: www.nasponline.org and www.apa.org.

Practice Within Competencies

The NASP Principles for Professional Ethics identify the ethical standard that school psychologists "engage only in practices for which they are qualified and competent" (NASP, 2010b, p. 6). Doing so requires a great deal of self-awareness, self-reflection, access to resources and peers for consultation, willingness to seek out additional supervision, and opportunities to participate in professional development.

The NASP Principles for Professional Ethics go on to say that school psychologists assume responsibility for the work of their supervisees. This offers some degree of protection for school psychology interns to continue practicing and developing a range of skills consistent with NASP's Model for Comprehensive and Integrated School Psychological Services (NASP, 2010b). In fact, when considering internship as a component of graduate preparation, school psychology interns may want to actively seek out opportunities during internship to practice in areas where they feel *less* competent, utilizing the availability of supervision. After all, according to the standards, the supervisors accept responsibility for "all professional practices of the supervisees" (NASP, 2010b, p. 13). In this vein, interns may rightfully be confused about whether they must practice within their competencies, particularly in situations where roles and expectations are not well defined.

Role Definition and Expectations

Given this year of transition, school psychology interns may sometimes feel as if they are straddling the line between graduate student and professional. In some instances, such as during individualized education program (IEP) meetings with a supervisor present, their role as a supervisee is apparent. In others, they may easily assume the role of a professional, such as when others in the building seek their input and advice and their supervisor is not present. All school psychology interns should remember that while they possess professional skills, the intent of the internship is to provide a structured supervised training experience. Taking on a role as a professional, while appealing, can create practical and ethical challenges.

Vignette 8.1

Regina is completing her internship at a school with a relatively small but growing population of English language learners (ELL). Recently, the district has had difficulties finding a bilingual school psychologist, and has instead been contracting with independent psychologists when ELL require an assessment. Given the relatively small number of these cases, the school has not pursued hiring a bilingual school psychologist with urgency. Regina speaks Spanish fluently, and her supervisors have asked her to help with some of the bilingual assessments this year on internship. After completing her first two assessments, she has been asked to spend approximately half of her time completing bilingual assessments for the district at various schools, with her supervisors signing off on the reports.

Establishing and defining expectations at the outset of the internship is critical to a successful experience. In Regina's case, the district attempted to leverage her bilingualism to fill a gap in service delivery for students in the district. This could create a situation where the intern ends up providing services without the benefit of a structured, supervised learning experience, and possibly providing services without an established basic level of knowledge and skills. Despite Regina's fluency in Spanish, it is unclear if she maintains competence in assessing ELL students. Additionally, this may compromise the best practice guideline of ensuring interns the opportunity to work with varying ages, ethnicities, backgrounds, abilities, and needs, and could impact the quality of the internship experience with half of Regina's time spent on a specific activity.

If the intern supervisor assumes responsibility for the intern's work, yet does not feel competent to provide bilingual assessments, this practice could be considered ethically irresponsible on the part of the supervisor. The ethical principle to practice within one's competence also applies to

136 • SECTION II: INTERNSHIP

supervisors. In this case, the intern supervisor should recognize his or her own limits and refer to others for assistance/supervision, or pursue additional professional development in order to effectively provide supervision. In Regina's district, without other practitioners that can provide appropriate supervision related to assessments with ELL students, the supervisor may consider contacting colleagues or working with the university supervisor to identify others who can provide support.

Vignette 8.2

Stephanie completed her specialist-level degree 3 years ago, and worked for 2 years in a district with assignments in elementary and middle schools. She decided to return for her doctorate, and is now on her doctoral internship in a high school. Given her prior experience and still current state school psychologist certification, her supervisor decides to give Stephanie half of her caseload and meet twice per week to review progress and offer case consultation.

Despite the presence of advanced skills among school psychology interns, the fundamental expectation of a culminating supervisory learning experience is unchanged. The supervisor, along with the intern and graduate program, should consider areas of competence and areas in need of development, and arrange for an experience that leads to professional growth for Stephanie. Professional supervision to ensure ongoing professional development should be available regardless of level of experience (Harvey & Struzziero, 2008). Having Stephanie independently offer services that she had mastered and applied in her previous job as a school psychologist would not fulfill the spirit or intent of the internship.

The APA's (2010) ethical standards also address this within Standard 2.05 related to delegating work to others. Specifically, the standard notes that a supervisor should only delegate work that the supervisee can reasonably perform competently. Further, the supervisor has the responsibility to ensure those services are being delivered effectively.

Additionally, consideration should be given to the NASP Standard 1.1.3 (NASP, 2010b), which states that services provided by interns are explained to individuals giving consent (i.e., parents/caregivers) and agreed to in advance, along with the nature of how the work will be supervised. Harvey and Struzierro (2008) note that anytime consent is obtained for work to be completed by a school psychology intern, the nature of who will do the work and the role and accessibility of the supervisor should be stated explicitly at the outset. Having Stephanie working somewhat independently may be misleading to parents, or possibly raise anxiety or concern over her qualifications without a supervisor present.

Vignette 8.3

Allan graduated from a program that emphasizes a problem-solving model, multi tiered systems of support, and a comprehensive role for school psychologists. He decides to go to an urban district for his internship to gain experience working with diverse populations. The district is regularly in crisis and has a more limited view of the role of school psychologists. Despite early conversations between the program and field site, by late winter, Allan finds himself spending the majority of his time engaged in special education evaluations and IEP meetings. His supervisors recognize his frustration, but feel this is an important reality for an intern to experience, and try to provide variety among the special education evaluation cases.

The role of any school psychology program is to ensure that its graduates demonstrate basic professional competencies across all domains of school psychological services consistent with the program's goals and objectives. Ideally, the intention is to prepare the intern to be a competent and effective school psychologist. The field-based supervisor, however, may have different views of what skills are needed to become an effective school psychologist. Despite efforts at collaboration between the program and field-based supervisor, conflicts can still arise as a result.

This situation is somewhat common, as many internship sites continue to emphasize assessment and offer a different emphasis or approach than the graduate program (Harvey & Struzziero, 2008; Newman, 2013). School psychology interns can, and should, help meet district needs during internship. However, this should balance with meeting the program's goals and intern's needs. The internship should provide opportunities to participate in a range of school psychological services, and in order "to ensure breadth of training, activities in no single major function [should predominate] the intern's time" (Prus, 2009, p. 31). This applies even within districts that have a narrow role for school psychologists, as the primary objective of internship is a culminating learning experience for the intern. Outlining opportunities ahead of time as part of an internship contract, described in more detail later in this chapter, can help document what experiences the intern should be receiving.

Vignette 8.3 also raises a potential issue for intern supervisors who must maintain responsibility for the work of their interns even though they may not have as much knowledge or skills in that area. In these situations, it can be perfectly acceptable for supervisors to work collaboratively with other colleagues with more knowledge in that area to provide supplemental supervision, or use the opportunity to develop new skills themselves.

Discussion Questions: Vignettes 8.1 to 8.3

1. What are some strategies that can be taken to resolve the concerns?
2. What is the responsibility of the university/program?
3. What are some steps that can be taken prior to internship to prevent problems like these?

Self-Advocacy

School psychologists, including graduate students and interns, maintain a responsibility to advocate for the profession and for their own roles in the setting in which they work. Such self-advocacy can significantly improve the internship experience by developing effective communication at the outset of the internship experience as well as when unforeseen concerns arise. The NASP Practice Model provides an excellent framework to advocate for a comprehensive role and identify the range of skills and activities that the internship should include. The Practice Model can also guide which services need development or require specific focus during the internship year. Developing these advocacy skills, ranging from self-advocacy to district, state, or federal advocacy, encompasses an important skill set that can be developed throughout one's professional career. NASP offers numerous advocacy resources (see www.nasponline.org/advocacy/advocacyresources.aspx) to help learn effective ways to communicate and advocate for a comprehensive role.

INTERNSHIP CONTRACT

Formal agreements or contracts prior to the beginning of internship can help clarify roles, expectations, and responsibilities, and offer a process when conflicts may arise (Harvey & Struzziero, 2008). Harvey and Struzziero go on to identify the following components of a well-written, individualized supervisory contract:

1. Credentialing requirements to be met by supervision, such as providing supervision by a doctoral-level practitioner licensed by a state board of psychology to allow eligibility for both school and independent credentials, or ensuring a certain total number of supervised hours are provided.
2. Supervision logistics such as regularity and process of face-to-face supervision, identification of the supervisee as an intern to school staff and families, and legal responsibilities of supervisors.
3. Supervisory process (e.g., models of supervision used, individual or group supervision).

4. Supervisory methods (e.g., case consultation, observation, audio or video recording).
5. Supervision goals that are aligned with the supervisee's developmental level (rather than a blanket set of predetermined supervisory goals).
6. Information regarding the extent and limits of liability of the supervisor for services provided by the supervisee.
7. Methods to evaluate the intern's performance, including the degree of involvement of the supervisee in the evaluation process and possibly opportunities for the intern to evaluate the quality of supervision.

Contracts may also identify the expectations of each individual or entity, including the intern, the supervisor(s), the school/district, and the university program, and should include minimum expected experience for the field-based supervisor (i.e., having a minimum of 3 years of experience as a practicing school psychologist). Table 8.1 provides some examples of identified responsibilities, although elements can be added or removed based on the individual circumstances.

TABLE 8.1 Sample Expectations Within Internship Supervisory Contracts

INTERN	INTERN SUPERVISOR(S)	INTERNSHIP SITE	UNIVERSITY PROGRAM
• Completing a certain number of evaluations or direct intervention cases • Developing intervention plans • Attending and participating in various school team meetings • Completing logs • Use of title such as "intern" or "resident"	• Ensuring a lower case load for the intern than a typical school psychologist • Providing a comprehensive experience to the intern (e.g., providing opportunities to engage in a range of services as described within the NASP standards; NASP, 2010b) • Regular supervision and evaluation • Limiting supervisors to no more than two supervisees	• Ensuring access to professional development • Providing opportunities to engage in research (including work on a dissertation) • Ensuring access to appropriate supplies (e.g., test kits, stationery, desk, computer, software, e-mail) • Administrative support • Providing opportunities to work with youth of varying ages, ethnicities, backgrounds, needs, and abilities • Limiting total school psychology interns at the site	• Consultation with district or site visits • Supervision and support to interns • Monitoring of logs • Ongoing instruction through seminars or other formats • Mechanism to facilitate evaluation of interns

NASP, National Association of School Psychologists.

Some school psychology interns have reported contracts that require the intern to apply for or accept an offer for employment upon completion of an internship, or maintaining a caseload that might otherwise restrict opportunities to provide comprehensive services. In these instances, interns should work collaboratively with their university-based internship coordinator to help navigate and negotiate those requirements. School psychology programs often provide copies of their internship contracts in their program handbooks. (Sample contracts [Exhibits 8.1 and 8.2] are also available at www.springerpub.com/school-psychology-practicum.)

Internship Plan

Newman (2013) draws a distinction between internship contracts or agreements, and internship plans. Internship plans, like contracts are formal, written documents shared between the program and internship site; however, the internship plan specifically identifies and maps out the activities and opportunities to help develop the range of knowledge and skills expected for the intern. Newman identifies numerous components as critical to a successful internship plan, such as including the intern in its development, identifying at least one area of professional focus, formative and summative evaluation, and promoting accountability.

CONFLICTS WITH SUPERVISORS

The development of personal conflicts between an intern and supervisor can occur, and perhaps is more common than one may think. Moskowitz and Rupert (1983) found that over one third of graduate clinical psychology students in their study experienced at least one conflict with a supervisor. Additionally, "conflicts in supervision are frequent, because advanced students are simultaneously trying to meet expectations of the training program and trying to be autonomous" (Harvey & Struzziero, 2008, p. 36).

Despite the apparent stress already on interns (e.g., applying for jobs, student loans, completing course work or theses/dissertations), interpersonal problems with supervisors are among the most frequent sources of stress (Harvey & Struzziero, 2008). Such conflicts can become particularly difficult for the student as the supervisor has evaluative authority, leading to fear of reprisal. As a result, most students do not express their concerns directly to their supervisors.

The lack of a positive working alliance can hamper progress for the intern (Patton & Kivlighan, 1997; Perrotto, 2006) and increase the likelihood of an intern withholding information from the supervisor (Yourman, 2003).

Despite the potential for negative experiences from conflict, handling the conflict well can actually become productive for both the intern and supervisor and lead to an improved relationship (Nellis, Hawkins, Redivo, &Way, 2011). Recognizing potential sources of conflict between an intern and supervisor is an important step in preventing negative outcomes. Some potential conflicts that may arise include:

- Different expectations regarding skill level or organization of the intern, the method or amount of supervision/feedback, adherence to timelines, or expectations for research activities associated with the graduate program
- Differing perspectives on effective service delivery, best practices, or what services should be provided
- Miscommunication, which can result from different communication styles, cultural differences, inherent power differential (Ramos-Sanchez et al., 2002), or overuse of electronic communication
- The evaluation process, which can include overly harsh criticism, minimizing the value of supervision, intern resistance, inexperience/difficulty expressing disagreement
- Different personalities or simply not getting along
- Power imbalance
- Organizational barriers that prevent a range of experiences or opportunities for face-to-face supervision

Vignette 8.4

Nikki, as a new intern, was asked to first observe her supervisor administer some cognitive assessments to ensure that expectations for appropriate assessment were consistent. Nikki noticed that the supervisor used specific, leading, and direct cues (e.g., "Take a closer look" or "Take another minute and think about it") that were not part of the standard queries. Nikki also noticed that the supervisor used this cuing technique for cognitive ability assessments but not during achievement testing, and the district utilized a discrepancy model.

Vignette 8.4 provides a unique challenge when the intern recognizes an ethical and professional practice concern with her supervisor who holds differential power. In this case, the supervisor appeared to be violating NASP's (2010a) ethical principles related to valid assessment (Standard II.3.5) and adhering to standardized administration procedures (Standard II.3.2). Other similar examples could include disagreements about eligibility decisions or a supervisor's inappropriate use of outdated assessment measures.

Discussion Questions:

1. What should Nikki do to resolve this concern?
2. What are the potential risks Nikki should consider?
3. What responsibility does Nikki have despite the potential risks?
4. What additional ethical principles (NASP or APA) should Nikki consider, if any?

Vignette 8.5

Oscar attends an internship placement, and within his first 2 weeks his supervisor is asked to work with a student identifying as transgender. The supervisor suggests that Oscar would be a good fit to work with the student instead. When Oscar asks why, the supervisor implies that he thinks Oscar is gay, but quickly backtracks and asks, "Don't you identify with the LGBTQ community?"

Vignette 8.5 represents a clear violation of the privacy of personal information. The supervisor made an assumption and put the supervisee in an uncomfortable place. APA's (2010) Ethical Standard 7.04 specifies that supervisees should not be required to disclose personal information regarding sexual history or orientation. Oscar has the right to respond honestly, or state that such information is personal. Nevertheless, he might fear that not responding will damage the supervisory relationship. Oscar could also simply deflect the question by stating he'd be comfortable or uncomfortable working with the student. Either way, he should certainly consult with his university supervisor on how to proceed.

Interns that work with more than one supervisor can expect that each supervisor will have his or her own unique approach to providing services and to the supervision process. Ideally, each intern can potentially learn new insights and approaches with this variety. This requires open dialogue, however. One method to address the potential for conflict is to discuss methods to handle such conflict before it happens. This can help normalize the experience, set expectations for how conflicts can be resolved, and potentially provide professional growth opportunities for the interns (Duff & Shahin, 2010; Nellis et al., 2011). Another strategy is for interns to express any foreseeable challenges at the outset, such as difficulties writing reports, lack of confidence in counseling skills, or a tendency to become anxious in meetings. This can help ensure these become goals of effective supervision as opposed to barriers or future conflicts.

Interns should also know what options or recourse they have when conflicts arise with their supervisor that can't be easily resolved, including due process protection in the threat of having the internship terminated. Such protections can be helpful as part of the agreement with the university prior to the start of the internship.

CONFLICTS IN LAWS AND AGENCY RULES OR POLICIES

Conflicts can arise among ethical standards, state/federal laws, and district/agency policies, often leading school psychologists to question how to proceed and which standards to follow. Ethics, laws, and policies all have the common purpose of protecting the rights of students and parents; however, differences exist in who creates them and who enforces them. Navigating these differences can be challenging, especially for school psychology interns.

Laws

Laws are a set of rules of conduct that are legally enforceable through the judicial system. Laws can be set through local, state, or federal legislative bodies. Federal law and the U.S. Constitution typically supersede state or local laws when regulating the same activity (Vaillancourt & Rossen, 2012), and conflicts can be decided in federal court. Generally speaking, local laws cannot be weaker or less strict than state laws—for example, a state law issuing a mandate that all reported cases of bullying require in-school suspension could not be lessened by a local jurisdiction; however, the local jurisdiction could mandate that all reported bullying cases are considered for expulsion as well. School psychology interns should identify laws that may impact practice, particularly when completing an internship in a different state from the university program, including laws related to identification of disabilities, bullying, and discipline.

Rules and Policies

Rules and policies typically describe expectations of conduct that are enforceable by the agency that created them. A school district has the right to create policies related to activities such as conduct, dress code, attendance, and employee conduct. Violation of these rules would be enforced by the agency (e.g., disciplinary action) although not necessarily subject to legal discipline. School psychologists and interns should always become familiar with the district rules and policies as soon as possible.

Ethics

Ethics represents a code of conduct designed to protect students and families. A violation of ethical standards does not necessarily lead to legal or agency discipline, although it could lead to action through a credentialing body or professional organization. Professional ethics explicitly note the expectation of practitioners to respect and know the law.

144 • SECTION II: INTERNSHIP

School psychology graduate students, interns, and practitioners should always consider and recognize what laws, policies, standards, and codes might apply in any situation. For example, child assent or confidentiality are ethical standards yet are not laws enforceable by the judicial system. The NASP's ethical standards make clear that in conflicts between ethics and law, school psychologists should make attempts to resolve the conflict responsibly and otherwise may follow the law as long as human rights are protected.

Vignette 8.6

Will is in the second semester of his internship, and has developed a good rapport with an elementary school student he has counseled for several months. During one of the counseling sessions, the student tells Will that he brings in his toy plastic gun to school a lot because it makes him feel safer walking home from school, even though he knows it's not real. Will later realizes that the school has a policy against bringing toy weapons to school, subject to suspension, with the expectation that staff notify administration when learning about this infraction.

Discussion Questions:

1. What ethical standards and school policies may be in conflict?
2. What is the role of the intern supervisor?
3. What other information might be needed?
4. How should Will proceed?

Vignette 8.6 highlights a clear conflict between a school policy and ethical standards related to confidentiality. Even by simply sharing information with his supervisor, information could get back to an administrator which could damage Will's counseling relationship with the student. However, by not sharing with his supervisor, he could make both himself and his supervisor liable and damage the supervisor–supervisee relationship. Other considerations might include whether Will views the student as a danger to himself or to others, or whether Will takes notes that may become part of the student's educational record.

The intern, Will, may make a judgment call that there is no imminent danger and choose to focus the counseling on the student's sense of fear and danger, generating alternatives to carrying a plastic toy gun. In purely ethical terms, there may not be any obligation to disclose this information to an administrator, although that will need to be balanced with the potential consequences of violating district policy.

The APA (2010) Ethics Code (Standard 1.03) notes that when ethical standards conflict with organizational demands or policies, the professional should clarify the conflict, make known the commitment to the ethical standards, and take reasonable steps to resolve the conflict.

Some viable courses of action for Will may be to discuss the policy with the student, including the mandate for staff to inform administration, and identify some immediate alternatives to bringing a toy gun to school. At that point, Will could discuss the issue with his immediate supervisor and review the relevant ethical principles and policies to consider.

On a systems level, Will and his supervisor may use this opportunity to reexamine the current policy. Standard IV.1.2 within the NASP Principles for Professional Ethics (NASP, 2010b) states that school psychologists "advocate for school policies and practices that are in the best interests of children" (p. 12). Within this process, they can pose questions such as:

- What data are available about the effectiveness of this policy?
- How is the policy enforced?
- What objectives does this policy meet?

This activity could help improve or clarify existing policies, offer a valuable learning experience for the intern, and further establish the role of the school psychologist within the school.

Vignette 8.7

Tricia has been providing direct academic interventions to a middle school student for several months and has developed a rapport. Despite the academic nature of the intervention, Tricia made sure to describe confidentiality and the boundaries and limits of confidentiality. One afternoon the student reveals that she used to have difficulty completing the homework assigned to her because she was afraid of her father as he used to get violent, but since her grades improved over the last few months that has subsided. The student begs Tricia not to tell anyone because her relationship with her father is finally starting to improve.

Similar to Vignette 8.6, Tricia has to determine a course of action amid conflict between the ethical principle of confidentiality, and legal mandates to report suspicion of child maltreatment. In this case, Tricia made the right move to describe the limits of confidentiality at the outset of the relationship with the student. As mentioned earlier, confidentiality is not a law, and when conflict exists between law and ethics, the law can be followed if human rights are not violated. Upon first hearing this, Tricia should be clear with the student that they cannot keep it a secret, although she did the right thing sharing that information. Tricia may even consider sharing with the student what may happen next and that information will be kept confidential from peers—being honest can ease the student's anxiety and help maintain trust.

Tricia should also talk to her direct supervisor and follow procedures for reporting a suspicion of child maltreatment.

Most states require only suspicion (not factual evidence) to justify a report, with educators typically considered mandated reporters and given immunity if reporting a suspicion in good faith. Tricia should avoid asking any leading questions (e.g., Has your father ever punched you?) as obtaining more information is unnecessary to make the report and may complicate any legal proceedings at a later date. Each state maintains state-specific laws related to reporting suspected maltreatment, which can be found by visiting the Child Welfare Information Gateway (www.childwelfare.gov/systemwide/laws_policies/state/can) or FindLaw (law.findlaw.com/state-laws/child-abuse). Some states may require interns to directly report, whereas in others the supervisor may become the mandated reporter.

Discussion Questions:

1. What ethical standards and laws may be in conflict?
2. What is the role of the intern supervisor?
3. What other information might be needed?
4. How should Tricia proceed?
5. If the previous violence is disclosed, who is a mandated reporter? Is that the responsibility of Tricia or Tricia's supervisor?

Record Keeping

Maintaining appropriate records and documenting work are critical to effective practice and protecting yourself as an intern. However, recognize that any documents or notes that contain any information identifying a particular student may be open to discovery, regardless of whether you store it in your own personal file or in the student's file in the main office of the school. This is one reason that some counselors/supervisors may recommend deidentifying clinical notes (e.g., assign a number to notes and keep a separate log of student names/numbers). Also, never alter a record after the fact as it's both illegal and more often than not, you will get caught (Smith, 2003). Hodges (2011) identifies a general guideline that "if it's not written in a file it didn't happen" (p. 45). Hodges notes that in the event you are subpoenaed, you do not need to immediately comply as that could represent an ethical violation. In this case, you should make known the ethical conflict, consult your supervisor, and likely the school or agency's attorney.

Title Conflicts

The NASP Principles for Professional Ethics (NASP, 2010a; Standard IV.4.2) make clear that interns should be identified as such during their internship experience (e.g., "school psychology intern"). Further, Prus (2009) recommends as a best practice that the site uses a title that accurately designates the training status of the intern. However, some states offer or even require interns to obtain a state-level credential to work as an intern, with varying titles associated with those credentials. For example, Arizona offers an "Interim School Psychologist" credential; Colorado offers a "Provisional License"; and Louisiana offers a "Provisional Certificate." An intern may have rightfully earned the credential interim school psychologist and the district may ask the intern to use this title, although this may not reflect the NASP ethical standard of conveying status as an intern. APA's guidelines are less specific, although note that psychologists avoid false, deceptive, or fraudulent claims about their training, experience, or credentials. Interns should consult with program faculty and internship supervisors to ensure that they are complying with ethical standards and any state laws or district policies regarding how they represent themselves.

Electronic Communication and Supervision

As school psychology interns continue to pursue competitive internships across the country, and often far from the home institution, the desire for effective electronic communication and telesupervision (i.e., synchronous supervision via video-conferencing) grows. Remote supervision using various technologies offers many benefits:

• Convenient.
• Software is cheap and often free.
• Reduces intern cost for traveling to campus.
• Allows for regular contact and easier scheduling.
• Face time improves quality of interaction rather than via telephone alone.
• Options for connecting with other expert colleagues outside of geographic area on an as-needed basis.
• Less intrusive and distracting than direct observation when providing direct services (Dudding & Justice, 2004).

Telesupervision can help facilitate the availability and viability of a more expansive option of internship sites. In fact, pursuing experiences beyond the vicinity of the home institution, or even out of state, may help provide an important perspective on the field that would be difficult if staying within local districts only. Importantly, some preliminary research suggests that telesupervision can be just as effective as traditional supervision or useful as a complement to traditional supervision (see Chipchase et al., 2014; Dudding, 2012).

Despite these benefits, some differences of opinion remain in the viability of telesupervision to completely replace traditional supervision models. The APA's Commission on Accreditation (2014) outlined various considerations, guidelines, and limitations on the use of telesupervision. Notably, the APA recommended that internship placements establish a formal policy considering rationale, logistics, and special circumstances; and imposed a limit of no more than 1 hour of minimum supervision time through telesupervision. In response, the Council of Graduate Departments of Psychology (n.d.) viewed the 1-hour limitation as "arbitrary." The Council of Directors for School Psychology Programs' (CDSPP) Internship Guidelines (2012) allow for up to 2 of the 4 total weekly hours of supervision to be met through synchronous audio and video communication. The Association of Psychology Postdoctoral and Internship Centers (APPIC) also weighed in on this issue, stating, "The required [supervision] hours shall be through face-to-face individual supervision (rural sites may use visual telecommunication technology in unusual circumstances and when face-to-face supervision is impractical, but must demonstrate that such technology provides sufficient oversight)." Additional consideration was given to the importance of having established interpersonal supervisory relationships prior to relying on telesupervision. Notably, these typically refer to field-based supervision rather than university-based supervision.

Several challenges may emerge when using technology to facilitate supervision, of which the most concerning is the potential for breaches of confidentiality given that much of the information is not completely secure or encrypted unless using specifically designed software. Some question also remains about who "owns" records of conversations or communications using various software. This is particularly true if using telesupervision *while* providing services (e.g., during a counseling session) as opposed to case consultation. Telesupervision may also lend itself to more frequent e-mail communications between interns and supervisors that may contain identifying information on students that could be considered part of a student's educational record, or not protected from discovery in court.

Some supervisors may ask interns to record administration of assessments or counseling sessions to help facilitate supervision. This practice can be an incredibly useful tool within supervision. However, consent and assent should be obtained prior to recordings, which would include information about maintenance and disposal of those recordings.

Written Electronic Supervision

E-mail as a specific method of clinical supervision can be helpful, either for individual or group supervision, particularly to augment face-to-face communication (Harvey & Struzziero, 2008). Online chatting can even provide instantaneous, synchronous supervision when video opportunities are not available. However, in addition to the concerns already identified related to telesupervision, written communications can easily be copied, forwarded, or even modified.

Steps can be taken to limit risks to confidentiality, including encryption software or avoiding inclusion of identifying information. However, these limitations can impact the quality and effectiveness of supervision. Additionally, these methods lead to loss of nonverbal cues and potential misunderstanding or incorrect interpretations.

CHAPTER REVIEW

This chapter helps graduate students and interns recognize the potential for ethical dilemmas and develop a course of action to take when they arise to ensure high-quality professional practices. This is particularly relevant for school psychology interns given the unique and complex position of being subject to the ethical principles while also under the supervisory authority of others. This chapter also provides tools to help interns work collaboratively with university and field-based supervisors to avoid pitfalls during internship by identifying expectations, developing plans, and generating contracts at the outset of the internship.

REFERENCES

American Psychological Association. (2010). *Ethical principles of psychologists and code of conduct with the 2010 amendments.* Washington, DC: Author. Retrieved from www.apa.org/ethics/code/index.aspx

American Psychological Association Commission on Accreditation. (2014). *Policy statements and implementating regulations.* Washington, DC: Author. Retrieved from http://www.apa.org/ed/accreditation/about/policies/implementing-regs.pdf

Chipchase, L., Hill, A., Dunwoodie, R., Allen, S., Kane, Y., Piper, K., & Russell, T. (2014). Evaluating telesupervision as a support for clinical learning: An action research project. *International Journal of Practice-based Learning in Health and Social Care.* doi: 10.11120/pblh.2014.00033

Council for Directors of School Psychology Programs. (2012). *Doctoral level internship guidelines.* Retrieved from https://sites.google.com/site/cdspphome/2012guidelines

Council of Graduate Departments of Psychology. (n.d.). *COGDOP response to proposed IR on telesupervision.* Retrieved from www.cogdop.org/page_attachments/0000/0141/TeleSupResponse.pdf

Dudding, C. C. (2012, December). Focusing on tele-supervision. *Access Academics and Research.* Retrieved from http://www.asha.org/Academic/questions/Focusing-in-on-Tele-Supervision/

Dudding, C. C., & Justice, L. M. (2004). An e-supervision model: Videoconferencing as a clinical training tool. *Communications Disorders Quarterly, 25*(3), 145–151.

Duff, C. T., & Shahin, J. (2010). Conflict in clinical supervision: Antecedents, impact, amelioration, and prevention. *The Alberta Counsellor, 31*(1), 3–8.

Harvey, V. S., & Struzzerio, J. A. (2008). *Professional development and supervision of school psychologists: From intern to expert* (2nd ed.; A joint publication with the National Association of School Psychologists). Thousand Oaks, CA: Corwin Press.

Hodges, S. (2011). *The counseling practicum and internship manual: A resource for graduate counseling students.* New York, NY: Springer Publishing Company.

Moskowitz, S. A., & Rupert, P. A. (1983). Conflict resolution within the supervisory relationship. *Professional Psychology: Research and Practice, 14*(5), 632–641. doi:10.1037/0735-7028.14.5.632

National Association of School Psychologists. (2010a). *Model for comprehensive and integrated school psychological services.* Bethesda, MD: Author. Retrieved from http://www.nasponline.org/standards/2010standards/2_PracticeModel.pdf

National Association of School Psychologists. (2010b). *Principles for professional ethics.* Bethesda, MD: Author. Retrieved from http://www.nasponline.org/standards/2010standards/1_%20Ethical%20Principles.pdf

National Association of School Psychologists. (2014). *Best practice guidelines for school psychology internships.* Bethesda, MD: Author. Retrieved from http://www.nasponline.org/trainers/documents/2014_Best_Practice_Guidelines_for_SP_Internships.pdf

Nellis, A. C., Hawkins, K. L., Redivo, M., & Way, S. (2011). *Productive conflict in supervision.* Ideas and Research You Can Use: VISTAS 2012. Article 81. Retrieved from http://www.counseling.org/resources/library/vistas/2012_Vol_1_67-104/2_2012-ACA-PDFs/Article_81.pdf

Newman, D. S. (2013). *Demystifying the school psychology internship.* New York, NY: Routledge.

Patton, M. J., & Kivlighan, D. M., Jr. (1997). Relevance of the supervisory alliance to the counseling alliance and to treatment adherence in counselor training. *Journal of Counseling Psychology, 44*(1), 108–115.

Perrotto, D. S. (2006). The working alliance as predictor of successful school psychology internships. *Dissertation Abstracts International, 66*(09), 5072B. (UMI No. AAI3187934)

Prus, J. S. (2009). Best practice guidelines for school psychology internships. *Communiqué, 37*(8).

Ramos-Sánchez, L., Esnil, E., Goodwin, A., Riggs, S., Touster, L. O., Wright, L. K., . . . Rodolfa, E. (2002). Negative supervisory events: Effects on supervision and supervisory alliance. *Professional Psychology: Research and Practice, 33*(2), 197–202. doi:10.1037/0735-7028.33.2.197

Smith, D. (2003). 10 ways practitioners can avoid frequent ethical pitfalls. *Monitor on Psychology, 34*(1), 50.

Vaillancourt, K., & Rossen, E. (2012). Navigating school safety law and policy. *Communiqué, 41*(1), 22–23.

Yourman, D. B. (2003). Trainee disclosure in psychotherapy supervision: The impact of shame. *Journal of Clinical Psychology: In Session, 59*, 601–609.

CHAPTER 9

Psychological Case Reports

LEARNING OBJECTIVES

At the conclusion of this chapter, readers should be able to:

1. Effectively delineate the core components of comprehensive case reports
2. Identify school-based report-writing strategies that facilitate problem-solving decisions
3. Understand how clinic-based therapy/treatment reports differ from school-based reports

This chapter discusses different types of comprehensive case reports to illustrate the key components essential to producing effective psychoeducational summaries that help inform schools, parents, and mental health professionals of an individual's needs. Report writing is a core skill competency area for the practice of school psychology and multiple writing exercises are often intertwined into the practica requirements. Generally, training programs will coordinate a master curricula plan to ensure that multiple assessment, intervention, and consultation assignments are embedded in course work with the case requirements facilitated through the practica setting, across the multiyear duration of the program.

The assignments build sequentially with graduated responsibilities and increasingly complex expectations. Therefore, initial psychoeducational *evaluation reports* may be limited to one particular assessment method that has been learned in class (e.g., conducting a functional behavioral analysis). Later report assignments often integrate multiple tests or methods of collecting performance data (e.g., IQ, achievement, and observations). Near the completion of the program's assessment and intervention course series, comprehensive cases are often required. These cases may include multiple domains (e.g., IQ, achievement, social–emotional measures, and *Diagnostic and Statistical Manual of Mental Disorders, Fifth Edition* [*DSM-5*; American

151

Psychiatric Association, 2013] diagnoses) and are intended to demonstrate a wide range of skills that are seamlessly integrated. Examples of sequentially graduated *intervention report* assignments may include an initial application of one intervention method (e.g., academic tutoring, implementation of a behavioral plan) with later assignment responsibility for intensive interventions (e.g., long-term individualized therapeutic counseling intervention), and a capstone case report (as noted in Chapter 3) might require a multifaceted and/or multiagency comprehensive service plan.

Thus, the report example (Example 9.1) included in this chapter and other sample reports available at www.springerpub.com/school-psychology-practicum (Exhibits 9.1 to 9.3) are offered as samples only. It will be important to clarify specific report-writing expectations with supervisors. Asking for sample report copies from instructors, advisors, and/or practicum sites also can be helpful in better understanding the preferred site formatting, style, length, and report components. Keeping a group of sample report templates available also may be helpful as you build your own professional style in report writing.

REPORT-WRITING PRINCIPLES

The overarching goal of psychological and psychoeducational report writing is to succinctly, accurately, and respectfully communicate the needs of an individual. It is easy for novice writers to focus on stating referral concerns and describing the technical aspects of complex scoring systems or data interpretation. As in the beginning, these are newly acquired skills and need some practice. However, astute parents and teachers generally know the referral concerns and low areas of performance prior to reading psychoeducational reports. The information they are seeking and expertise they are expecting is a refined distillation of specific skill deficits with solutions on how to effectively remediate them so that the child can succeed. Any school psychologist who can consistently deliver insight on academic and behavioral needs with solutions will be highly respected and sought out. Following are two brief summaries: The first focuses on stating the referral needs and describing scores; the second focuses on elucidating specific skill gaps and linking those to interventions.

REPORT-WRITING VIGNETTES

Vignette 9.1

Utilizing the perspective of a concerned parent or teacher, which of the following two report summaries is most helpful? What thoughts do they elicit as the section is read?

Summary 1:

Maria was referred for evaluation due to concerns for low math performance, high absences, and low self-esteem as noted by self-derogatory statements that seem to interfere with work effort. Records review indicates she has missed 16 days of school this year and has earned a grade of D in math class since the spring of the past school year. Observations indicated she was on-task 85% of the time and made self-disparaging remarks when presented with her weekly math test. A measure of self-esteem indicates low-average self-efficacy. Her Broad Math composite was in the low average range with a standard score of 88 (20th percentile, 82–93 confidence band at 95%). Math Problem Solving as well as Math Fluency for Addition and Multiplication were all in the average range (SS = 86, 18th percentile; SS = 95, 36th percentile; SS = 87, 19th percentile, respectively). Numerical Operations were in the low-average range (SS = 79, 8th percentile) and Math Fluency for Subtraction was below average (SS = 77, 6th percentile). Review of these data for educational planning, counseling to increase self-efficacy, parental consult to improve attendance, and remediate of math skill deficits is recommended.

Discussion Questions:

1. Is there much information, beyond scores, in this summary that the parents and teachers did not already know before the evaluation?
2. Does the summary provide clear direction on specific skills to target for intervention?

Summary 2:

Maria was referred for evaluation due to concerns for low math performance, high absences, and low self-esteem as noted by self-derogatory statements that seem to interfere with work effort. Review of records and parent interview indicate she has a long-standing history of good attendance except for missing 16 days this semester due to her father's prolonged rehabilitation following an accident and the family's need to stay in the city for his intensive physical therapy. He is currently recovering and her mother assures school personnel that Maria will again attend regularly. Maria's math grades have generally been Cs in the past and her mother notes math was never Maria's best subject but she did manage to make passing scores. With the spring semester, grades in math declined to Ds. The lower grades coincide with the onset of her father's health needs; her mother and teachers also note that Maria began making self-derogatory comments about the same time as well as giving up more easily on math items she found difficult. Observations indicated she was on-task 85% of the time but did make self-disparaging remarks when presented with her weekly math test ("I'm stupid," "I can never do good on math—I'm gonna fail"). Interviews and observations indicate the nature of Maria's self-derogatory comments are catastrophizing and labeling, related to math, and are becoming more habitual. Her Broad Math composite was in the low-average range with Math Problem Solving as well as Math Fluency for Addition and Multiplication all in the average range. Numerical Operations were in the low-average range with most errors in subtraction functions that required borrowing or carrying forward, especially for problems with numbers of two digits or more. Consistent with this skill deficit, the area of Math Fluency for Subtraction was below average and error analysis indicates most wrong answers involved either borrowing or carrying forward functions. Test observations also indicated Maria would become frustrated on these types of problems and seems to become discouraged and give up easily on them. Review of these data for educational planning is recommended and although recent attendance is improving it will be important to continue monitoring. Home–school collaboration regarding the family's stressors also is important as the school remains a support resource. Counseling for Maria to address cognitive restructuring of catastrophizing and labeling statements as well as replacement strategies for frustration such as relaxation training and positive self-affirmations is recommended. A classroom reinforcement plan that also encourages effort on items she finds difficult and encourages the use of her replacement coping strategies taught in counseling may assist in generalizing those new skills. Remediation of math skill deficits in the functions of carrying forward and borrowing in subtraction is recommended. In addition to review of these skills, practice to build automaticity will be important as Maria had difficulty with completing simple subtraction problems with speed. Facilitating factors for Maria's continued success include her desire to achieve, her fondness for school, her strong family support, and her history of consistently good achievement across other academic areas.

Discussion Questions:

1. What new information in Summary 2, beyond the original referral concerns, adds insight into this child's needs?
2. Does Summary 2 provide clear direction on specific skills to target for intervention?
3. How could this summary be further improved?

Guiding principles for quality school psychology reports include expertise in understanding the tenets of psychology and pedagogy, guarding the confidentiality of information, remaining cognizant of the audience for the report, and being well-organized. Expertise in educational systems and psychological precepts will ensure that critical elements are included that will answer referral questions and inform services needed. Within a school system, reports will be utilized to make intervention plans, special education eligibility decisions, Section 504 disabilities accommodation provisions, gifted or enrichment program placements, and sometimes diagnoses. Thus, it is important that individuals writing these reports are knowledgeable regarding the purpose, the types of information required to access specific services, the federal disability laws and eligibility rules, as well as state criteria for educational services. Additionally, it is incumbent upon the school psychology examiner to have awareness of local school district programs, special programs, and community services for families. Connecting youth and families to the appropriate services can have significant positive effects on long-term outcomes. Reports bring the most value to schools and families when they reflect this level of in-depth knowledge of the field.

Sometimes knowing what information to exclude also is important to make reports clear, succinct, and to the point in addressing the referral question and also assisting problem-solving teams in making well-informed decisions. Nonpertinent information can hinder the reader from focusing on the essential components that will best inform intervention needs and may sometimes be counterproductive to building rapport between parents and school personnel. One of the goals of psychological evaluation is to provide thorough data in the least invasive manner. At times it is difficult to resist including what may be interesting or even intriguing information but it is essential to do so. Examples of nonpertinent information may include whom the parent is dating, divulging high profile extended family member identities, identifying diagnoses of relatives (e.g., stating that a second cousin has AIDS), stating incomes, noting the child's home address or neighborhood, revealing personal cell phone numbers of staff as contact sources, or detailing students' preferences for specific teachers. In fact, there are times when revealing some information is illegal; for example, personally identifiable health information should be protected, revealing information for persons who are not the subject of the evaluation may breach ethical guidelines, and a number of occupations (e.g., judges, police officers) have restricted disclosure given the safety considerations for their job.

After the legality and ethical issues of information disclosure have been decided, a good way to test the *necessity* of information is to ask the following questions: (a) Is this information important and directly related to decisions for intervention or educational placement decisions? and (b) Does the benefit of documenting this information outweigh the potential negative impact? If the answer to both questions is yes, then the next consideration is how to most diplomatically and respectfully phrase the content for the report.

156 • SECTION II: INTERNSHIP

Examples of negative consequences for documenting uncomplimentary statements about teachers and their classroom strategies may include undermining the trust parents or guardians have in the school, destroying teacher rapport with a child, and lowering the probability that a teacher may be forthcoming in the next interview a school psychologist has with her or him. To the extent possible, it is prudent to be judicious with sensitive information in reports. Remember, some information has the option of being shared outside the report. As an example, consulting privately with teachers to discuss classroom management skills may be more productive than noting the teacher's name and skills in the report. Alternately, information can be shared about the structure a child benefits from rather than a negative portrayal of classrooms that are less effective.

Vignette 9.2

Consider the two following report approaches to establishing a need for structure in a student's environment.

Oscar was on-task an average of 85% to 90% of the time in his language arts, science, and algebra classes, which provided teacher-directed and interactive discussion formats or lab experiments. It was noted that he checked his assignment schedule on the class whiteboard several times during the classes. In contrast, he was off-task 40% of the time in Ms. Walter's art class where activities are less structured, students were told to finish their own projects, and there was no assignment schedule on the board. However, in comparison to other students in the class, his off-task behavior was typical as most of the students were disengaged. Additionally, he was late to lunch and some classes due to wandering around socializing and also had difficulty attending to his homework during study hall.

Discussion Questions:

1. Is there a more productive way to state this information?
2. What might the long-term consequences be for teacher rapport in sharing this wording in a formal school report meeting?
3. Is there another way to discuss classroom structure with Ms. Walters outside of the report?

Oscar was on-task an average of 85% to 90% of the time in classrooms when instruction was teacher-directed coupled with interactive discussion formats or lab experiments. He seemed to maintain alertness better when provided regular teacher interaction, guided hands-on activities, and a posted assignment schedule he could view periodically throughout the class time. In contrast, he was more off-task (i.e., 40% of the time) when independent, self-directed work was expected and a visual reminder of task requirements was not available. Additionally, he demonstrated a tendency to wander around the campus socializing with others during class transitions, which at times made him late for class.

Discussion Questions:

1. How does this description focus on the student's need for structure?
2. What might the long-term consequences be for teacher rapport in sharing this wording in a formal school report meeting?

REPORT-WRITING BASICS

Psychoeducational school-based assessment and evaluation reports generally contain the following common elements (Sattler, 2014): They are placed on letterhead for the agency providing the evaluation and have a dominate confidentiality statement at the beginning or on each page as a footer/header. They typically follow a format that includes personal demographic information regarding the student's name, date of birth, age, grade, and parent names as well as the examiner's name and credentials. Often the reason for referral is noted next, which includes the presenting concerns and referring individual, educational team, or agency. This is followed by background history, which is presented chronologically and includes medical and developmental history, family composition, educational information (e.g., attendance, grades, state testing scores, retentions, interventions, disability classifications), and current status of vision, hearing, and speech/language screenings. As some of this information is acquired through interviews, notes on discussions with the teachers, parents, and the child or adolescent also may be included as well. Observational data follow with information utilizing both formal and informal methods. These data may be collected during classroom activities or testing circumstances. Assessment results often make up the bulk of the report and will include domains of interest to the referral questions. When diagnoses are included, those may follow the assessment section and provide *DSM-5* codes. A summary with recommendations completes the report and are followed by a signature. It is important for any practica or internship student signatures to be designated as such and accompanied by the signature of a credentialed supervisor. Some practitioners choose to add score tables and resources following the signature, whereas others may integrate this information into the text of the report.

Example 9.1 provides a sample psychoeducational report for a student with a specific learning disability and social skills as well as inattention difficulties (also available as Exhibit 9.1 at www.springerpub.com/school-psychology-practicum).

EXAMPLE 9.1 SCHOOL-BASED PSYCHOEDUCATIONAL CASE REPORT

PSYCHOEDUCATIONAL REPORT

This report contains privileged and confidential information and may only be released with written parental consent, except as provided by law.

Child's Name: Shanila Price	Parent(s)/Guardian(s): Mr. and Mrs. Price
Date of Birth (DOB): xx/x/xxxx	Dates of Evaluation: 2/5/2015 through 4/2/2015
Chronological Age (CA): 9 years, 1 mo	Sex: Female
Grade: 3rd	Evaluator(s): Ms. Maggie Zuker, BS
Date of Report: May 2, 2015	Supervisor: Maria Rodriguez, EdS, NCSP

INSTRUMENTS ADMINISTERED AND INTERVIEWS

Review of Educational Records
Developmental History
Interviews With Parent and Teachers
Observations
Wechsler Individual Achievement Test, Third Edition (WIAT-III)
    Kaufman Assessment Battery for Children, Second Edition (KABC-II)
    Behavioral Assessment System for Children, Second Edition (BASC-2)
    Social Skills Improvement System (SSIS)

BACKGROUND INFORMATION

Reason for Referral

Shanila was referred for a comprehensive reevaluation to assess her academic progress and social–emotional functioning due to continued concerns regarding her academic performance and interactions with peers and adults. The Student Success Team (SST) recommended academic and social–emotional functioning information to inform educational planning and interventions support services. Parental consent for evaluation was obtained on February 4, 2015. Shanila passed her hearing, vision, and speech/language screenings on February 5, 2015.

Social/Developmental History

Shanila is a 9-year-old, third-grade student that has attended Rolling Oak School since kindergarten. A developmental history interview with Shanila's mother and father noted that she had a full-term birth without complications. Although her height was somewhat low from the ages of 3 to 6, she currently has average range weight and height. Reportedly, Shanila reached motor developmental milestones within normal

(continued)

EXAMPLE 9.1 SCHOOL-BASED PSYCHOEDUCATIONAL CASE REPORT (*continued*)

developmental expectations (e.g., sitting up at 6 months, speaking first words at 8 months, walking at 13 months, using short sentences at 13 months, potty trained at 2 years). She does not have a history of serious illnesses or injuries and does not take any medications.

Shanila currently lives with her mother, father, and baby brother. Mrs. Price noted that Shanila is very organized, enjoys listening to music, playing outside, and interacting with siblings. In regard to Shanila's academic performance, Mrs. Price described her as a student who works hard and wants to do well, but has some difficulty paying attention at times. In particular, she stated that Shanila's performance in math is "okay" and she has more difficulty with reading comprehension. Mrs. Price expressed that Shanila is generally confident, but she sometimes expresses negative self-comments (e.g., "I'm failing) regarding her academic performance. Furthermore, Shanila can become frustrated and give up when she has trouble successfully completing her academic work. Mrs. Price indicated that Shanila has a hard time expressing herself with people who are new to her and socializing with other students/staff, although she is talkative at home and when attending synagogue.

Regarding her social relationship with her parents, Mrs. Price explained that Shanila requires a lot of supervision. Specifically, Shanila prefers to be involved in everything her mother does (e.g., cooking). In addition, Shanila sometimes yells if frustrated; deliberately disobeys; has a short attention span; doesn't seem to listen or follow directions; and doesn't respond well to criticism.

ACADEMIC AND BEHAVIORAL HISTORY

Academic History

Shanila did not meet grade-level benchmarks in reading and math during her kindergarten school year. Due to her academic deficits on progress monitoring measures, she began to receive supplemental small group instruction in reading and language in addition to attending the school's Summer Adventures in Literacy (SAIL) program. Shanila appeared to benefit from supplemental small group reading instruction and SAIL attendance, as she demonstrated grade-level proficiency in reading throughout her first-grade school year. However, she continued to experience difficulties in math and began receiving intensive math intervention during the second half of her first-grade school year. Because Shanila continued to experience difficulties in reading, math, and writing during her second-grade school year, she received intensive reading and math interventions, and attended the SAIL program again. At the end of her second-grade school year, Shanila met grade-level benchmarks for Oral Reading Fluency (ORF), but she did not meet grade-level benchmarks in reading comprehension, vocabulary, and math problem solving. A review of her current academic data indicates that reading comprehension, vocabulary, writing, and math problem solving remain a concern. She does, however, demonstrate strengths in basic math calculation. Shanila

(continued)

EXAMPLE 9.1 SCHOOL-BASED PSYCHOEDUCATIONAL CASE REPORT (*continued*)

continues to receive intensive reading and math supports due to her difficulties in these academic areas.

Kindergarten

Academic data demonstrate that Shanila's academic skills in reading and math were generally below grade level during her kindergarten school year.

Kindergarten Curriculum–Based Measures

	JANUARY	MARCH	JUNE
Reading	Below Grade Level	Below Grade Level	Below Grade Level
Math	Below Grade Level	Below Grade Level	On Grade Level

First Grade

Shanila demonstrated grade-level proficiency in reading during her first-grade school year. She continued to experience difficulties in math. Her performance on math curriculum-based measures shows that her math skills were below grade level throughout most of the school year.

First-Grade Curriculum–Based Measures

	FALL	JANUARY	MARCH	JUNE
Reading	On Grade Level	On Grade Level	On Grade Level	On Grade Level
Math	On Grade Level	Below Grade Level	Below Grade Level	On Grade Level

Second Grade

Academic data show that Shanila's academic skills in reading, math, and writing were below grade level during her second-grade school year.

Second Grade Curriculum–Based Measures

	FALL	WINTER	SPRING
Reading	Below Grade Level	Below Grade Level	Below Grade Level
Writing	Below Grade Level	Below Grade Level	Below Grade Level
Math	Below Grade Level	Below Grade Level	Below Grade Level

(continued)

EXAMPLE 9.1 SCHOOL-BASED PSYCHOEDUCATIONAL CASE REPORT (continued)

Second-Grade Stanford Achievement Test–Second Edition (SAT-10)

	PERCENTILE RANK	EXPECTED GRADE-LEVEL PERCENTILE
Reading		
Comprehension	21st	39th
Vocabulary	3rd	39th
Math		
Problem Solving	1st	39th
Math Procedures	40th	39th

SAIL Second-Grade Curriculum–Based Measures

	END YEAR	END SUMMER PROGRAM	EXPECTED LEVEL
Dynamic Indicators of Basic Early Literacy Skills (DIBELS) Oral Reading Fluency	106 wpm	119 wpm	90 wpm
SAT-10 Reading Comprehension	21st percentile	24th percentile	39th percentile

wpm, words per minute.

Third Grade (Current)

Current academic data indicate that Shanila continues to struggle in the areas of reading comprehension, vocabulary, writing, and math problem solving. Shanila's performance on math curriculum-based measures (CBMs) demonstrates that she has strong math calculation skills.

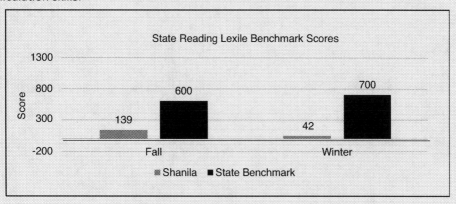

(continued)

162 • SECTION II: INTERNSHIP

EXAMPLE 9.1 SCHOOL-BASED PSYCHOEDUCATIONAL CASE REPORT (*continued*)

Third-Grade Curriculum–Based Measures

	FALL	FALL BENCHMARK	WINTER	WINTER BENCHMARK
Reading				
Gates-MacGinitie Reading Vocabulary	19th Percentile	39th Percentile	22nd Percentile	39th Percentile
Gates-MacGinitie Reading Comprehension	42nd Percentile	39th Percentile	27th Percentile	39th Percentile
State Test Practice			11	24
Writing				
Narrative Prompt	1	2	1	2.5
Expository Prompt			1.5	2.5
Math				
Math Facts +0–9	26	25	26	26
Math Facts +10–18	24	15	36	20
Math Facts −0–9	30	10	27	15
Math Facts −10–18	19	10	14	10
Everyday Math			77%	80%

Tiered Academic Support

KINDERGARTEN	
Tier 1	*Reading:* Daily 90-minute reading block (Fall, Winter, Spring) *Math:* Daily core math instruction (Fall, Winter Spring)
Tier 2	*Reading:* Daily small group instruction (Winter, Spring)
FIRST GRADE	
Tier 1	*Reading:* Daily 90-minute reading block (Fall, Winter, Spring) *Math:* Daily core math instruction (Fall, Winter Spring)

(*continued*)

EXAMPLE 9.1 SCHOOL-BASED PSYCHOEDUCATIONAL CASE REPORT (*continued*)

Tiered Academic Support (*continued*)

Tier 2	*Math:* Daily small group instruction (Winter, Spring)
Tier 3	*Math:* Daily intensive small group instruction (Winter, Spring)
SECOND GRADE	
Tier 1	*Reading:* Daily 90-minute reading block (Fall, Winter, Spring) *Math:* Daily core math instruction (Fall, Winter Spring)
Tier 2	*Reading:* Daily small group instruction for decoding (Fall, Winter, Spring) *Math:* Daily small group instruction (Winter, Spring)
Tier 3	*Reading:* Daily intensive instruction for reading comprehension (Winter) *Math:* Daily intensive small group instruction (Winter, Spring)
THIRD GRADE (CURRENT)	
Tier 1	*Reading:* Daily 90-minute block *Math:* Daily core math instruction
Tier 2	*Reading:* Daily small group instruction and one-to-one instruction as needed *Math:* Daily small group instruction *Language:* Small group language support
Tier 3	*Reading:* Daily intensive instruction for reading comprehension *Math:* Daily intensive instruction *Language:* Push in one-to-one support

Behavioral History

Kindergarten

A review of Shanila's records indicates that Shanila's classroom behaviors and social skills were a concern. Specifically, Shanila engaged in limited interactions with others. In regard to Shanila's classroom participation, Shanila frequently provided verbal responses that were wrong or disconnected from conversations and demonstrated difficulties paying attention and understanding/remembering directions for independent activities.

First Grade

Shanila began receiving small group counseling during the spring due to concerns regarding her social interactions. The Second Steps Curriculum was utilized to help Shanila develop adaptive social skills, including empathy building and emotional

(*continued*)

164 • SECTION II: INTERNSHIP

EXAMPLE 9.1 SCHOOL-BASED PSYCHOEDUCATIONAL CASE REPORT (*continued*)

regulation. Due to limited progress, recommendations were made for Shanila to continue tiered behavioral support in the following school year.

Second Grade

Shanila received small group and individual counseling to further improve her social skills. The Second Step Curriculum was utilized to help Shanila recognize emotions, develop appropriate social skills to help her meet new people, initiate/end conversations, and engage in active listening. Furthermore, goals were established to help Shanila learn to improve her reciprocity skills in social interactions, give/receive compliments, and problem solve when unsure how to complete an activity. Recommendations were made for her to continue individual counseling supports targeting peer interaction skills.

Third Grade (Current)

Shanila is currently receiving individual counseling to address social skills difficulties and inappropriate classroom behaviors. The Second Steps and Social Skills Improvement System (SSIS) curricula were utilized to help Shanila build affective vocabulary; gain empathy skills and perspective taking; improve her conversational and active listening skills; and learn how to appropriately join a group and ask for help. Additional counseling goals included teaching Shanila positive self-affirmation statements and strategies to cope with shifting routines. She has demonstrated the ability to express her feelings with visual prompts and maintain conversations about preferred topics. Additionally, Shanila has skill knowledge regarding how to join a group/maintain friends and demonstrate appropriate classroom behaviors (e.g., listening to instructor, attending to lesson, and asking for help). Overall, Shanila has made progress; although slowly and she still exhibits significant intervention needs at this time.

Tier Social–Emotional and Behavioral Supports

KINDERGARTEN	
Tier 1	Teacher implemented classroom wide social–emotional curriculum
Tier 2	N/A
Tier 3	N/A
FIRST GRADE	
Tier 1	· Teacher implemented classroom wide social–emotional curriculum
Tier 2	Small group counseling to address social skills (Spring)
Tier 3	N/A

(*continued*)

9: PSYCHOLOGICAL CASE REPORTS • 165

EXAMPLE 9.1 SCHOOL-BASED PSYCHOEDUCATIONAL CASE REPORT (*continued*)

Tier Social–Emotional and Behavioral Supports (*continued*)

SECOND GRADE	
Tier 1	Teacher implemented classroom wide social–emotional curriculum
Tier 2	Small group counseling to address social skills (Fall, Winter)
Tier 3	Individual counseling (Spring)
CURRENT	
Tier 1	Teacher implemented classroom wide social–emotional curriculum
Tier 2	Counseling–small friendship group
Tier 3	Individualized counseling to address social skills and appropriate classroom behaviors (Fall, Winter, Spring)

PREVIOUS EVALUATIONS

Shanila was referred for a psychoeducational evaluation in the spring of 2013 as a result of her slow academic progress in language and early reading skills. Her shyness and social skills also were areas of concern. Therefore, an interview with Shanila's mother and a classroom observation were conducted. A review of the results of the evaluation indicates that Shanila experienced difficulties with peer and adult interactions: limited conversation; teasing others; listening and following directions; difficulty with speech and expression; and paying attention. In addition, the following results were reported based on an administration of the Early Diagnostic Reading Assessment (ERDA): Overall, Shanila demonstrated strengths in phonological awareness, fluency (measured by reading target words in context), and reading comprehension. She experienced difficulties with syllables and rhyming, letter recognition, receptive and expressive vocabulary, and story retell.

Due to continued concerns regarding Shanila's academic and behavior performance and language skills, a comprehensive psychoeducational and speech and language evaluation was conducted in the spring of 2013. Shanila's achievement in reading and math were assessed with the WIAT-III and the KeyMath-3, respectively. The results of the evaluation indicated that Shanila's ORF was a strength, but she demonstrated difficulties with pseudoword decoding and reading comprehension. Shanila's total math abilities fell in the below-average range with significant deficits in numeration skills, computation, and numerical problem solving. Her nonverbal cognitive ability, as measured by the KABC-II, fell within the average range.

(*continued*)

166 • SECTION II: INTERNSHIP

EXAMPLE 9.1 SCHOOL-BASED PSYCHOEDUCATIONAL CASE REPORT (*continued*)

CURRENT EVALUATION

Teacher Interviews

Shanila's third-grade teacher and two interventionist teachers were interviewed. They described her as a student who loves horses, running, and outdoor activities. Regarding Shanila's skills and performance in academic domains, the following accounts were provided. According to one of the teachers, Shanila enjoys reading. Although she has improved in her ability to make predictions related to written text, all of Shanila's teachers noted that she has difficulty with reading comprehension. Shanila's teachers explained that she enjoys basic math computations and quickly answers math facts with automaticity. However, she tends to exhibit greater difficulty with math problem solving. In respects to Shanila's skills in writing, Shanila's teachers reported that she typically writes concrete and basic facts as opposed to providing descriptive statements/words, and her writing generally lacks creativity. Overall, Shanila has difficulty comprehending abstract content. She performs better when presented with concrete material with picture references and with one-on-one, step-by-step, and structured instructions.

In regard to Shanila's work habits, one of her teachers explained that she reads quickly. However, her reading is not always accurate and she often fails to stop for errors. Her teachers indicated that Shanila does not like to be wrong. When working alone during higher order thinking tasks, she may refrain from asking for help and pretend to complete her work or copy other students' work instead. Teachers also mentioned that she participates more in group discussions, especially with peer prompting.

Shanila's teachers commented on her peer interactions noting she seems to be playing with and talking more to other students since counseling. However, she does not appear to have built significant friendships with other students and her peer interactions are sometimes inappropriate. Shanila's teachers indicated that she does not always seem to know how to respond to students' attempts to include her in games, and her play sometimes seems developmentally inappropriate (e.g., following students around to join play group and hitting students to get their attention).

With regard to classroom behaviors and adult interactions, Shanila's teachers reported that she sometimes yells out of turn and laughs at inappropriate times. Furthermore, she occasionally exhibits oppositional behaviors such as refusing to do nonpreferred work, talking out of turn, and slow compliance with teachers' requests. When asked to describe classroom interventions implemented to address Shanila's behaviors, her current third-grade teacher stated that she has tried verbal warnings, writing plans, and Tier I class-wide prosocial curricula.

Behavioral Observations

Shanila was observed on six occasions during structured classroom time. On average, Shanila was on-task 70% of the time. Off-tasks behaviors frequently occurred during

(continued)

EXAMPLE 9.1 SCHOOL-BASED PSYCHOEDUCATIONAL CASE REPORT (*continued*)

independent and nonteacher-led small group activities, especially during the reading block. Staring-off and talking at inappropriate times occurred most often. Across observations, Shanila appeared easily distracted by others' movement resulting in inappropriate talking and also often appeared to be daydreaming or staring. Other low frequency behaviors were noted including inappropriate statements (e.g., telling peer that his work was incorrect) and slow compliance with the teacher requests.

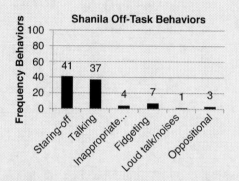
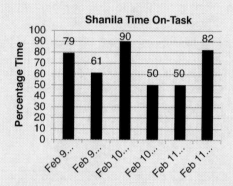

Test Session Behaviors

Shanila was talkative and maintained good eye contact throughout test administrations. Hence, rapport was easily established and maintained. She also was cooperative and attentive, eager to speak and provide answers; as she frequently asked the examiner to let her know what was coming up next. The examiner utilized reinforcement during both test administrations to maintain Shanila's engagement. This consisted of allowing Shanila to earn and place stickers on a sheet of paper after each subtest, so that Shanila could visually see her progress. The reinforcers seemed to motivate Shanila to persist with testing, as she often stated that she was aiming to fill the sheet.

Shanila generally persisted with difficult items and frequently used strategies to help her answer the questions (e.g., thinking aloud and using visual stimuli for cues). Although, she showed some signs of frustration on one subtest during the KABC-II administration, Shanila was eager to successfully complete the tasks presented and generally showed care in responding. Therefore, results of this evaluation should be considered a valid estimate of abilities at this time.

Reading

Reading Composite

The WIAT-III was administered to assess Shanila's academic achievement in the area of reading. On the Early Reading Skills subtest, she performed significantly below average (SS = 69, 2nd percentile). She was able to recognize and produce rhyming words, identify the onset sounds of words, and encode words. However, she had difficulties

(*continued*)

EXAMPLE 9.1 SCHOOL-BASED PSYCHOEDUCATIONAL CASE REPORT (*continued*)

identifying paired words beginning with the same single/two sounds and paired words ending with the same single sound. On the Total Reading composite, which reflects performance in reading comprehension, word reading, pseudoword decoding, and ORF, Shanila performed in the below average range (SS = 89, 23rd percentile). While overall reading scores can be helpful to understand general reading performance, more specific information was gathered to identify areas of strength and weakness in the five key benchmarks of reading acquisition noted in the following and to determine the need for instructional supports.

Phonics

Phonics refers to the ability to understand letter/sound relationships in text. On the WIAT-III Basic Reading composite, which reflects performance in real word and nonword reading, Shanila performed in the average range (SS = 93, 32nd percentile).

Fluency

Fluency refers to one's ability to quickly and accurately read text. The results of the WIAT-III further examined Shanila's ORF. Her score was in the high average range (SS = 113, 81st percentile) with oral reading rate also in the high average range (SS = 112, 79th percentile) and reading accuracy below average (SS = 83, 13th percentile). Administration observations indicated that Shanila made errors by trying to rush the task and omitting words as she read, which negatively impacted her level of reading comprehension.

Comprehension

Comprehension refers to the ability to understand the meaning of text. On the WIAT-III Reading Comprehension subtest, Shanila performed in the below range (SS = 72, 3rd percentile). The reading comprehension measure involved asking Shanila to silently read passages and answer questions that were all orally presented to her. She also had the opportunity to refer back to the passage while answering the questions, which she took advantage of during the testing session. Although Shanila generally performed better on explicit questions, she made frequent errors regarding the recollection of specific, concrete details specified explicitly within the passages. Additionally, Shanila did not successfully answer any of the questions that required her to make inferences about the text based on background knowledge and related information provided in the passages.

Writing

The WIAT-III was administered to assess Shanila's academic skills in the area of writing. On the Written Expression composite of the WIAT-III, which reflects performance in sentence composition, essay composition, and spelling, Shanila performed in the below-average range (SS = 85, 16th percentile). Her performance on the subsections of grammar and mechanics as well as word count were at the average range (SS = 92,

(continued)

EXAMPLE 9.1 SCHOOL-BASED PSYCHOEDUCATIONAL CASE REPORT (*continued*)

30th percentile; SS = 111, 77th percentile, respectively). Theme and development of her essay text indicated neglect to provide an identified thesis and conclusion, and her entire essay was a run-on sentence (SS = 89, 23rd percentile). Furthermore, Shanila made a few spelling errors that appeared to reflect difficulties with phonemic awareness related to hearing sounds in words (e.g., sockter vs. soccer).

Shanila's performance on the sentence composition tasks corresponded with the below-average range (SS = 71, 3rd percentile). The sentence composition subtest consisted of two components, including sentence building and sentence combining. Shanila performed within the significantly below to below-average range with corresponding percentile ranks of 5 and 14, respectively. Specifically, she experienced difficulties combining two to three sentences into one. During the sentence building tasks, Shanila was asked to write a sentence that included a presented word. She demonstrated appropriate mechanic skills during these tasks. However, she frequently misused the word provided in her constructed sentences due to confusing the words with similar sounding words (e.g., an vs. and; of vs. off; and or vs. our). Shanila's performance in spelling was average range (SS = 93, 32nd percentile).

Math

Broad Mathematics

The WIAT-III was chosen to assess Shanila's academic achievement in the area of mathematics including problem solving, numerical operations, and math fluency. For broad mathematics, Shanila performed within the below-average range (SS = 87, 19th percentile).

Numerical Operations

Shanila's performance on the Mathematics composite of the WIAT-III reflects average skills on the numerical operations subtest, with a score that corresponds to the 63rd percentile rank. She demonstrated strengths in single to triple digit addition, single to double digit subtraction, and single digit multiplication.

Math Fluency

Math fluency is an area of strength for Shanila including skills in her rate and accuracy when completing addition, subtraction, and multiplication problems (Addition SS = 132, 98th percentile; Subtraction SS = 105, 63rd percentile; Multiplication SS = 136, 99th percentile).

Problem Solving

Math Problem-Solving skills appear to be the only area of skill struggle within the math subtests. She performed within the below-average range (SS = 72, 3rd percentile). Overall, Shanila demonstrated strengths in answering questions that required her to solve basic addition and subtraction problems presented in the form of word problems.

(*continued*)

170 • SECTION II: INTERNSHIP

EXAMPLE 9.1 SCHOOL-BASED PSYCHOEDUCATIONAL CASE REPORT (*continued*)

However, she had difficulty with some specific types of problems (i.e., completing complex patterns; telling the time on an analog clock; analyzing basic features on a bar graph; and identifying differences in monetary value of coins).

Intellectual Functioning

The KABC-II was administered to obtain an estimate of Shanila's cognitive abilities. The Fluid-Crystallized Index (FCI) measures five broad abilities (sequential, simultaneous, learning, planning, and knowledge) and is considered an overall measure of one's general cognitive ability. Shanila obtained a FCI within the below-average range of cognitive functioning (SS = 72, 3%). Her Nonverbal Index (NVI) was in the low average range (SS = 84, 14%).

Sequential

Shanila's ability to replicate sequential or serial ordered items to solve problems is in the average range (SS = 94, 34th percentile). Tasks assessing this skill required her to remember sequences of information and recall this information to answer questions. During these tasks, Shanila demonstrated use of metacognitive strategies to remember and recall information presented to her (e.g., repeating the information quietly to herself).

Simultaneous

Shanila's ability to manipulate abstractions, rules, generalizations, and recognize patterns is in the below-average range (SS = 87, 19th percentile). Tasks assessing this skill required Shanila to solve problems using visual stimuli, spatial manipulations, and nonverbal reasoning. When asked to solve complex mazes with manipulatives, Shanila appeared to impulsively respond to some of the items. Furthermore, Shanila frequently noted that she could not successfully complete the task presented ("I'm a failure at this"), when asked to recreate a series of modeled or pictured designs using triangle-shaped manipulatives.

Learning

Shanila's ability to store and efficiently retrieve newly learned or previously learned information is in the significantly below-average range (SS = 70, 2nd percentile). Tasks assessing this skill required her to memorize names of pictures and be able to identify them when they were presented in various ways.

Planning

Shanila's ability to solve novel problems by using reasoning abilities such as induction and deduction is in the significantly below-average range (SS = 69, 2nd percentile). Tasks assessing this skill required Shanila to place pictures in order of sequential events and identify patterns in groups of pictures presented to her. Shanila enjoyed these tasks and often commented about the sequential order of items.

(*continued*)

EXAMPLE 9.1 SCHOOL-BASED PSYCHOEDUCATIONAL CASE REPORT (*continued*)

Knowledge

Shanila's ability to demonstrate the breadth and depth of knowledge acquired from one's culture is in the below-average range (SS = 72, 3rd percentile). Tasks assessing this skill required Shanila to identify pictures that best exhibited the meaning of various words presented to her as well as solve riddles. Shanila was able to identify pictures of words that she was familiar with; however, she demonstrated difficulties solving increasingly complex riddles.

Social–Emotional Assessments

The Behavioral Assessment System for Children, 2nd Edition (BASC-2) was administered to Shanila's mother and two of her teachers. The BASC-2 is an omnibus behavior rating scale designed to broadly assess children's and adolescents' emotional and behavioral functioning. Shanila's mother and current third-grade teacher also completed the SSIS rating scales. The SSIS rating scales use a multirater approach to identify students suspected of having significant social skills deficits, and provides a brief assessment of problem behaviors.

Social–Emotional: BASC-2 Parent Ratings

Shanila's mother completed the BASC-2, Parent Rating Scale and indicated at-risk concerns for anxiety. At-risk concerns also were indicated for hyperactive behaviors, aggression, conduct problems, and attention. Specifically, items noted were that Shanila often cannot wait her turn; interrupts others; disobeys; and gets into trouble. Furthermore, she is sometimes dishonest to escape responsibility for her actions, deceives others, and sneaks around. Mrs. Price reported concerns in the clinically significant range for withdrawal with specific concern for her hesitancy to make new friends.

With respect to Shanila's adaptive skills, Mrs. Price reported that Shanila generally demonstrates normal range leadership skills, functional communication, activities of daily living, and overall adaptibility. In contrast, she rated difficulty with social skills in the clinical range, an indication that Shanila is sometimes easily annoyed by others and generally does not display behaviors that will help her maintain friendships.

Social–Emotional: BASC-2 Teacher Ratings

Two of Shanila's teachers also completed the BASC-2 Teacher Rating Scale indicating at-risk to clinically significant concerns for externalizing behaviors (hyperactivity, conduct problems, and aggression), school problems (learning and attention), and behavioral symptoms (atypicality and withdrawal). With respects to externalizing behaviors, Shanila's teachers noted concerns about her sitting still; interrupting others; defying

(continued)

EXAMPLE 9.1 SCHOOL-BASED PSYCHOEDUCATIONAL CASE REPORT (*continued*)

teachers; and annoying/teasing other children. Shanila's teachers generally reported inconsistent ratings for internalizing behaviors (anxiety and depression), ranging from average to at-risk concerns. Although Shanila's teachers reported inconsistent ratings for anxiety and depression, both teachers noted that Shanila worries often; says she's afraid to make mistakes; worries about the opinions of other students; seems lonely at times; is easily upset and negative about things; sometimes states that she does not have any friends; and complains about being teased. Teacher ratings also indicate that Shanila's problems in school may be attributed to learning problems and attention, as these ratings were both in the at-risk range.

In regard to Shanila's social interactions, Shanila's teachers noted that she is easily annoyed with others and exhibits clinically significant withdrawal and atypical behaviors. According to Shanila's teachers she sometimes refuses to talk; has trouble making new friends; takes a longer time processing information; does not seem to understanding body language and social cues; laughs excessively in a high pitch tone; stares at others; says things that make little sense; and acts confused. The teachers also reported at-risk to clinically significant concerns regarding her adaptive behaviors. Specifically, she has difficulties with functional communication, adjusting to changes in routine, and demonstrating adequate leadership and social skills.

Social Skills Improvement System

Because Shanila's mother and teachers endorsed items that suggest that Shanila lacks adequate social skills on the BASC, the SSIS Parent Rating Form and Teacher Rating Form also were given to Mrs. Price and Shanila's current third-grade teacher. At the subscale level, the result of the ratings shows a general agreement between their perceptions of Shanila's social skills. Both raters reported that Shanila's Communication, Assertion, Empathy, Engagement, and Self-Control are all in the below-average level. In contrast, Shanila's mother indicated that Shanila's Responsibility is at the average level, while Shanila's teacher indicated that her Responsibility is at the below-average level. Shanila's teacher rated her Cooperation level as falling within the average range, compared to Mrs. Price who reported Shanila's Cooperation level as falling within the below-average range.

Reflecting on Shanila's strengths, the following behaviors were reported on the parent and teacher rating forms. Shanila is generally responsible with other people's things, makes eye contact when talking to others, and speaks in the appropriate tone of voice. Furthermore, she pays attention to her mother's instructions and follows household rules. Mrs. Price reported that Shanila almost always expresses her feelings when wronged and often questions unfair rules. Shanila's teacher's ratings also reveal that Shanila demonstrates the following strengths in the classroom: asking for help more often than not; staying calm when teased; participating in games/group activities; and starting conversations.

Overall, Mrs. Price reported that Shanila's Social Skills (SS = 64, 1st percentile) are well below-average range. Similarly, Shanila's teacher's ratings indicate that her

(continued)

EXAMPLE 9.1 SCHOOL-BASED PSYCHOEDUCATIONAL CASE REPORT (*continued*)

Social Skills (SS = 58, 1st percentile) fall within the below-average range. These results suggest that Shanila has significant difficulties exhibiting appropriate social skills.

SUMMARY AND RECOMMENDATIONS

Shanila is a 9-year-old third-grade student that has attended Rolling Oak School since kindergarten. Her mother noted that Shanila enjoys listening to music, playing the piano, being outside, and interacting with siblings. Although Shanila is experiencing difficulties, Mrs. Price expressed that Shanila wants to do well in school. Similarly, Shanila's teachers described her as a student who loves horses, running, and outdoor activities. Shanila was evaluated during the spring of her first-grade school year and documentation indicates that she did not meet criteria for special education at that time. Successively more intensive interventions have been implemented for Shanila since first grade to address academic difficulties in the areas of reading and math. While Shanila has demonstrated proficiency levels in basic reading skills and math calculations, her WIAT-III and classroom CBM performance indicates that she continues to experience difficulties with reading comprehension, vocabulary, math problem solving, and writing.

Previous interventions have also been implemented since her first-grade year to address inappropriate classroom behaviors and social skills. These interventions have included Tier 1 prosocial classroom curricula and inclusion in small friendship group counseling as well as individualized counseling. Overall, Shanila has made gradual progress. Although she is engaging in more peer interactions and generally follows directions, Shanila's teachers noted that she sometimes disobeys, refuses to comply with teachers' requests, talks/laughs at inappropriate times, is easily distracted, stares at others, and can withdraw at times from other students. In general, on the BASC, Shanila's mother noted at-risk to clinically significant ratings in withdrawal and at-risk concerns for hyperactivity, aggression, conduct problems, attention, anxiety, and social skills. Shanila's teachers reported at-risk to clinically significant concerns for hyperactivity, conduct problems, aggression, school problems, learning, attention, atypicality and withdrawal. Furthermore, Shanila's teachers reported at-risk to clinical ratings for adaptability, social skills, leadership, and functional communication. Parent and teacher ratings on the SSIS also demonstrate that her social skills are well below the average level.

Furthermore, the current estimate of her general cognitive abilities are in the below-average range of functioning. Within her cognitive profile, sequential learning is a relative strength, which may explain Shanila's increased performance with concrete, step-by-step structured tasks, particular those presented with visual cues. Based on these assessment results, her slow response to the interventions provided suggests a significant lack of response to intervention. Any special education placement considerations remain a parent/school personnel team decision. Therefore, the recommendations noted in the following are made to support Shanila's academic

(continued)

EXAMPLE 9.1 SCHOOL-BASED PSYCHOEDUCATIONAL CASE REPORT (*continued*)

progress, reduce inappropriate classroom behaviors, and improve her social and problem-solving skills. Facilitating factors for her success include her desire to perform well in school, her positive regard for classes, and her parental supports for educational achievement.

Reading

Continued intervention utilizing explicit instruction with immediate feedback is recommended. Given that Shanila performs better with structured tasks, graphic organizers and story maps could be used to help her identify important text elements; arrange words to make sentences; identify the sequence of events, grammar, setting, characters, problems, and resolutions; practice organizing information to gain understanding; and restating the main idea using her own words. Shanila also may benefit from explicit and systematic vocabulary instruction by decreasing the amount of information she has to infer. Shanila would benefit from being exposed to word-rich stories and target words in varied and meaningful contexts. She would also benefit from being provided direct and incidental vocabulary instruction with multiple opportunities to practice and use target words. The following specific skills gaps were noted: difficulty differentiating paired words beginning or ending with the same sound, reading accuracy, difficulty making inferences, and errors in remembering concrete factual details in stories. It is important to note that some of her errors appeared to be related to rushing through tasks. Thus, prompts to *slow down, stop-and-think*, or *take her time reviewing* may be helpful.

Math

Continued intervention to address math problem solving is recommended. Explicit instruction can be delivered with immediate feedback. The following seven-step process may help Shanila improve her math problem-solving skills: (a) read the problem, (b) paraphrase the problem (orally or in print), (c) draw the problem, (d) create a plan (with support) to solve the problem, (e) predict the answer, (f) compute the answer, (g) check the answer. Regarding complex numerical operations, Shanila may benefit from having ongoing access to a number line and a calculator, in addition to one-to-one supports.

Writing

Shanila may benefit from intensified intervention to address writing skills. She may benefit from the direct use of graphic organizers to help her plan her writing. Additionally, writing instruction targeting sentence construction, combining sentences, the use of descriptives, and how to develop a thesis and a conclusion are warranted.

(continued)

EXAMPLE 9.1 SCHOOL-BASED PSYCHOEDUCATIONAL CASE REPORT (*continued*)

Individualized Social Skills Counseling

Because Shanila continues to demonstrate social skills needs despite some prior progress toward intervention goals, individualized counseling in this area is warranted. The following specific needs are noted: replacement behaviors for staring at others, use of appropriate tone, reciprocity in conversation, scripts for introducing herself and kindness in communications, as well as some empathy-building exercises to help her understand how others may feel when criticized or stared at. Additionally, there are some aggression and conduct problems. Therefore, problem-solving curricula addressing these needs are recommended.

Self-Affirmation Statements and Immediate Feedback

Given that Shanila frequently comments on her failures and seems to worry about her academic progress and peer relationships, it is important to teach her self-affirmations and write these on an index card for reference (e.g., "I am a hard worker," "I can do my best," "I can play well with other children") or a reminder bracelet may be helpful.

Classroom Behavior

Throughout test and counseling sessions, Shanila displayed more appropriate behaviors with the use of a sticker reinforcement sheet. Therefore, she may benefit from positive reinforcement strategies using visual stimuli. Because Shanila responds to one-to-one feedback and is at times inattentive and off-task, she may also benefit from discreet cues or signals including teacher monitoring in close proximity to remind her to stay on task. Furthermore, Shanila appeared to understand the content in counseling sessions when presented visually. Hence, she may also benefit from visual cues regarding appropriate classroom behaviors.

Intellectual Functioning

Based on teachers' reports and Shanila's performance on the KABC-II, Shanila may benefit from step-by-step, concrete, structured tasks. Because Shanila experienced difficulties retrieving newly learned or previously learned information, she may also benefit from the use of memory aids and strategies to help her recall greater amounts of information (e.g., rehearsal/repetition; visual aids; break procedures down into smaller tasks; and lesson summaries using graphic organizers).

Maggie Zuker, BS	Maria Rodriguez, EdS, NCSP
School Psychology, Practicum Student	Certified School Psychologist # 12345

(continued)

EXAMPLE 9.1 SCHOOL-BASED PSYCHOEDUCATIONAL CASE REPORT (*continued*)

SHANILA'S ASSESSMENT RESULTS
Wechsler Individual Achievement Test, Third Edition (WIAT-III)

COMPOSITES/SUBSCALES	STANDARD SCORE	PERCENTILE	DESCRIPTIVE CATEGORY
Total Reading	89	23	Below Average
Early Reading Skills	69	2	Significantly Below Average
Basic Reading	93	32	Average
Word Reading	90	25	Average
Pseudoword Decoding	97	42	Average
Reading Comprehension and Fluency	90	25	Average
Reading Comprehension	72	3	Below Average
Oral Reading Fluency	113	81	High Average
Oral Reading Accuracy	83	13	Below Average
Oral Reading Rate	112	79	High Average
Written Expression	85	16	Below Average
Alphabet Writing Fluency	119	90	High Average
Spelling	93	32	Average
Essay Composition	101	53	Average
Grammar and Mechanics	92	30	Average
Word Count	111	77	Average
Theme and Development and Text Organization	89	23	Below Average
Sentence Composition	71	3	Below Average
Sentence Building	84	14	Below Average
Sentence Combining	61	.5	Significantly Below Average
Mathematics	87	19	Below Average
Math Problem Solving	72	3	Below Average

(*continued*)

9: PSYCHOLOGICAL CASE REPORTS • 177

EXAMPLE 9.1 SCHOOL-BASED PSYCHOEDUCATIONAL CASE REPORT (*continued*)

SHANILA'S ASSESSMENT RESULTS (*continued*)

COMPOSITES/SUBSCALES	STANDARD SCORE	PERCENTILE	DESCRIPTIVE CATEGORY
Numerical Operations	105	63	Average
Math Fluency	127	93	Above Average
Math Fluency—Addition	132	98	Above Average
Math Fluency—Subtraction	105	63	Average
Math Fluency—Multiplication	136	99	Above Average
Total Achievement	82	12	Below Average

KAUFMAN ASSESSMENT BATTERY FOR CHILDREN (KABC-II)

SCALE INDEXES	STANDARD SCORE	CONFIDENCE INTERVAL	PERCENTILE	DESCRIPTIVE CATEGORY
Sequential/Gsm	94	84–104	34th	Average
Number Recall	10		50th	Average
Word Order	8		25th	Average
Simultaneous/Gv	87	78–98	19th	Below Average
Rover	6		9th	Below Average
Triangles	10		50th	Average
Learning/Glr	70	63–79	2nd	Significantly Below Average
Atlantis	6		9th	Below Average
Rebus	3		1st	Significantly Below Average
Planning/Gf	69	62–78	2nd	Significantly Below Average
Story Completion	4		2nd	Significantly Below Average

(*continued*)

EXAMPLE 9.1 SCHOOL-BASED PSYCHOEDUCATIONAL CASE REPORT (*continued*)

KAUFMAN ASSESSMENT BATTERY FOR CHILDREN (KABC-II) (*continued*)

SCALE INDEXES	STANDARD SCORE	CONFIDENCE INTERVAL	PERCENTILE	DESCRIPTIVE CATEGORY
Pattern Reasoning	5		5th	Below Average
Knowledge/Gc	72	64–82	3rd	Below Average
Verbal Knowledge	6		9th	Below Average
Riddles	4		2nd	Significantly Below Average
Nonverbal Index	84	78–90	14th	Below Average
Fluid-Crystalized Index	72	66–78	3rd	Below Average

BEHAVIOR ASSESSMENT SYSTEM FOR CHILDREN, SECOND EDITION–PARENT RATING FORM

	T SCORE	PERCENTILE
Clinical Scales		
Hyperactivity	66*	93
Aggression	64*	91
Conduct Problems	69*	96
Anxiety	60*	84
Depression	41	17
Somatization	36	3
Atypicality	52	71
Withdrawal	75**	99
Attention Problems	68*	94
Adaptive Scales		
Adaptability	43	27

(*continued*)

9: PSYCHOLOGICAL CASE REPORTS • 179

EXAMPLE 9.1 SCHOOL-BASED PSYCHOEDUCATIONAL CASE REPORT (*continued*)

BEHAVIOR ASSESSMENT SYSTEM FOR CHILDREN, SECOND EDITION–PARENT RATING FORM (*continued*)

	T SCORE	PERCENTILE
Social Skills	25**	1
Leadership	49	44
Activities of Daily Living	58	78
Functional Communication	45	26
Externalizing Problems	69*	95
Internalizing Problems	45	33
Adaptive Skills	43	22

*, at risk; **, clinically significant.

BEHAVIOR ASSESSMENT SYSTEM FOR CHILDREN, SECOND EDITION–TEACHER RATING FORM

	TEACHER 1		TEACHER 2	
	T score	Percentile	T score	Percentile
Clinical Scales				
Hyperactivity	73**	96	73**	96
Aggression	71**	95	66*	92
Conduct Problems	70**	94	65*	91
Anxiety	61*	86	51	62
Depression	54	76	65*	92
Somatization	42	19	50	64
Attention Problems	62*	85	68*	94
Learning Problems	68*	93	64*	89
Atypicality	77**	97	67*	94
Withdrawal	86**	99	75**	97

(*continued*)

EXAMPLE 9.1 SCHOOL-BASED PSYCHOEDUCATIONAL CASE REPORT (*continued*)

BEHAVIOR ASSESSMENT SYSTEM FOR CHILDREN, SECOND EDITION–TEACHER RATING FORM (*continued*)

	TEACHER 1		TEACHER 2	
Adaptive Scales				
Adaptability	30**	3	30**	3
Social Skills	28**	1	30**	2
Leadership	34*	4	36*	8
Study Skills	45	31	35*	9
Functional Communication	19**	1	28**	3
Externalizing Problems	73**	97	69*	95
Internalizing Problems	53	70	57	80
School Problems	66*	93	67*	94
Adaptive Skills	29**	2	29**	3

*, at risk; **, clinically significant.

SOCIAL SKILLS IMPROVEMENT SYSTEM, PARENT AND TEACHER RATING SCALES

	STANDARD SCORE / %	DESCRIPTIVE
Parent Scores		
Social Skills	64 / 1st	Well Below Average
Communication		Below Average
Cooperation		Below Average
Assertion		Below Average
Responsibility		Average
Empathy		Below Average
Engagement		Below Average
Self-Control		Below Average

(continued)

EXAMPLE 9.1 SCHOOL-BASED PSYCHOEDUCATIONAL CASE REPORT (*continued*)

SOCIAL SKILLS IMPROVEMENT SYSTEM, PARENT AND TEACHER RATING SCALES (*continued*)

	STANDARD SCORE / %	DESCRIPTIVE
Teacher Scores		
Social Skills	58 / 1st	Well Below Average
Communication		Below Average
Cooperation		Average
Assertion		Below Average
Responsibility		Below Average
Empathy		Below Average
Engagement		Below Average
Self-Control		Below Average

Intervention Case Reports

In addition to psychoeducational assessment reports, school psychologists also will generate intervention reports and summaries as well. The purpose of these reports is generally to document tiered intervention services and outcomes to inform further educational decisions for students. The reports focus on describing the duration, frequency, and types of specific intervention services provided, sometimes by delineating goals and activities for each session. Data tend to be related to preintervention baseline measures, progress monitoring data throughout intervention, and postintervention information to test the efficacy of intervention. When the services are highly effective, recommendations may include dismissal from services. When the results are not optimal, recommendations may include problem solving different approaches to the interventions, adding additional services, or increasing the frequency and duration of services.

Intervention reports created within clinical settings often document treatment regimens and patient response. Outpatient treatment documentation for insurance reimbursements also may be a reason that intervention reports are required. In some circumstances, intervention reports may be mandated by juvenile justice for adjudicated youth provisions and by courts for truancy or custody decisions. It will be important to consider the intended audience for each report as highly specific information may need to be included. For example, adjudicated youth stipulations may require documenting case numbers, date of offense, court decisions, and terms of treatment. An example of an intervention report providing very short-term, individualized counseling intervention for a student with test anxiety is provided at www.springerpub.com/school-psychology-practicum (Exhibit 9.2).

Clinic-Based Case Reports

Although the goals of reports generated in clinical settings are similar to those in school settings, some differences do exist. Clinical reports are written for an audience of parents and guardians but in addition need to meet the standards insurance providers require so that families can be reimbursed for the evaluation costs. Thus, the reports may have a greater focus on medical terms and establishing criteria for *DSM-5* diagnoses. A broader emphasis on in-depth social–developmental history is typically included and recommendations are more likely to include outside service providers. When clinical reports have a purpose of supporting transitioning for inpatient hospital treatment back to school or when collaboration between outpatient services and school services are anticipated, educational elements also may be presented in the clinical reports. It is important to note that, generally, professionals in the medical community are not as familiar with the Individuals with Disabilities Education Improvement Act (IDEIA) or state educational regulations; therefore, they may recommend school services without adequate criteria. This is an opportunity for school psychologists to bridge the two fields, and practicum experience in both school and clinical settings can help facilitate this set of skills. In particular pediatric school psychology programs are designed to offer extensive knowledge across the domains of medical- and school-based intervention (see Exhibit 9.3 for an example of a clinic-based report; www.springerpub .com/school-psychology-practicum).

Legal and Ethical Guideline Considerations

A number of converging national laws and ethical codes also address guidelines for writing psychological reports and service recommendations. The specific laws and standards will most likely be covered in detail in the program's ethics and law course work. However, the following are mentioned briefly as each provides important areas of guidance for report writing.

- Individuals with Disabilities Education Improvement Act (2004); 20 United States Code section 1400 et seq.
  - Provide appropriate services to students with disabilities in the regular classroom when appropriate
- Federal Register, Offices of Special Education and Rehabilitative Services, Department of Education (2006) 34 Code of Federal Regulation, section 300 et seq.
  - Utilize assessments that inform educational needs
- National Association of School Psychologists, Principles for Professional Ethics (2010)
  - Respect individual's privacy
  - Assessments are valid, fair, and utilize a variety of measures and methods
  - Report test results in clear and understandable terms
- American Psychological Association (APA) Ethics Code (2010)
  - Assessors indicate limitation of their evaluation interpretations and only provide opinions based on examination that is adequate to support the opinion
  - Utilize instruments and measurements within the limits supported by research
- APA Standards for Educational and Psychological Testing (2014)
  - Provide interpretations appropriate for the audience in simple language
  - Use only test that are valid for the intended purpose

Diversity Considerations

Best practices in assessment, intervention, and subsequent report writing also emphasize the need for diligence in the selection of methods and measures that are nondiscriminatory and appropriate for the population to whom they are administered. Additionally, personal awareness of the influence of one's own cultural heritage when interpreting and reporting data is important. This may be especially true of psychology methods that rely on qualitative sources of information (e.g., interviews, observations). Acknowledging that individuals will interpret their life experience based on their culture, as well as being cognizant of the limitations in fully understanding another's culture, also are important considerations when writing psychological reports (McGoldrick, Giordano, & Garcia-Presto, 2005, pp. 36–37). A detailed review of these standards is typically given in the program's core curricula, often through diversity classes and/or ethics and law course work. Guidance on these factors is provided through a number of national publications (e.g., *Guidelines for Providers of Psychological Services to Ethnic, Linguistic, and Culturally Diverse Populations* [APA, 1990]; *Guidelines on Multicultural Education, Training, Research, Practice, and Organizational Change for Psychologists* [APA, 2002]).

CHAPTER REVIEW

This chapter has reviewed the basic components of psychological evaluation and intervention report writing. Although the core elements in reports (e.g., referral concern, assessment data review, recommendations) are the same across settings, there also are a number of differences between school-based and clinic-based evaluations. School-based reports will attend closely to educational history and academic interventions, special education eligibility criteria, and recommendations that can be implemented in classroom settings. Differences for clinical reports may include a greater emphasis on medical history and psychopharmacology regimens, as well as inclusion of diagnostic codes for insurance billing. Both types of reports focus on meeting the needs of the child or adolescent and strive to facilitate access to appropriate services. Intervention case reports have less focus on history and assessment with a greater emphasis on describing the services provided and the child's responsiveness to the treatment or intervention. Recommendations within intervention reports typically note the youth's current functioning level and discuss whether continued services are warranted. If so, the type of intervention needed also will be indicated.

REFERENCES

American Psychiatric Association. (2013). *Diagnostic and statistical manual of mental disorders* (5th ed.). Arlington, VA: American Psychiatric Publishing.

American Psychological Association. (1990). *Guidelines for providers of psychological services to ethnic, linguistic, and culturally diverse populations*. Washington, DC: Author.

American Psychological Association. (2002) *Guidelines on multicultural education, training, research, practice, and organizational change for psychologists*. Washington, DC: Author.

American Psychological Association. (2010). *Ethical principles of psychologists and code of conduct with the 2010 amendments*. Washington, DC: Author.

American Psychological Association. (2014). *Standards for educational and psychological testing*. Washington, DC: Author.

Federal Register, Offices of Special Education and Rehabilitative Services, Department of Education 34 CFR §300 (2006).

Individuals with Disabilities Education Improvement Act 20 U.S.C. § 1400 (2004).

McGoldrick, M., Giordano, J., & Garcia-Presto, N. (2005). *Ethnicity and family therapy* (3rd ed.). New York, NY: Guilford.

National Association of School Psychologists. (2010). *Principles for professional ethics*. Bethesda, MD: Author.

Sattler, J. M. (2014). *Foundations of behavioral, social, and clinical assessment of children* (6th ed.). San Diego, CA: Jerome M. Sattler.

CHAPTER 10

Preparing for Career Positions

LEARNING OBJECTIVES

At the conclusion of this chapter, readers should be able to:

1. Develop a professional curriculum vita for entry-level career positions
2. Identify appropriate postdoctoral sites or institutions with positions that meet professional goals
3. Apply strategies to prepare for interviews

Preparing applications for your first career position is the culminating event of years of professional training and competency building. This is the launch point for a career track that will most likely span the next 30 years. Keeping this in mind, this chapter offers tips and strategies for searching and acquiring career positions that are most likely to satisfy your life-long aspirations. Although the chapter reviews some aspects found in Chapter 6 such as vita preparation and interview skills that will be necessary in the job search process, the perspective is from the needs of a professional seeking career opportunities rather than from that of an intern seeking culminating competency-building and training experiences.

IS A POSTDOC IN YOUR FUTURE?

For some individuals with doctoral-level training, an intermediary step between internship and the first career position may be an important consideration. The American Psychological Association (APA; 2014a, 2014b) defines the postdoctoral fellowship as a temporary period in which postdoctoral graduates receive highly individualized mentoring and supervised training to obtain essential skills for one's chosen career path. For individuals who are anticipating a research-intensive position or a

186 • SECTION II: INTERNSHIP

highly complex clinical specialization, having postdoctoral or fellowship experience can be beneficial. Although many employers will not require such experience, a postdoc can help you establish your professional identity early as an independent researcher or an expert treatment provider, and may provide an advantage for highly competitive positions. The postdoc may be especially valuable for acquiring academic positions at nationally funded research centers, one-of-a-kind clinics that require technical expertise, and during economic downturns that may result in fewer job openings and therefore greater competition among job applicants. Likewise, a postdoctoral teaching appointment can expand your competency as a faculty member by broadening experiences in presenting varied course topics, participating on college committees, attending leadership meetings, and involvement in program development.

For those interested in pursuing a career in an independent practice outside of schools, many states mandate at least 1 year of licensed supervision following internship. This supervision requirement may be acquired through the first year of independent work or can be arranged as an additional benefit of a formalized postdoc experience. Postdoctoral supervision for those seeking a license to practice psychology also may permit individuals to obtain specialty credentialing (APA, 2014b). Planning for postdoc positions should occur well before completing your graduate program to allow adequate time to identify postdoc options and acquire graduate school experiences that help prepare you for your desired position.

Finding a Postdoc

If you aspire to obtain a postdoc position, multiple resources are available through national professional organizations. The APA website maintains a list of psychology postdoc opportunities through its PsycCareers webpage that offers keyword searches by location and specialty (www.psyccareers .com/jobs). The Association of Psychology Postdoctoral and Internship Centers (APPIC) also lists postdoctoral psychology training opportunities (www.appic.org/About-APPIC/Postdoctoral). Additionally, following are a variety of highly specialized postdoc training sites:

- The American Association for the Advancement of Science (sciencecareers .sciencemag.org)
- The Association of Postdoctoral Programs in Clinical Neuropsychology (www.appcn.org)
- The National Postdoctoral Association (NPA; www.nationalpostdoc.org)
- The Society of Behavioral Medicine (www.sbm.org)

- The Society of Clinical Child and Adolescent Psychology (APA Division 53; www.clinicalchildpsychology.org/internships_postdocs)
- The Society of Pediatric Psychology (APA Division 54; www.apa.org/about/division/div54.aspx)
- *Rehabilitation Psychology* (APA Division 22; www.apadivisions.org/division-22)

Each of these specialized opportunities will have strict prerequisite course work and skill expectations, another reason to plan early. Many of the specialized psychology postdocs may be best suited to hybrid school psychology programs that offer cross-disciplinary approaches (e.g., pediatric school psychology; clinical school psychology).

Additional listings of postdoctoral openings may be found in several journal and professional organization publications such as the *Chronicle of Higher Education* and the *APA Monitor*. Advertisements tend to be easily accessible both in online and in printed formats. Because not all postdoctoral positions are well advertised, networking and self-advocacy also can be advantageous. Thus, you may want to reach out to your program faculty, clinicians, your internship supervisor, and members of your state's professional psychology-related organizations to help identify additional potential opportunities.

Quality of the Postdoc

Bailey (2004) advises students to choose between formal and informal training programs. Formal programs such as those accredited by the APA or affiliated with the APPIC can provide students with focused training and specialized experience. Nationally, there are generally fewer vacancies for formalized accredited psychology postdoc sites. Nevertheless, school psychology graduates from rigorous programs with appropriate prerequisites can successfully compete for these openings. It is important to note that the informal postdocs can also still offer high-quality specialized training experiences although there is more variability. These opportunities may include working as a psychological assistant or unlicensed psychologist for a private practitioner. If you choose this option, you want to confirm that the position is structured in a manner that meets your goals and state licensure requirements, and perhaps offers employment opportunities after completing the postdoc.

Several organizations offer guidelines and principles for high-quality postdoc experiences including the APA, the Council of Specialties in Professional Psychology (cospp.org/resources/accreditation), and the NPA (NPA, www.nationalpostdoc.org). Collectively, their guidelines and principles emphasize the importance of purposefully structuring the postdoctoral

188 • SECTION II: INTERNSHIP

experience to include the following key components (APA, 2012; Nathan, Piacentini, Spririto, & King, 2014):

- Licensed supervision with a senior faculty member or psychologist that can ensure the state requirements for number of supervision hours per week and duration of the postdoc (e.g., 1 year, 2,000 hours) are met.
- Significant one-on-one collaboration and mentorship with the supervisor offering both didactic and experiential learning.
- Institutional or agency sponsorship and resource allocation with an operating budget that supports residents' office space, equipment, technology, resource materials, and salary/benefits needs to foster a high caliber training experience.
- Location in institutional infrastructures with provision of psychological services or training programs that facilitates access to populations for treatment or research activities consistent to the postdoctoral training goals.
- Systematic, formally documented, and consistently implemented procedures that foster respect for linguistic, cultural, and individual diversity as well as responsible and ethical practice/research.
- Written roles and responsibilities, policies, employment contracts, performance feedback/evaluation measures, due process, and grievance procedures.
- A cohesive, written philosophy of training that offers graduated complexity and responsibilities for the resident's experiences for building competencies and expertise.
- Socialization into the profession through mentoring, role modeling, and collaborative scholarship (e.g., coauthoring, copresenting, and participation in organizational leadership forums).

The APA website delineates guidelines for two types of postdocs: research and practice (www.apa.org/education/grad/post-fellow.aspx). With respect to research-based postdoc positions, Pelham (2014) suggests that you consider whether the postdoctoral position will permit you to acquire new skills and publish meaningful research papers. If the postdoc experience does not offer expanded opportunities beyond your internship experience, it may not have added value for the time invested and potentially reduced salary. You may also want to determine if you will be afforded the opportunity to work alongside a highly recognized faculty or research mentor whose expertise, skills, and interests are a good match to yours. The postdoc experience should foster a productive, healthy, and collaborative relationship between the mentor(s) and the fellow who needs additional research experience. Publications and national presentations are an added benefit of a research postdoc; thus, reviewing the number and type of publications and presentations of the mentor will be helpful in determining her or his productivity and the likelihood of coauthoring or copresenting.

Fairness and adherence to ethical guidelines in crediting coauthors will also be an important consideration. Expectations for coauthorship are delineated in several publications and generally following guidelines regarding the source of original data, the level of contribution and project grant funding considerations (American Psychological Association Science Student Council, 2007; Barker, 2002). It would be important to be familiar with the guidelines and to also explore the expectations postdoc supervisors may have regarding coauthoring during interviews. This conversation can help clarify the willingness of the supervisor to facilitate coauthorship, first-authorship opportunities, and potential funding for regional and national presentations.

For those students seeking postdoctoral training to obtain licensure and a practice specialization, acquainting yourself with your state's licensing requirements and any specialized certification processes is highly recommended. The postdoc may need to be specifically structured in client service contact hours to qualify for the state's specialized credentialing mandates. Specialization also may require skills in specific assessment instruments or treatment modalities that are not typically taught in graduate programs; thus, attendance at professional development workshops and rotations to work with specialized populations may be a point of negotiation for a clinical postdoc. Having a substantial amount of meaningful responsibilities coupled with the autonomy to pursue your individualized specialization interests is recommended as well. Of note, some postdoctoral positions may be very narrow in scope; thus, explicit expectations for both the breadth and depth or experiences should be established in the postdoc contract to ensure that agreed opportunities are facilitated. Other factors to consider include benefits and salary. Because postdocs have a high level of experience and are often hired as employees, salaries are generally higher than for internships and benefits (e.g., insurance) will be offered, although postdoc salaries are often lower than typical staff positions.

CAREER LISTING RESOURCES

In selecting application sites, start by conceptualizing both short- and long-term career aspirations and deciding what trajectory will most likely facilitate those goals. This is often called a *big picture approach* and it is okay to let yourself visualize a *dream job* scenario. Contemplating what you wish to accomplish in the next 5 years, 10 years, and perhaps 20 is essential to guiding application choices. Identifying the type of sites that align with your professional growth needs will help to narrow the search and save time wasted in applying to sites that are unlikely to facilitate your personal development. Also consider the type of institutions that offer purposeful opportunities for advancement. As it is unlikely that the first entry-level position will encompass all your career aspirations, jobs that offer clear promotion steps and a tiered progression toward higher rank are valuable structures for your achievement. Often institutions' and agencies' websites will provide information on salary structure and promotion criteria. It is more likely that large institutions (e.g., urban school districts, government agencies, universities) will have a clear hierarchical infrastructure for career growth and specialization compared with small organizations. For example, some very rural school districts may have only one to two school psychologists. In those cases, salary and rank advancement based on years of service or the ability to cross to administrative roles will be important over time.

The National Association of School Psychologists (NASP) online career center service and the APA Monitor on Psychology website provide career seekers with a diverse range of job openings. For example, the NASP online career center services include district openings for school psychologists, school psychology vacancies within private agencies, and academic positions that are primarily situated in school psychology programs. Likewise, the APA Monitor on Psychology website includes multiple types of postings such as research and practice openings, available academic positions across a range of psychological fields, and clinical jobs in public and private institutions. If you have a specific agency to which you would like to apply, consider looking at the agency's website for career opportunities; as many career listing sites charge fees, some agencies opt to limit listings for career opportunities.

Some prospective employees desire to settle in or relocate to a specific region, state, city, or county. This decision may be influenced by several factors, such as financial obligations, family responsibilities, preferred climate, and so forth. For that reason, you also are encouraged to review your local state school psychology and psychology organizational websites. Visiting your local school district's human resource office and/or website can be helpful as well.

As noted by the National Career Fairs (2014), every meeting with a potential employer is an opportunity for you to learn about current and anticipated openings while making a lasting impact. Consequently, job fairs serve as another means for you to acquire knowledge about job openings. Job fairs may be held at national and state conferences (e.g., NASP's and APA's annual conventions) or on specified dates in your state or local community. If you choose to identify job availabilities through career fairs, the National Career Fairs (2014) website includes several helpful tips that you may want to review. One tip encourages prospective employees to present a professional appearance, smile, and make eye contact. Furthermore, prepare a few open-ended questions to ask in advance. These questions should demonstrate your knowledge of the company and enthusiasm to work for the agency. Speak clearly, refrain from interrupting the speaker or existing conversations, be brief, and offer a word of thanks at the end of your interaction.

You also might consider sending a follow-up e-mail or note thanking the employer for his or her time and expressing your interest in the position. Doing so can strengthen the employer's chances of remembering you and it makes a great impression.

In addition to specific organizational, institutional, and district websites, there are a host of general job vacancy websites that can be reviewed as well. For academic jobs, one frequently visited site is HigherEdJobs (www .higheredjobs.com). This website permits job seekers to search for vacant positions by field of study, category (e.g., faculty vs. administrative), location, and type of postsecondary academic institution (e.g., community college, 4-year university). The *U.S. News and World Report* website is another helpful resource for specific school psychologist positions (money.usnews .com/careers/best-jobs/school-psychologist). Lastly, several websites post international jobs, including:

- International Schools Services
  - www.iss.edu/school-services/staffing-a-school/school-recruiting-with-iss/open-positions
- International School Psychology Association
  - www.ispaweb.org
- InternationalSchoolJobs.com
  - www.internationalschooljobs.com/category/psychology.html

Finally, the power of networking cannot be stressed enough and there are a number of social network sites (e.g., LinkedIn) that facilitate this process. Your graduate faculty can be an excellent networking resource as well. They have a national trainer's listserv and receive regular academic job postings that can be forwarded to you (Networking [Def. 1], 2014). Informal inquiries through professors, internship supervisors, or prior employees of an institution can also provide important qualitative information on the work climate and quality of professionalism at an organization, which will be important deciding factors in selecting sites. Networking with your peers and colleagues can also be utilized as a means to gain information about vacant positions. Aside from graduate faculty, colleagues, and internship supervisors, some school psychology students have developed long-standing relationships with professional mentors outside of academia. These individuals can also alert career seekers to unfilled job positions.

WRITING A CAREER COVER LETTER AND VITA

Many employers will request applicants to also submit a cover letter. This may be the first item they read and serves as your introduction or first impression. Cover letters should be concise, point out your most notable accomplishments, and link your abilities directly to the criteria of the position, perhaps even including some of the specific phrases or language from the job advertisement that demonstrate how well you match their criteria (e.g., experience with low-incidence disabilities, license eligible). It will often be necessary to tailor cover letters to specific sites (National Association of School Psychologists [NASP], 2008). For examples of tailored cover letters for academia and practice see Appendix B, Exhibits B.10 and B.11, and see Chapter 6 for more details on writing a statement of professional goals.

You will also want to consider reconstructing your curriculum vita to highlight recent professional competencies and skills acquired on internship and to drop earlier, less relevant experiences, especially those not directly related to your professional goal. It also may be necessary to align the vita with the position that you aspire to obtain, which may require creating more than one version (for academic and professional practice vita samples see Exhibits 10.3 and 10.4, at www.springerpub.com/school-psychology-practicum). In pursuing a practitioner position, it is most important to highlight readiness for state certification or practitioner licensure, school-based service delivery, or clinical experiences, and obtain references from school psychologists and supervisors. In pursuing an academic position, it will be more important to highlight research, publications, presentations, or teaching accomplishments and to include references from research faculty.

The career vita (CV) is a professional document that provides a detailed description of your academic credentials and accomplishments. You want to develop a strong CV, which means paying careful attention to how the content is presented. This is important, given that your CV is often the first source of information that employers will acquire about you to make interview or employment decisions. Reviewing some of the information in Chapter 6 as well as a recent guide or text on broad professional résumé style/formatting for high-impact résumés might be helpful. These resources may include suggestions regarding the use of colored paper, font sizes, margins, and action verbs. Consideration is also given for the nuances of electronic submissions (e.g. submitting a PDF rather than a Word file can prevent altered formatting if the file is opened in a different software version).

In addition to basic formatting, the content included in your vita is essential. As noted, it is most appropriate to only include relevant information. Since you'll probably have a vita that you have utilized since your matriculation into graduate school, regular updating is crucial. Hence, remove the undergraduate or graduate school experiences that highlighted nonspecific personal accomplishments that are not psychological service/researched focused. This includes but is not limited to part-time jobs, civic awards unrelated to psychology, generic volunteer services, and conferences *attended* rather than presented. If your vita includes a laundry list of tests administered, consider regrouping them as categories of measurement, such as cognitive, achievement, low incidence disabilities, behavioral, and so forth. These elements all served as a bridge in prior résumés to demonstrate "work" experience and efforts toward professional development. This vita needs to communicate specific, strong, targeted areas of expertise. Table 10.1 compares and contrasts the general content of internship versus CVs.

Finally, the CV needs to be tailored to the audience (e.g., academic position, clinical position, school position). Some positions will require employees

TABLE 10.1 Comparing and Contrasting Content of the Internship and Career Vita (CV)

INTERNSHIP (MAY BE APPROPRIATE ON INTERNSHIP VITA BUT NOT ON CV)	CAREER (MORE APPROPRIATE FOCUS FOR CV)
Early volunteer, job, and leadership experiences that are not strongly related to psychology (e.g., child care, nanny, sorority/fraternity officer, band/school club memberships, extracurricular school activities)	Only volunteer experiences related to direct services for children and adolescents (e.g., Boys/Girls Club, youth mentoring, camp counselor); work experiences related to psychology (e.g., teaching or research assistantships), and leadership roles related to psychology (e.g., student committee member; school psychology representative)
Conferences and workshops attended, class papers presented	Conference presentations, manuscripts published or in press, ad-hoc reviewer, student journal reviewer or contributor
Lists of tests learned or administered	Types of assessment batteries administered (e.g., cognitive, learning disabilities, low incidence, early childhood, mental health, neuropsychological)
List of course work completed	Note expected degree attainment date and any additional certifications, licenses, or endorsements obtained
Practica settings, hours, or number of tests administered	Detailed review of internship responsibilities and competencies; note only specialized practica experiences
Guest class lectures	Courses taught
Peer mentoring	Scaffolded supervision responsibilities for other graduate or undergraduate students
General awards, general undergraduate scholarships, travel awards	Teaching or research awards, grants
All publications, significant research contributions, peer-reviewed conference presentations, teaching or research assistantships, fellowships, dissertation funding, specialized training (e.g., low-incidence disabilities, inpatient or outpatient provision of treatment, and direct provision of school-based interventions)	

to hold or work toward licensure, so you want to note your eligibility for licensure as well. Like the cover letter, multiple versions of your vita may be beneficial if you are applying to very different types of positions. Doing so can prevent you from including arbitrary information on a site-specific vita. After you create your vita, have two to three professionals read and edit it (NASP, 2008). This is critical, as they have fresh insight and also can offer valuable suggestions related to appropriately structuring your final draft. You may want to visit professional organizations' websites to get started. The NASP website offers a number of résumé template resource sites and multiple articles with strategies on showcasing competencies for a powerful school psychology résumé (e.g., www.nasponline.org/students/ Curriculum%20Vitae.pdf). Tips for constructing a high-impact vita also can be found on the APA website (APA, 2014a; www.apa.org/education/grad/ career-development.aspx).

CAREER INTERVIEWS

Being invited to interview for a position can be a celebratory, exciting, albeit anxiety-provoking, experience. The impression you make on your prospective employer during the interview is one of the most significant determining factors regarding whether you will be viewed as a viable candidate. Similarly, the interview helps you to decide if the hiring agency is in fact a suitable match for your goals, skills, knowledge, and perhaps personality. Because the career interview is a two-way process with potentially great benefits for the employer and candidate, it should not be taken lightly. Hence, it's important to be well prepared. As a starting point, you are encouraged to visit the APA of Graduate Students (APAGS) website to review helpful resources, including quick web videos on interviewing (www.apa.org/apags). It is critical to practice, practice, practice prior to the interview. Rehearsing responses to typical interview questions multiple times can help you accomplish a fluent interview by facilitating prior response choices and also lessening the surprise or anxiety of a new high-stakes situation. Videotaping yourself and/or asking a colleague or friend to conduct a mock interview can alert you to areas of strength and areas for growth. A few sample interview questions that you can utilize during your preparation for academic and psychological practice positions are listed in Tables 10.2 and 10.3. Additional questions can be found through the NASP Career Center (2011) and Vitae (2014).

Although a number of laws since the early 1960s prohibit some types of personal questions, these may still be encountered during interviews. The provisions for employment fairness include the Title VII of the Civil Rights Act of 1964, which prohibits discrimination based on race, color, religion, sex, and national origin (U.S. Equal Employment Opportunity

TABLE 10.2 Practice Interview Questions for Research/Academic Positions

Research
- Tell us about your current research line and how you expect to expand that over time.
- What do you think are your most significant research accomplishments?
- What will be your major focus as an independent researcher?
- What statistical data analysis methods and software are you most familiar with?
- How will this job help you achieve your long-term research goals?
- How do you plan to mentor graduate students in research?

Grant Funding
- What experience do you have in writing grant proposals?
- What experience do you have in managing budgets for large projects?
- If you get this position, how do you hope to fund your research line?

Publications
- Tell us about your publications.
- What contributions did you make to coauthored articles?
- How do you organize your time to ensure an active publication record?
- What journals do you plan to submit to?

Presentations
- Tell us about your conference presentations topics.
- Tell us about your presentation skills.
- What presentation proposals do you have outstanding?
- Have you copresented with students?

Teaching
- Describe your teaching experience and level of responsibility (e.g., grading, guest lectures, text selection, reading selections, complete responsibility for course).
- What courses would you prefer to teach?
- How prepared are you to teach [specific course]?
- What is your teaching philosophy?
- How would you respond to a student who is upset about a grade?
- How would you respond to a student in crisis?

Professional Skills
- Tell us about your experiences with collaboration. What cross-discipline projects have you been involved in.
- What cross-discipline opportunities would you like to foster?
- What experiences do you have with supervision of graduate students?
- Tell us about your experiences mentoring others.
- Why do you think you are the right person for this position?
- In what ways, other than research and teaching, could you contribute to this department?
- What leadership roles have you held?
- What professional associations are you a member of?
- What awards have you received?
- Tell us about your work ethic, your time-management skills.
- What are your 5-year goals?

Commission, 2015). The Americans with Disabilities Act (ADA) prohibits workplace discriminations for people with physical disabilities (ADA, 1990, 2008), and the Older Workers Benefit Protection Act (OWBPA, 1990) prohibits inquiries regarding a person's age. Additionally, the Pregnancy Discrimination Act (PDA, 1978) forbids discrimination based on pregnancy,

196 • SECTION II: INTERNSHIP

TABLE 10.3 Practice Interview Questions for Professional Practice Positions

General Questions
- Why do you want to be a school psychologist?
- Describe your internship experiences.
- What do you plan to be doing in 5 years?
- What kind of cases did you encounter in your internship?
- Why do you want to work in our district (or other clinical site)?
- What do you know about our school district (or other clinical site)?
- How do you plan on juggling the demands of our district (or other clinical site)?
- What additional professional growth opportunities would you like to pursue?
- Tell us about your supervision experiences.
- Are you interested in pursuing additional credentials, licensure?

Clinical Skills
- What types of assessments are you familiar with?
- Describe a recent consultation and your interpersonal style when working with teachers.
- Share an intervention that you designed and found highly successful.
- Tell us about your participation in leadership roles within schools.
- Tells us about your contributions to problem-solving teams.
- How would you describe your approach to collaborating with families?
- What ages, disabilities have you worked with?
- Have you provided program-level evaluation, consulted with principals on school-wide data?
- Tells us about your experience in delivering professional development training in schools.
- Tell us about your experiences with manifestation determination or crisis intervention.
- What progress monitoring measures do you utilize?
- How do you decide on the efficacy of an intervention or treatment?
- What diagnoses are you most familiar with?
- How familiar are you with our state's special education eligibility rules and statutes?

Professional Skills
- Tell us about your experiences with collaboration.
- Why do you think you are the right person for this position?
- In what ways would you ideally like to contribute to this district?
- What leadership roles have you held?
- What professional associations are you a member of?
- Tell us about your work ethic, your time-management skills, and your interpersonal skills?
- What are your 5-year goals?

The Scenario
Sometimes school districts may pose *scenario questions* as an interview technique. Sometimes this involves providing the interviewee with data and background information on a student, providing time to review the materials, and then discussing your thoughts and recommendations for the child with the interview committee. Another variation of the *scenario question* is to ask the interviewee to conduct a mock parent or problem-solving team discussion. This version also provides the applicant with student data, time to review and reflect on the presenting needs of the child, and then committee members assume the role of a parent or teacher and the interviewee presents his or her insights and recommendations.

childbirth, or related medical conditions. A sample list of illegal questions that employers should not ask is provided in Table 10.4. There are several choices when illegal questions are presented and the response will be a personal choice for the applicant. Response options include pausing long enough to signal the interviewer that it would be best to retract the

TABLE 10.4 Sample Illegal Questions

ILLEGAL QUESTIONS	SUBTLE WORDING TO CIRCUMVENT ILLEGAL QUESTIONS
Are you married?	Are spousal hire considerations needed? (Should we plan a tour of the area for your spouse to assist in his or her decision?)
Do you plan on getting married?	Do you anticipate needed information on spousal insurance options in the near future?
Do you have children? Do you plan to have any more children?	Would you like information on the schools in a specific neighborhood? We can review maternity leave policy if you'd like.
What's your nationality?	Tell us where you are from and your early childhood school experiences. You have such a lovely accent, where is that from?
What is your age?	What year did you start kindergarten, graduate from high school?
What is your sexual orientation?	Do you need information on the employee diversity plan for LGBT?

LGBT, lesbian, gay, bisexual, transgender.

question, noting that it is an illegal question and declining to answer, ignoring the question, or answering with a redirected question. If the incident is grievous or thought to have interfered with opportunity to acquire the job, a more formal complaint can be filed with the U.S. Equal Employment Opportunity Commission (www.eeoc.gov/field).

From the time your interview begins, every response and question you pose is noted and remembered. Additionally, every individual encountered in the interview process is a source of opinion regarding your suitability as a potential hire for their institution. Respectful and courteous interactions are as equally important with office staff, students, and auxiliary personnel as they are with the direct interviewing team as each of the individuals can ultimately attest to your interpersonal skills and influence the hiring decision. Even during less formal components of a job interview (e.g., meals, site visit tours) information is being gathered by the site to determine hiring potential. For practitioner or mental health agency interviews the format will generally include a formal interview with a team or individual and then possibly introductions to key stakeholders within the organization (e.g., lead school psychologist, medical director). The interviewing process may last 1 to 3 hours.

For academic and researcher positions, the interview format is more typically a 2- to 3-day process and may adhere to the following schedule:

- First day: travel, transportation to the hotel, and dinner with the search committee
- Second day: breakfast with faculty; hourly interviews with core program as well as department faculty; a 1-hour presentation or meeting with

program students, a 1-hour colloquia presentation by the applicant on her or his area of research for a broad college audience with candidate rating forms (see Exhibit 10.5 for a sample, at www.springerpub.com/school-psychology-practicum); and lunch and dinner with select faculty
• Third day: breakfast with select faculty; additional interviews with administrators (e.g., department chair, college dean, university provost); tours of university clinics or labs; tour of the local housing options with a realtor; and lunch with faculty; transportation to the airport for return flight.

When significant travel is involved, especially for academic positions, the hosting institution will usually reimburse all travel costs and make all travel arrangements (e.g., flight, hotel, and meals). Once a hiring offer is made, it is not unusual for colleges and universities to also fund a visit to the area for partners/spouses as part of the recruitment effort so the partner can view the local housing options and community as part of the decision-making process.

It is important to note that academic interviews can be very long, 12-hour days and all interactions including transportation and meals are opportunities for you and the site to learn more about each other. Given the variety of personnel you are likely to encounter, it is important to be familiar with their profiles in addition to being knowledgeable regarding the program. It also is helpful to be prepared with questions specific to the role of administrators. For example, program faculty may discuss teaching/research/service/advising expectations or work load as well as the tenure or promotion processes. Deans may best discuss broad faculty opportunities or research office support infrastructures and shared faculty governance. Deans also typically make the final hiring decisions and negotiate salaries, thus are aware of available financial supports. Provosts and administrators outside of the college may best address university-wide resources, cross-discipline collaboration supports, and the university's long-range vision. One mechanism for becoming more familiar with the academic hiring process is to attend any applicant colloquia that are presented in your college while you are still a student, volunteering to be an applicant escort as the individual moves between interviews, and volunteering to be a student representative on any search committee opportunities. These experiences can provide a broader understanding of the process and also afford models for job talk presentations.

Regardless of the type of career position, reviewing information on the organization prior to the interview is beneficial because demonstrating your knowledge about the site can attest to your interest in and potential commitment to the position. Obtaining knowledge about the site can also help develop meaningful questions that you could ask during your interview. Areas to focus on include but are not limited to: Who works at the site? What are their accomplishments? What is their practice model/theoretical orientation? What other relevant positions might they hold? Information about your prospective employer and colleagues can be found by perusing the site's website and/or discussing the job with professional contacts.

Some employers might request the interviewee to bring specific documents to the interview. If not, a few suggestions are offered with respect to documents that you may want to carry with you. First, you may want to have extra copies of your vita and cover letter. Some members of the hiring committee may not review your documents before interviewing with you. Providing these individuals with a copy of your profile can help guide the conversation if necessary. Furthermore, your information might have changed since you applied for the job (e.g., additional publications, completed graduation), and some employers would prefer a more updated copy of your vita. Career interviews afford candidates the opportunity to discuss their training and experiences, and showcase their work. As such, bring reports or publications from your professional portfolio as well. Reports that range in scope and focus on needs of specific populations can demonstrate both the breadth and depth of your training. Suggested reports include comprehensive psychoeducational evaluations, targeted evaluations (e.g., academic vs. social–emotional and behavioral), direct intervention summary reports (e.g., counseling, classroom behavior intervention plans), and indirect intervention summary reports (e.g., consultation).

Be prepared to discuss your future goals during the interview. Employers elect to ask candidates about their future goals for several reasons. First, your response informs the hiring committee of the compatibility between your career goals and the position. This is important, as candidates are hired when they are determined to be a good fit. Second, many employers prefer to hire a candidate who is serious about the position and desires longevity in the institution or district. Therefore, your response also helps the committee gauge your commitment. Your passion for the position and motivation to perform the responsibilities which the position entails will also be ascertained through this question. Although specific career goals do not necessarily need to be shared at the time of your interview, providing the search committee with a general layout of your long-term goals is highly recommended.

As emphasized in previous paragraphs, interviewing is a reciprocal exercise. Keeping this is mind, it is equally important for you to ask questions during the interview. The following is a list of sample questions that you might want to consider to aid you with your preparation:

- What type of support, mentoring, or supervision for early career personnel will be provided?
- What are the expectations for obtaining licensure or national certification?
- How are faculty (or psychologists) evaluated?

200 • SECTION II: INTERNSHIP

- What opportunities are there for personnel to attend conferences and other professional development activities?
- Academic positions: What does the work load consist of in terms of courses, advisees, research, service, and so forth? What are the program's needs or expectations for the new faculty member?
- School or clinical positions: What percentage of time will be spent in assessment? Consultation? Counseling? Other activities? How are work assignments structured?

Financial Considerations for Salary and Benefits

Remember, the purpose of the career interview is also for you to gain additional insight about the position to determine if it is a good fit for you as well. Accordingly, it is acceptable to ask questions about the salary, benefits, vacations, and support and resources (NASP Career Center, 2011) during the later stages of your interview. This conversation may include a negotiation of the position's salary structures. For instance, you may want to ask if there are built-in pay increase steps by years of experience and stipends for specialized experience or holding the national certification as a school psychologist. Know the range of salaries at the institution or district before interviewing. This information is usually available online. If not, familiarize yourself with the national salary norms for the specific position. This information is listed on the NASP website or in the Occupational Outlook Handbook available online.

With respect to the benefits package, you may choose to inquire about health, dental, vision, disability, and other insurance packages. Questions about available retirement programs (e.g., guaranteed state pension plans vs. investment plans, number of employment years required to be vested in retirement) are appropriate and informative as well. Given that you may be employed with the institution or district for a substantial period of time, you also may want to ask if professional growth stipends are offered such as travel funding for conferences, paid leave, reimbursement for license fees, and so forth. Additional information that you may consider gathering includes whether you will be afforded sick and personal days leave. If you plan to obtain licensure and the state requires supervision during the first career year, you should also ask if licensed supervision is available. Although licensed supervision can be obtained privately, this is often expensive and more difficult than supervision that is structured within the personnel agreement.

Negotiating

Negotiating options for salaries and benefits will vary by institution so it is good to have a plan for exploring these details prior to accepting an employment contract. For school-based positions, salaries are often formalized in union contracts and delineated by specific annual income for numbers of years of experience or degree. For example, a specific entry-level salary is set for persons with a specialist degree with a modest additional amount for a doctoral degree; the salary is then increased systematically with years of service and every employee in that classification earns the same salary. Some districts may add salary supplements for specializations (e.g., neuropsychology, applied behavioral analysis certification, supervision responsibilities, NCSP). Hospitals and agencies often offer a salary range for specific titles and accompanying responsibilities, which permits the administrator presenting the offer a small range of latitude in the negotiated salary. Within academia, salaries generally have a range and are based on rank (e.g., assistant professor, associate professor, and professor; assistant scholar, associate scholar, and scholar) and experience. The range of salary tends to be substantial for higher level positions and individuals the institution is eager to recruit; therefore, discussing a negotiation strategy with a mentor prior to agreeing to a contract for academic positions is highly advisable. Additionally, academic employment offers may include *start-up packages* that can include funds for a variety of expenditures that assist in launching a career (e.g., furniture, equipment, lab resources, hiring a graduate assistant, travel, and curricula materials). The institution may ask applicants to submit a line-item budget for what expenses they think are important during the first year.

Finally, some colleges and universities acknowledge that recruiting and retaining faculty members is contingent upon the hiring of a spouse or domestic partner. Therefore, if you are seeking an academic position and this is a consideration, you may also want to ask the search committee if the university has a spousal hire policy. Final spousal hiring decisions are typically made at the college or university administrative level and may take a lengthy inquiry time to establish, thus a search committee may not be able to offer details but can certainly let a candidate know if this type of opportunity has historically been available at their institution. Spousal hires come in a variety of forms including a full second hire within the same department or college or a shared-cost opportunity. Shared-cost arrangements may be funded by the provost's office and permit a department (even outside the college the initial candidate is hired in) to benefit from a limited time and/or partial salary allocation as an incentive for the unit to hire the spouse. For example, a math department interested in the spousal hire may receive funding for half of the person's salary for the first 2 years. The details of a spousal hire option will most likely be revealed once a formal job offer has been proposed and the salary negotiation phase has been entered. In many cases, the institution also will arrange interviews for the spouse with programs that are a potential match and cover all expenses for a visit to the campus.

CHAPTER REVIEW

After years of professional training and competency building, you are now preparing for your first career position. Identify your short- and long-term career goals and aspired positions that will help you reach your goals. Upon finding vacant positions and narrowing down your search to specific jobs, it is time for you to prepare to land your dream job. Such preparation entails developing a strong vita (or résumé) and an appropriate cover letter. If you are invited for an interview, practice, practice, practice! This includes practicing your responses to typical questions and how you would articulate the questions that you might want to ask to gain additional information about the position. Seek support, feedback, and suggestions from your graduate faculty or other professional mentors throughout the process, as guidance from experienced professionals is invaluable.

REFERENCES

American Psychological Association. (2012). *Guidelines and principles for accreditation of programs in professional psychology.* Washington, DC: Author.

American Psychological Association. (2014a). *Career development.* Retrieved from http://www.apa.org/education/grad/career-development.aspx

American Psychological Association. (2014b). *Postdoctoral fellowships.* Retrieved from http://www.apa.org/education/grad/post-fellow.aspx

American Psychological Association Science Student Council. (2007). *A graduate student's guide to determining authorship credit and authorship order.* Washington, DC: Author.

Americans with Disabilities Act of 1990. 42 U.S.C.A. § 12101 et seq.

Americans with Disabilities Amendments Act of 2008, Pub. L. No. 110-325, 42, U.S.C.A. § 12101–12102.

Bailey, D. S. (2004). The skinny on the postdoc: When to get started, how to get one and what you can do to make the most out of it. *gradPSYCH Magazine, 2.* Retrieved from http://www.apa.org/gradpsych/2004/01/postdoc-skinny.aspx

Barker, K. (2002, November). Accountability and authorship. *Science.* Retrieved from http://sciencecareers.sciencemag.org/career_magazine/previous_issues/articles/2002_11_08/nodoi.191412875531467470

Nathan, S., Piacentini, J., Spirito, A., & King, C. (2014). *Guidelines and principles: Accreditation of postdoctoral training programs in clinical child psychology.* Retrieved from https://www.clinicalchildpsychology.org/internships_postdocs

National Association of School Psychologists. (2008). *Bringing your vita to life: Preparing for internship and early career positions.* Retrieved from http://www.nasponline.org/students/Curriculum%20Vitae.pdf

National Association of School Psychologists Career Center. (2011). *Getting and keeping your first job as a school psychologist* [PDF document]. Retrieved from http://www.nasponline.org/conventions/2011/handouts/unstated/Hill,%20Kubick,%20York%202011.pdf

National Career Fairs. (2014). *Ready to make an impression?* Retrieved from http://www.nationalcareerfairs.com/advice

Networking [Def. 1]. (2014). In *Merriam-Webster Online.* Retrieved from http://www.merriam-webster.com/dictionary/networking

Older Workers Benefit Protection Act of 1990, 29 U.S.C. § 623; 29 CFR § 1625.22 (1990).

Pelham, B. (2014). *Doing postdoctoral work—should I?* Retrieved from http://www.apa.org/careers/resources/academic/postdoc-work.aspx

Pregnancy Discrimination Act, 42 U.S. Code § 2000e (1978).

U.S. Equal Employment Opportunity Commission. (2015). *Title VII of the Civil Rights Act of 1964.* Retrieved from http://www.eeoc.gov/laws/statutes/titlevii.cfm

Vitae. (2014). *Commonly asked questions in academic interviews.* Retrieved from https://www.vitae.ac.uk/researcher-careers/pursuing-an-academic-career/applying-for-academic-jobs/commonly-asked-questions-in-academic-interviewsh

APPENDIX A

Resources: Professional Organizations and Standards

EXHIBIT A.1 PROFESSIONAL ORGANIZATIONS

ORGANIZATION	WEBSITE
National Association of School Psychologists (NASP)	www.nasponline.org
American Psychological Association (APA)	www.apa.org
American Psychological Association—Division 16	www.apa.org/about/division/div16.aspx
State School Psychology Associations	www.nasponline.org/about_nasp/links_state_orgs.aspx
International School Psychology Association (ISPA)	www.ispaweb.org
The Association of State and Provincial Psychology Boards (ASPPB)	www.asppb.net

EXHIBIT A.2 PROFESSIONAL STANDARDS AND GUIDELINES FOR SCHOOL PSYCHOLOGY

ORGANIZATION	RESOURCE	WEBSITE
National Association of School Psychologists (NASP)	Model for Comprehensive and Integrated School Psychological Services	www.nasponline.org/standards/2010standards/2_PracticeModel.pdf
	Principles for Professional Ethics	www.nasponline.org/standards/2010standards/1_%20Ethical%20Principles.pdf
	Standards for Graduate Preparation of School Psychologists	www.nasponline.org/standards/2010standards/1_Graduate_Preparation.pdf
	Standards for the Credentialing of School Psychologists	www.nasponline.org/standards/2010standards/2_Credentialing_Standards.pdf
	Best Practice Guidelines for School Psychology Internships	www.nasponline.org/trainers/documents/2014_Best_Practice_Guidelines_for_SP_Internships.pdf
	Best Practices for Intern Supervision	www.nasponline.org/trainers/documents/2014_Best_Practice_Guidelines_for_Intern_Supervision.pdf
American Psychological Association (APA)	Ethical Principles for Psychologists and Code of Conduct	www.apa.org/ethics/code/index.aspx
	Guidelines and Principles for Accreditation of Programs in Professional Psychology	www.apa.org/ed/accreditation/about/policies/guiding-principles.pdf
	Guidelines on Multicultural Education, Training, Research, Practice, and Organizational Change for Psychologists	www.apa.org/pi/oema/resources/policy/multicultural-guidelines.aspx
Council for Directors of School Psychology Programs (CDSPP)	Doctoral-Level Internship Guidelines	sites.google.com/site/cdspphome/2012guidelines

(continued)

EXHIBIT A.2 PROFESSIONAL STANDARDS AND GUIDELINES FOR SCHOOL PSYCHOLOGY (*continued*)

ORGANIZATION	RESOURCE	WEBSITE
The Association of State and Provincial Psychology Boards (ASPPB)	ASPPB Code of Conduct	www.asppb.net/resource/resmgr/Guidelines/Code_of_Conduct_Updated_2013.pdf
	ASPPB Guidelines on Practicum Experiences for Licensure	c.ymcdn.com/sites/asppb.site-ym.com/resource/resmgr/guidelines/final_prac_guidelines_1_31_0.pdf
	ASPPB Supervision Guidelines	c.ymcdn.com/sites/asppb.site-ym.com/resource/resmgr/guidelines/current_asppb_supervision_gu.pdf

Note: Some resources identified may have restricted access.

APPENDIX B

Chapter Exhibits

EXHIBIT B.1 SAMPLE PRACTICA LOG

SCHOOL PSYCHOLOGY PROGRAM PRACTICA LOG
HORATIO MARTINEZ

DATE	TIME	AGE	GENDER	ETHNICITY	DISABILITY	LANGUAGE	ACTIVITY	THERAPY	INTERVENTION	CONSULTATION	INTERVIEWS	OBSERVATION	ASSESSMENT	SUPERVISION	PROBLEM-SOLVING MTGS	TOTAL
1/9	11:30–1:30						Practicum Seminar – Group Supervision							2		2
1/10	8:00–10:30	10	M	NA		Eng.	Administered RIAS; observed WJ Ach and WJ Cog.						2.5			2.5
1/10	10:30–12:30						Problem-Solving Team Mtg – Data Review								2	2
1/10	1:00–2:00	8	F	AA	SLD	Span.	Reading Tutoring – Error Analysis		1							1
1/10	2:00–2:30	6 6 7	M M M	W	NA	Eng.	Counseling – Social Skills Group	.5								.5
1/10	2:30–3:00	12	F	H	InD	Eng.	Behavioral Observations					.5				.5
Total hours								.5	1	0	0	.5	2.5	2	2	8.5

210 • APPENDICES

EXHIBIT B.2 SAMPLE SITE SUPERVISOR EVALUATION OF PRACTICA STUDENT FORM

Student: _____   Year in Program: _____

Practicum Site: _____   Supervisor: _____

Please utilize the following ratings matrix when completing this form. The purpose of this rating is to document applied competencies, measure professional attributes, and inform professional progress needs. Evaluations should be based on observed behaviors of the student during performance at the site. The results will be shared with the student and determine the practica course grade, as well as utilized in composing his or her annual evaluation.

RATING	DESCRIPTOR
1	Unsatisfactory: The candidate requires significant supervision of this activity and is not yet prepared to demonstrate this skill.
2	Developing: The graduate student is developing this competency and still requires close supervision to be successful in this endeavor.
3	Satisfactory: The student demonstrates emerging baseline-level skills in this area with a moderate level of supervision and feedback.
4	Accomplished: The graduate student can demonstrate this skill in routine situations with minimal supervision required.
5	Exceptional: The student consistently demonstrates high skill competency requiring minimal supervision and can modify this skill across situations.
N/O	Not observed (Given the degree track and/or the student's year in the program, this item may not have yet been required.)

Assessment/Data-Based Decision Making and Accountability
1. Knowledge of assessment methods and data collection   1 2 3 4 5 N/O
2. Utilizes data for effective decision making/problem solving   1 2 3 4 5 N/O
3. Evaluates response to services based on outcome data   1 2 3 4 5 N/O

Consultation and Collaboration
4. Knowledge of consultation/collaboration and communication   1 2 3 4 5 N/O
5. Utilizes consultation/collaboration to promote effective services 1 2 3 4 5 N/O
6. Demonstrates skills in consultation design, implementation   1 2 3 4 5 N/O

Interventions and Instructional Support to Develop Academic Skills
7. Knowledge of cultural and social influences on academics   1 2 3 4 5 N/O
8. Knowledge of evidence-based curriculum/instructional strategies 1 2 3 4 5 N/O
9. Utilize outcome data to evaluate services   1 2 3 4 5 N/O

Interventions and Mental Health Services to Develop Social/Life Skills
10. Knowledge of cultural and social influences on behavior   1 2 3 4 5 N/O
11. Knowledge of evidence-based behavioral/mental health strategies 1 2 3 4 5 N/O
12. Utilize outcome data to evaluate mental health supports   1 2 3 4 5 N/O

(continued)

EXHIBIT B.2 SAMPLE SITE SUPERVISOR EVALUATION OF PRACTICA STUDENT FORM (*continued*)

School-Wide Practices to Promote Learning
13. Knowledge of systems' structure, organization, and resources   1 2 3 4 5 N/O
14. Analysis of school-wide data to identify need patterns   1 2 3 4 5 N/O
15. Promotion of positive behavioral and learning strategies   1 2 3 4 5 N/O

Preventive and Responsive Services
16. Knowledge of evidence-based prevention strategies   1 2 3 4 5 N/O
17. Utilize screening data to identify early warning risk factors   1 2 3 4 5 N/O
18. Implementation of crisis responsive services   1 2 3 4 5 N/O

Family and School Collaboration Services
19. Knowledge of family systems, strengths, needs, and culture   1 2 3 4 5 N/O
20. Utilizes evidence-based strategies to support families/children   1 2 3 4 5 N/O
21. Applies methods to develop collaboration with families   1 2 3 4 5 N/O

Diversity in Development and Learning
22. Knowledge of individual differences, abilities, and disabilities   1 2 3 4 5 N/O
23. Utilizes principles and research related to diversity factors   1 2 3 4 5 N/O
24. Demonstrates understanding and respect for diversity   1 2 3 4 5 N/O

Research and Program Evaluation
25. Demonstrates knowledge of systems-level research   1 2 3 4 5 N/O
26. Knowledgeable of methods of program evaluation   1 2 3 4 5 N/O
27. Effectively implements program evaluation   1 2 3 4 5 N/O

Legal, Ethical, and Professional Practice
28. Knowledge of ethical, legal, and professional standards   1 2 3 4 5 N/O
29. Utilizes responsive ethical and professional decision making   1 2 3 4 5 N/O
30. Safeguards confidentiality in reports and interactions   1 2 3 4 5 N/O

Professional Attributes
31. Demonstrates effective interpersonal skills   1 2 3 4 5 N/O
32. Demonstrates accountability, personal responsibility   1 2 3 4 5 N/O
33. Completes work in organized, timely manner   1 2 3 4 5 N/O

Please elaborate on performance items rated 1 or 2: _____

Additional comments: _____

SIGNATURES: Practicum Student: _____

                Site Supervisor: _____

                Date: _____

The signatures acknowledge that ratings in this form were reviewed with the student. However, the practicum student has the right, at any time, to file a response explaining any discrepancies with the Program Director for placement into his or her permanent file. Please return the completed form to the University Practicum Coordinator.

EXHIBIT B.3 STUDENT CONSENT FOR EXCHANGE OF INFORMATION

Graduate Student Name: _____ (Please Print)
School Psychology Practicum
Consent for Exchange of Information

I hereby agree that personally identifiable performance information regarding my work at practica, including academic and professional qualifications, skill competencies, and character, may be provided by my academic program to my practicum site. I further agree that, during any practica, similar information may be provided by the practicum site supervisor to my graduate program. I understand that such exchange of information shall be limited to my graduate program and any practica site and such information may not be provided to other parties without my consent.

_____ Date _____
School Psychology Graduate Student Signature
_____ Date _____
Practicum Site Supervisor Signature
_____ Date _____
Practicum Seminar Instructor Signature
_____ Date _____
School Psychology Practicum Coordinator Signature

EXHIBIT B.4 STATEMENT OF INTEREST—DOCTORAL, SCHOOL SETTING

Dear Internship Selection Committee:

I am writing to express my interest in a school psychology predoctoral internship position at the Applebee School District. I believe that my graduate course work and varied supervised training experiences make me a strong candidate for an internship position within the CDE Department. I am especially excited by the opportunity to support the CDE Department's focus on providing training to school professionals, collaboratively focusing on systemic needs, and engaging in school consultation and behavioral interventions through your internship program.

My training and field-based supervised experiences have enabled me to deliver a range of services to children of varying backgrounds and abilities. I have had the opportunity to conduct functional behavioral assessments (FBAs) and behavior intervention plans (BIP), utilize a variety of assessment tools, and communicate evaluation results to parents and school professionals. I participated in practicum across ten different schools over the course of 4 years, where I learned how to quickly connect with staff, immerse myself in school communities and work with different supervisors, and transition to new settings. I have had extensive training in multitiered systems of support model (MTSS) and positive behavioral interventions and supports

(continued)

EXHIBIT B.4 STATEMENT OF INTEREST—DOCTORAL, SCHOOL SETTING (*continued*)

(PBIS) and was fortunate to be involved in the initial stages of implementation at one of my school placements. I am confident that this knowledge and experience can be applied and expanded upon at Applebee School District. I also believe that my abilities to work as part of a collaborative team, function independently in professional settings, seek supervision when needed, and engage in best practices are strengths that could be an asset to your department.

During my predoctoral internship, I would like to further develop my skills in supporting children with challenging behavioral and neurodevelopmental needs through FBAs, BIP, and a school consultation model based on evidence-based practice. I am also hoping to advance my training through the delivery of behavioral services based on applied behavior analysis. The CDE Department maintains a strong reputation and focus in all of these areas; thus, I believe this internship is ideally suited for my professional goals.

Applebee School District's CDE Department has made clear efforts to actively engage in systems-level interventions to support school-wide prevention efforts. Last year, I completed over 200 practicum hours at the Diner School District to explore my interest in systems-level work. I believe that experience and my doctoral course work have prepared me to be a change agent in schools and I seek to explore this aspect of the school psychologist role during internship. It is evident that Applebee School District would meet these training goals and also increase my knowledge through a breadth of supervised experiences.

My commitment to providing services to diverse populations drove me to train and work in an urban city like Metropolis, and also motivates me to pursue an internship in a setting like Applebee School District. In addition to my breadth of experience, I have excellent interpersonal skills, a great work ethic, and a strong desire to help students succeed.

I feel strongly that a position with Applebee School District will provide me with a rich and challenging opportunity. It would be a pleasure to meet with you and discuss how my qualifications and interests match the expectations of your site. I very much look forward to hearing from you and the possible opportunity to interview with the CDE Department at Applebee School District. Thank you for considering my application.

Sherlock Huges, MEd, BCBA

EXHIBIT B.5 STATEMENT OF INTEREST—SPECIALIST LEVEL, SCHOOL SETTING

[Date]
[Name]
[Address]

(continued)

214 • APPENDICES

EXHIBIT B.5 STATEMENT OF INTEREST—SPECIALIST LEVEL, SCHOOL SETTING (*continued*)

Dear Mr. Gonzo,

I am writing to apply for a School Psychology internship with Q Public Schools. I believe that the supervision Q Public Schools can provide, combined with the variety of opportunities and experiences offered to all of your interns, is an ideal setting to further my training. Additionally, your school system has been highly recommended to me by my professor, Dr. Simon Frederick. I believe my graduate preparation and supervised experiences combined with my work ethic and desire to grow professionally would contribute to the excellent reputation forged by the Department of Psychological Services in Q Public Schools.

As you will see from my curriculam vita (CV), all of my past work experiences have involved working with children. I have worked with children as young as 3 and as old as 18 in various locations around the country. I am very proud to have worked with children who come from various ethnic and socio-economic backgrounds. I am very dedicated to promoting diversity, which is evidenced by the leadership positions I held during my undergraduate studies at Indiana University. In fact, my commitment to multicultural settings drove me to move to Metropolis for graduate school and also motivates me to apply to a system like Q Public Schools.

I am particularly drawn to Q Public Schools given the leadership role that school psychologists play in crisis prevention and intervention. Having gone through NASP's comprehensive PREPaRE training, I feel that I can help hone the skills I learned, develop new skills, and help contribute to the processes already in place.

I believe that through the course work I have completed, my experience working with children, and my current involvement in evaluation and research adequately prepares me for an internship position. In addition to my strong background, I have excellent interpersonal skills, a great work ethic and a strong desire to improve my skills and my surroundings. I am excited to develop my independence as a school psychologist and I am confident that I would be suitable for Q Public Schools' internship program. Thank you for your time and consideration. I look forward to hearing from you soon.

Sincerely,

Homer Sanders

EXHIBIT B.6 INTERNSHIP LOG SAMPLE 1

Internship Log

										Group Therapy	Individual Therapy	Intervention	Intervention Support	Consultation	Consultation Support	Systems/Organization	Assessment	Assessment Support	Supervision	Supervision of Peers	Professional Development	Total Hours
SCHOOL PSYCHOLOGY INTERNSHIP ACTIVITIES LOG – WEEKLY																						
INTERN NAME:																						
DATES OF WEEK LOGGED:																						
DATE	TIME	LOCATION	AGE	GENDER	ETHNICITY	DISABILITY OR DIAGNOSIS	LANGUAGE	ACTIVITY	ACTIVITY CODE/HOURS													

EXHIBIT B.7 INTERNSHIP LOG SUMMARY—GRAPHS SAMPLE

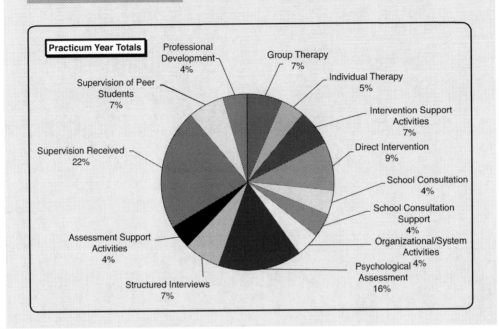

EXHIBIT B.8 NORM-REFERENCE DISTRIBUTION CURVE

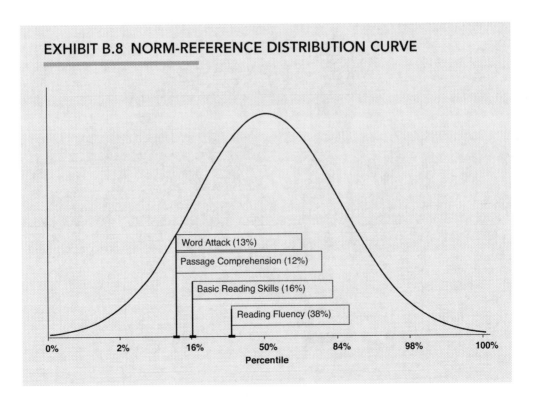

B: CHAPTER EXHIBITS • 217

EXHIBIT B.9 INTERNSHIP EVALUATION FORM—SAMPLE 1

Internship Evaluation Form

Intern: _____   Field Supervisor: _____

Internship Location: _____

University Supervisor: _____

Directions: Please rate the intern on each competency area based on actual observations and/or other appropriate sources (e.g., parents, teachers, and students). Rate each category independently, using the following scale points:

1. *Unsatisfactory*: The candidate demonstrates little knowledge of how to align practice with national and state standards at the appropriate level of rigor. The candidate is not yet prepared to demonstrate this skill in a practical setting.
2. *Developing*: The candidate is developing the ability to align practice with national and state standards at the appropriate level of rigor. The candidate requires coaching and supervision to implement this skill in the practical setting.
3. *Accomplished*: The candidate usually aligns practice with national and state standards at the appropriate level of rigor in a practical setting. The candidate is independent in routine situations with minimal to no supervision required.
4. *Exceptional*: The candidate consistently aligns practice with national and state standards at the appropriate level of rigor in a practical setting. The candidate can alter and implement this skill in various situations with minimal to no supervision required.

ND (*No Data*): Competence not evaluated due to insufficient data to make a rating at this time.

I. DATA-BASED DECISION MAKING AND EVALUATION OF PRACTICES	ND	1	2	3	4
1. Demonstrates knowledge of theories and research on methods of assessment and data collection to identify student strengths and needs, develop effective services, and/or measure outcomes.					
2. Analyzes multiple sources of qualitative and quantitative data across domains (cognitive, academic, and social/emotional/behavioral) to inform decision making and to design/implement services.					
3. Uses data to monitor student progress (academic, social/emotional/behavioral, mental health) and to evaluate the effectiveness of services and programs.					
4. Shares results of assessments in appropriate and understandable ways (orally and in written reports) with students, parents, and other stakeholders (e.g., teachers, administrators, and school teams).					
5. Applies technology to analyze, organize, and integrate assessment results.					

(continued)

218 • APPENDICES

EXHIBIT B.9 INTERNSHIP EVALUATION FORM—SAMPLE 1 (*continued*)

II. CONSULTATION AND COLLABORATION	ND	1	2	3	4
1. Demonstrates knowledge of theories and research on methods of consultation, collaboration, and communication applicable to individual, families, groups, and systems.					
2. Uses a systematic and comprehensive collaborative problem-solving framework to promote effective implementation of services and programs that permeates all aspects of service delivery.					
3. Collaborates with school-based and district-level teams to develop and/or maintain a multitiered continuum of services.					
4. Consults and collaborates at appropriate levels (individual, family, group, and systems) to implement effective services and programs.					
5. In collaboration with others, uses assessment and data collection methods to implement and evaluate the effectiveness of services and programs (cognitive, academic, social, and life skills).					
6. Collaborates with teachers and administrators to develop and implement school-wide positive behavior supports.					
7. Collaborates with school personnel to foster student engagement and appropriate school behavior.					

III. DIRECT INTERVENTIONS	ND	1	2	3	4
1. Demonstrates knowledge of theories and research on influences (e.g., biological, developmental, cultural, and social) on academic/social–emotional functioning and considers them in interventions.					
2. Plans and designs instruction/interventions based on data and aligns efforts with school and district improvement plans as well as state and federal mandates.					

(*continued*)

EXHIBIT B.9 INTERNSHIP EVALUATION FORM—SAMPLE 1 (*continued*)

III. DIRECT INTERVENTIONS	ND	1	2	3	4
3. Applies evidence-based practices to implement and evaluate student instruction/interventions that support cognitive and academic skills.					
4. Applies evidence-based practices to implement and evaluate student interventions supporting socialization and mental health.					
5. Identifies, provides, and refers for supports designed to help students overcome learning barriers.					

IV. INDIRECT INTERVENTIONS (DIRECT SERVICES TO CHILDREN AND YOUTH)	ND	1	2	3	4
1. Demonstrates knowledge of theories and research on school structure, organization, and theory; general and special education.					
2. Develops intervention support plans that help the student, family, or community agencies and systems of support to create and maintain effective and supportive learning environments that enhance critical thinking and maximize the learning potential of all children.					
3. Demonstrates knowledge of theories and research on resilience and risk factors, prevention, and crisis intervention.					
4. Appropriately engages parents and community partners whenever appropriate in the planning and design of instruction/interventions for a variety of student outcomes.					
5. Develops and implements prevention services and programs that enhance learning, mental health, safety, and physical well-being through protective and adaptive factors.					
6. Provides a continuum of crisis intervention services (crisis prevention, response, and recovery).					
7. Promotes safe school environments.					

(*continued*)

220 • APPENDICES

EXHIBIT B.9 INTERNSHIP EVALUATION FORM—SAMPLE 1 (*continued*)

V. DIVERSITY IN DEVELOPMENT AND LEARNING	ND	1	2	3	4
1. Demonstrates knowledge of theories and research on individual differences and diversity factors for children, families, and schools.					
2. Promotes multicultural understanding and dialog that facilitates family school partnerships.					
3. Respects cultural and linguistic background of students, parents, teachers, and stakeholders.					
4. Maintains a climate of fairness and support among students, parents, teachers, and stakeholders.					
5. Modifies assessments and testing conditions to promote reliable and valid assessment of children and youth from diverse backgrounds and with diverse learning needs.					
6. Adapts and designs instruction/interventions based on assessment data and the differing needs and diversity of students.					
7. Promotes effective functioning for students, parents, teachers, and other stakeholders with diverse characteristics, cultures, and backgrounds.					

VI. RESEARCH AND PROGRAM EVALUATION	ND	1	2	3	4
1. Demonstrates knowledge of research design, statistics, measurement, varied data collection and analysis techniques, and program evaluation methods.					
2. Demonstrates skills to evaluate and apply research as a foundation for service delivery.					
3. Independently, and in collaboration with others, uses data to monitor student progress and adjust instruction/interventions and programs when necessary.					
4. Uses various current techniques and technology resources for data collection, measurement, analysis, and program evaluation to support effective practices.					

(*continued*)

EXHIBIT B.9 INTERNSHIP EVALUATION FORM—SAMPLE 1 (*continued*)

VII. LEGAL, ETHICAL, AND PROFESSIONAL PRACTICE	ND	1	2	3	4
1. Knowledge of relevant legal, ethical, and professional standards.					
2. Engages in responsive ethical and professional decision making.					
3. Complies with national and state laws, district/agency policies, and professional standards.					
4. Develops a personal and professional growth plan that enhances professional knowledge, skills, and practices as well as addresses areas of need.					
5. Engages in targeted professional growth opportunities and reflective practices.					
6. Implements knowledge and skills learning in professional development activities.					

VIII. PROFESSIONAL WORK CHARACTERISTICS	ND	1	2	3	4
1. Respect for human diversity					
2. Oral communication skills					
3. Written communication skills					
4. Effective interpersonal skills					
5. Responsibility					
6. Adaptability/flexibility					
7. Initiative					
8. Creativity					
9. Dependability					
10. Cooperation					
11. Independence					
12. Personal stability					
13. Professional self-image					

IX. OVERALL INTERN RATING	NO DATA	UNSATIS-FACTORY	DEVELOPING	ACCOMPLISHED	EXCEPTIONAL
	ND	1	2	3	4

(*continued*)

222 • APPENDICES

EXHIBIT B.9 INTERNSHIP EVALUATION FORM—SAMPLE 1 (*continued*)

Please attach a separate letter to summarize the intern's key strengths and weaknesses. Where weaknesses are indicated, describe the kinds of experiences needed to strengthen them to a level of competence where little or no supervision is required.

Intern's Signature _____ Date _____

Field Supervisor's Signature _____ Date _____

University Supervisor's Signature _____ Date _____

EXHIBIT B.10 SAMPLE ACADEMIC POSITION COVER LETTER

11-25-15
Dr. Rubin Martin
Search Committee Chair
University of Edgewater
4949 Walter Hall
PO Box 85964
Charleston, SC 29401

Dear Dr. Martin and Search Committee Members:

I am writing to express my interest in the Assistant Professor position for the School Psychology program in the Professional Educators Department at the University of Edgewater. As you will note on my vita, my graduate training and recent internship experiences align well with the skill areas noted in your job announcement: teaching intervention course work, research related to internalizing disorders, and supervision contributions to the program's clinic. In addition, I have met early supervision requirements for licensure as a psychologist in your state and plan to take the Examination for Professional Practice in Psychology (EPPP) exam this summer, thus will soon be eligible to offer services in your program's outpatient clinic.

At this time, I have two published journal articles and one manuscript in review. Each publication is based on original research findings related to effective school-based interventions for generalized anxiety disorder in adolescents. The first publication reviews a study investigating a 12-week cognitive behavioral therapy (CBT) program focusing on empowering students with self-defeating thought patterns and low self-esteem. In the second publication, this work was extended to include a 4-week intervention protocol utilizing Socratic questioning methods to challenge and restructure cognitive distortions. As noted, positive outcomes were indicated for both studies. My long-term research interests include refining this line of inquiry to include school-based CBT intervention protocols for students with depression and bereavement. I also hope to further

(continued)

EXHIBIT B.10 SAMPLE ACADEMIC POSITION COVER LETTER (*continued*)

contribute in these areas of interest through my research and professional presentations. To date, I have presented research findings at two state and two national conferences.

In addition, I have taught two sections of an undergraduate child development course that included full responsibility for lectures, course exams, and student mentorship. Student ratings for these courses have consistently remained high. During my internship at the Walter's Medical Center for children, I provided intake psychological assessments for children and adolescents receiving outpatient therapy for a range of both internalizing and externalizing disorders. As part of a multidisciplinary team my responsibilities also included co-facilitating counseling sessions and collaborating with school district's as students transition from inpatient back to school.

In reviewing your program's handbook, website, and clinic services, I am excited about the research opportunities and caliber of training program offered. A copy of my vita and manuscripts are enclosed. Please feel free to contact me if you have any questions or require any further information. I look forward to the opportunity to meet with you and the search committee.

Sincerely,

_____

Name, credentials

E-mail address

EXHIBIT B.11 SAMPLE SCHOOL DISTRICT POSITION COVER LETTER

2-6-15
Elizabeth Sanchez, EdS, NCSP
Lead School Psychologist
Briley Public School District
5555 Providence Circle, Building H
Iowa City, IA 52243

Dear Ms. Sanchez and Colleagues:

I am writing to express my strong interest in the School Psychologist position opening in your school district. Your job advertisement emphasizes a number of training perspectives and skills that I believe align well with my educational background and professional experiences. The primary focus on providing

(continued)

EXHIBIT B.11 SAMPLE SCHOOL DISTRICT POSITION COVER LETTER (*continued*)

indirect interventions to students through teacher collaboration and systems-level universal screening data-analysis consultation with school administrations are key components of my graduate training. Additionally, my vita reflects 2 years of practica experience working within a MTSS school engaging in these activities. My internship placement in the Des Moines School District also provided extensive opportunities to participate in school leadership meetings, MTSS problem-solving team discussions, and systems-level collaboration on tiered interventions for both academic and behavioral needs.

As you will note on my vita, my internship experiences also have included providing assessments across cognitive, adaptive, academic, and social–emotional realms. Direct intervention service delivery experiences include providing small group and individual counseling for social skills and anger management, as well as designing and implementing behavioral contracts and supports. My professional engagement activities have included student membership in the National Association of School Psychologists (NASP) and the Iowa School Psychologists Association (ISPA), as well as attendance and volunteer participation in the conferences for both organizations. Additionally, I recently co-presented a teachers' professional development workshop, in my internship school district, on graphing and interpreting progress monitoring data.

In reviewing your school district's website, county educational programs, and online psychological services guide for parents, I have noted the pervasive consideration for strong prevention and early intervention services. I am excited about the potential opportunity to interview with your district and perhaps become a member of this type of service delivery model. A copy of my transcripts, vita, reference letters, and the requested sample reports are enclosed. Please feel free to contact me if you have any questions or require additional information. I look forward to the opportunity to meet with you and your colleagues.

Warmest regards,

_____

Name, credentials

E-mail address

Index

abuse, suspicion of, 27
ACA. *See* American Counseling Association
academic employment, salaries for, 201
academic interviews, 198
academic knowledge, 4
academic positions, 11, 186, 190, 192
   interview format for, 197–198
   practice interview questions for, 194, 195
   websites for, 191
accommodations, 70–77
acquisition, of knowledge and skills, 39–41
   capstone cases, 43–44
   competency ratings, 42, 50
   professional work products review, 42–43
ADA. *See* Americans with Disabilities Act
Adam Walsh Child Protection and Safety Act
   of 2006, 13
ADHD. *See* attention deficit hyperactivity
   disorder
administration of tests, 58–63
administrative interactions, 128
advanced practicum. *See* practicum
AHEAD. *See* Association on Higher Education
   and Disability
American Association for the Advancement of
   Science, 186
American Counseling Association
   (ACA), 125
American Psychological Association (APA),
   84, 97–98, 104–105, 118, 130, 133, 185
   accreditation, 3
   accredited internships, 103–104
   APA of Graduate Students (APAGS), 194
   Commission on Accreditation, 148
   competency, 39–41
   documentation, 3
   Ethics Code, 42, 125, 134, 142, 144, 183
   guidelines, 122

Monitor on Psychology, 190
Standards for Educational and
   Psychological Testing (2014), 183
supervision strategies, 47–48
Americans with Disabilities Act (ADA),
   75–76, 195
APA. *See* American Psychological Association
APAGS. *See* APA of Graduate Students
APPIC. *See* Association of Psychology
   Postdoctoral and Internship Center
application of research, 41
application sites, selection of, 189
ASPPB. *See* Association of State and Provincial
   Psychology Boards
assessment, 41, 58–60, 70
   scoring, 63–64
   social–emotional, 171–172
   techniques, 72
assignments, reports, 151, 152
Association of Postdoctoral Programs in
   Clinical Neuropsychology, 186
Association of Psychology Postdoctoral and
   Internship Centers (APPIC), 35, 105,
   113, 114, 148, 186, 187
   application process, 106
   internship, 99, 102–104
Association of State and Provincial
   Psychology Boards (ASPPB), 102, 119
Association on Higher Education and
   Disability (AHEAD), 72
attention deficit hyperactivity disorder
   (ADHD), 73, 129

background checks, 13, 14, 19
Behavioral Assessment System for Children,
   Second Edition (BASC-2)
   Parent Rating Scale, 171, 178–179
   Teacher Rating Scale, 171–172, 179–180

226 • INDEX

behavioral orientation, supervisor, 46
behaviors, 32, 57
   classroom, 175
   test session, 167
Best Practice Guidelines for School
   Psychology Internships, 134
boundaries for professional practice,
   setting, 125–126

capstone case format
   multidomain, 43
   multimethod, 43
   multiprovider, 44
capstone cases, 43–44
   report, 152
career interviews
   academic interviews, 198
   career position types, 198
   colloquia presentation, 198
   cover letter and vita, 191–194, 199
   financial considerations for salary and
      benefits, 200
   hiring committee, 199
   illegal questions, sample list of, 196–197
   negotiation, 200–201
   practice interview questions, 194–196
   reports/publications from professional
      portfolio, 199
   reviewing information on organization,
      198–199
   sample questions, 199–200
career position
   career interviews. *See* career interviews
   career listing resources, 189–191
   cover letter and vita, 191–194, 199
   postdoc, 185–189
   type of, 198
CDSPP. *See* Council of Directors of School
   Psychology Programs
Child Abuse Prevention and
   Treatment Act, 27
child records, 29
Child Welfare Information Gateway, 146
civil cases, 81
Civil Rights Act of 1964, Title VII of, 31, 194
classroom, 43
   behavior, 175
   management skills, 156
   securing accommodations in, 77
client contact considerations, 24

emergencies and crisis intervention, 27–29
   health issues, 26–27
   personal safety, 24–26
   suspicion of abuse and neglect, reporting, 27
clinical reports, 182, 184
coauthorship, expectations for, 189
code of conduct, 143
Code of Federal Regulations, Title 29 of, 31
college-level transition evaluations, 71, 72
colleges
   accommodations, assessing, 71–73
   administration, working with, 76–77
   spousal hiring policy, 201
college student evaluations, 70–71
   Americans with Disabilities Act, 75–76
   assessing college accommodations, 71–75
   college administration, working with, 76–77
communications
   electronic, 147–148
   with parents, resources for, 129–130
   written, 149
competencies, 41, 130–131, 134
   ratings, 42, 50
comprehensive psychoeducational
   report, 12, 64
conflicts, 44–46
   in laws and agency rules/policies, 143–149
   in supervisor evaluation and students, 44–48
   with supervisors, 140–142
   title, 146–147
consent
   forms, 14
   to share information, 42
   written, 122
constructive feedback, 56–57
consultation and collaboration, 41
contingency-based leadership for
   mentor–mentee relationship, 57–58
contracts, 139
   internship, 138–140
   sample expectations within internship
      supervisory, 139
Council of Directors of School Psychology
   Programs (CDSPP), 40, 99, 102, 104, 148
Council of Graduate Departments of
   Psychology, 148
Council of Specialties in Professional
   Psychology, 187
cover letters, 191–194, 199
credentialing requirements, 118, 119, 138

INDEX • 227

credentials, 81
  for graduate students, 98
  supervisors, 48
criminal cases, 80, 81
crisis intervention services, 27–29
cross-disciplinary approaches, 187
curriculum vita (CV), 192
  credentials and awards, 98
  definition of, 95–96
  education, 96
  experiences, 96–97
  header and contact information, 96
  professional association membership, 98
  professional publications and
    presentations, 97
  skills/areas of proficiency, 97–98

Department of Education (2006) 34 Code of
  Federal Regulation, 183
Diagnostic and Statistical Manual of Mental
  Disorders-5, 71
  classification models beyond, 87–88
  codes, 157
  diagnoses, 182
direct student considerations, 24
  emergencies and crisis intervention, 27–29
  health issues, 26–27
  personal safety, 24–26
  suspicion of abuse and neglect,
    reporting, 27
disability classifications, 23
disability documentation, 71, 72, 76
Disability Resource Center (DRC), 76
disability services, 73, 88
  for college students, 75–76
Disability Supports Services (DSS), 76
disagreements, 47, 141
distal data, acquisition of knowledge and
  skills, 39–40
diversity, 41
  considerations, 183
doctoral students, 103
  APPIC application process for, 106
  internships, 102
documentation of internship, 117–118
  personal and professional benefits of,
    119–120
  and psychologist licensure, 118–119
  and school psychologist credentialing, 118
documentation of practicum activities, 33

documents
  career interviews, 199
  career vita, professional, 192–194
  internship plan, written, 140
DRC. *See* Disability Resource Center
drug testing, 15
DSS. *See* Disability Supports Services
dual enrollment, 69

Educational Testing Service (ETS), 72
Education Amendments of 1972, Title IX of, 32
EEOC. *See* Equal Employment Opportunity
  Commission
electronic communication, 147–148
electronic supervision, 147–148
emergency procedures, 27–28
employment fairness, provisions for, 194
entry-level position, 189–190
  entry-level salary, 201
entry procedures considerations, 21
  acclimation to the hierarchy and culture
    within schools/clinics, 23
  building rapport, 21–22
  expectations and boundaries, setting, 22
  IDEIA and state classification systems and
    local programs, 23–24
Equal Employment Opportunity Commission
  (EEOC), 31–32
Ethical and Professional Practices Committee,
  NASP, 134
ethical practice, setting expectations for,
  125–126
ethical standards, 48, 134
  American Psychological Association
    (APA), 136
  National Association of School
    Psychologists (NASP), 144, 147
  violation of, 143
ethics, 41, 143–144
  code, school psychology interns' obligations
    to. *See* school psychology interns
  supervisors, 47
ETS. *See* Educational Testing Service
evaluation forms, 131
evaluation process, 42, 50, 131, 141
expectations for ethical practice, 125–126
expert testimony, 80, 81

face-to-face communication, augment, 148
face-to-face individual supervision, 148

228 • INDEX

Fair Employment Practice Agency, 32
Family Educational Rights and Privacy Act
    (FERPA), 31, 85, 121–122
federal disability laws, 155
Federal Register, 183
feedback
    constructive, 56
    positive, 56
    scoring assessments, 63
FERPA. *See* Family Educational Rights and
    Privacy Act
FindLaw, 146
fingerprinting, 14–15
forensic psychology, 79
    evaluation, 79–80
    expert testimony, 81
    professional credentials, 81

goal conflicts, 44–45
group review, 45
Guidelines and Principles for Accreditation
    of Programs in Professional
    Psychology, 130

harassment
    student-to-student, 32
    types of, 32–33
health, 88
    issues, 26–27
Health Insurance Portability and
    Accountability Act of 1996 (HIPAA),
    29–30, 85, 122
HIPAA. *See* Health Insurance Portability and
    Accountability Act of 1996
hiring committee, career interviews, 199
hiring of forensic expert testimony, 81
hostile work environment, 32–33

*ICD. See International Classification of
    Diseases*
ICD-10–Clinical Modification (ICD-10-CM),
    87–88
*ICF. See International Classification of
    Functioning*
IDEIA. *See* Individuals with Disabilities
    Education Improvement Act
identification, 15
IEP. *See* individualized education program
illegal questions, sample list of, 196–197
illness, 26

imposter phenomenon, 114
incident responses, 28
individualized education program (IEP), 71,
    129, 135
individualized social skills counseling, 175
Individuals with Disabilities Education
    Improvement Act (IDEIA), 23–24, 71,
    86, 182, 183
infectious disease, 26
Institutional Research Board (IRB), 82–84
institutions' websites, 190
insurance. *See* student liability insurance
insurance reimbursements, outpatient
    treatment documentation for, 181
interdisciplinary meetings, 129
International Classification of Diseases (ICD),
    87–88
*International Classification of Functioning
    (ICF)*, 88
international jobs, websites for, 191
International School Psychology
    Association, 191
International Schools Services, 191
internship, 117, 133, 142, 144, 186
    accreditation, 103–104
    APPIC, 99, 102–104
    application process, 105–106
    and career vita, 193
    clinical settings, 102–103
    contract, 138–140
    coordinator, university-based, 140
    curriculum vita. *See* curriculum vita
    decision, 114
    documentation, personal and professional
        benefits of, 119–120
    e-mail communications between, and
        supervisors, 148
    evaluation forms, sample, 131
    evaluation measures and competencies,
        130–131
    imposter phenomenon, 114
    interview. *See* interviews, internship
    letters of recommendation, 112–113
    log data and implications for, 34–35
    performance, evaluating, 139
    personal conflicts between, and supervisors,
        140, 141
    school psychology, 133, 137, 140, 143, 147
    setting boundaries and expectations,
        125–126

site selection, 99–105
standards and guidelines, 99–101
statement of interest, 106–107
stipends, 104–105
supervisory contracts, sample expectations within, 139
time management for, 122–125
transitioning to role of professional, 126–130
interpersonal skills, 41, 128
interpersonal supervisory relationships, 148
intervention, 41
competencies, 43
medical-based, 182
school-based, 182
intervention case reports, 181–182, 184
interviews
career
academic interviews, 198
documents, 199
financial considerations for salary and benefits, 200
hiring committee, 199
illegal questions, sample list of, 196–197
list of sample questions, 199–200
negotiation, 200–201
position types, 198
practice interview questions, 194–196
reports/publications from professional portfolio, 199
reviewing information on organization, 198–199
videotaping, 194
internship, 107–112
basic, 108–109
interviewer and, 109–110
log data and implications for, 34–35
questions for school psychology, 110–111
IRB. *See* Institutional Research Board

Jessica Lunsford Act, 13
job fairs, 190
job interview, formal components of.
See interviews
job search process, 185
job vacancy, websites, 191

laissez-faire leadership for mentor–mentee relationship, 57
laws, conflicts in, 143
leadership, 41

mentor–mentee relationship, for supervising, 57–58, 68
multiple styles of, 57–58, 68
letters of recommendation, 112–113
liability insurance, 15–16, 19
licensed supervision, 188, 200
licensure requirements, 118, 119
logs, 34, 117–118
data and implications for internships, 34–35
sample, 121

major life activities, ADA, 76
medical-based intervention, 182
medications, access to, 25
Megan's Law, 13
mental health, settings of, 85–87
mentoring, peer. *See* peer mentoring
mentor–mentee relationship, leadership approaches to, 57–58
mentorship, 55, 188
metacognitive abilities, supervisors, 48
method conflicts, 45
miscommunication, 141
Model Act for State Licensure of Psychologists, 118
Model for Comprehensive and Integrated School Psychological Services, NASP's, 134
modifications, curriculum, 71
multidomain capstone case format, 43
multimethod capstone case format, 43
multiple progress monitoring measures, 4
multiprovider capstone case format, 44
multiyear practica curricula sequence, 5
multiyear practica placement options, 7

NASP. *See* National Association of School Psychologists
NASP Practice Model, 138
NASP Principles for Professional Ethics, 134, 145, 146
NASP Standards for Graduate Preparation of School Psychologists (2010), 4
National Association of School Psychologists (NASP), 129, 133, 134, 183, 192, 200
and APA domains, 40
approval and accrediting processes, 39
Ethical and Professional Practices Committee, 134
ethical principles, 84, 125, 144, 147

230 • INDEX

National Association of School Psychologists
    (NASP) (*cont.*)
  guidelines, 130
  internship standards, 99
  Model for Comprehensive and
    Integrated School Psychological
    Services, 134
  NCSP credential, 118
  online career center, 190
  online resources and handouts, 28–29
  practicum, 3
  PREPaRE: School Crisis Prevention
    and Intervention Training
    Curriculum, 98
  resources for communication with
    parents, 119
  school setting, 101
  student strategies, 45–47
  supervision strategies, 47–48
national college test accommodation
    applications, 73
National Joint Committee on Learning
    Disabilities (NJCLD), 72
Nationally Certified School Psychologist
    (NCSP), 118
  credential of, 134
national professional organizations, 186
NCSP. *See* Nationally Certified School
    Psychologist
neglect, suspicion of, 27
negotiating salary, 200–201
negotiation, career interviews, 200–201
networking, power of, 191
NJCLD. *See* National Joint Committee on
    Learning Disabilities
NPA. *See* National Postdoctoral Association

Occupational Outlook Handbook, 200
Offices of Special Education and
    Rehabilitative Services, 183
Older Workers Benefit Protection Act
    (OWBPA), 195
online career center, 190
organizational barriers, 141
organization management skills, 11–13
outpatient treatment documentation for
    insurance reimbursements, 181
overcommitted schedules, 12
OWBPA. *See* Older Workers Benefit
    Protection Act

patient considerations, 24
  emergencies and crisis intervention, 27–29
  health issues, 26–27
  personal safety, 24–26
  suspicion of abuse and neglect, reporting, 27
PDA. *See* Pregnancy Discrimination Act
pediatric school psychology, 182
peer mentoring, 53. *See also* peer supervision
  levels of support, 55–56
  positive effects of, 53
  process of, 55, 67–68
  proofing common writing errors, 64–65
  relationship, 55
peer review form, 59, 63
peer supervision, 53–54, 65–67
  levels of support, 55–56
  models of, 57–58
  positive interactions, facilitating, 56–57
  proofing common writing errors, 64–65
  roles and responsibilities, 54–55
  scoring protocols, 63–64
  test administration, critiquing, 58–63
performance competency, 48–49
personal benefits, of internship
    documentation, 119–120
personal career goals, 6
personal conflicts, development of, 140
personalized supervision, 4
personal liability insurance, 16
personal questions, types of, 194
personal safety considerations, 24–26
personal skills, 41
PHI. *See* Protected Health Information
policies, rules and, 143
portfolios, work products review, 42–43
positive interactions, of supervisors, 56–57
postdoc positions, planning for, 186
postdocs, 185–186
  benefits of research, 188
  experience, 188
  finding a, 186–187
  informal, 187
  quality of, 187–189
  types of, 188
postdoctoral fellowship, 185
postdoctoral openings, listings of, 187
postdoctoral positions, applications for, 120
postdoctoral psychology training
    opportunities, 186
postdoctoral supervision, 186

postdoctoral teaching appointment, 186
postdoctoral training, 189
postdoc training sites, 186–187
postsecondary educational experience, vital components of, 53
postsecondary student evaluations, 70
practica competencies, 41, 42
practica coordinators, role of, 5–6
practica evaluation/counseling room, 25
practica program structure, 4–6
practica site placements, 6–7
practica supervision, 47
practica syllabi, 4
practice interview questions
  for professional practice positions, 194, 196
  for research/academic positions, 194, 195
practicum
  advanced practicum, 69–70, 77–79
    forensic psychology, 79–81
    mental health settings, 85–87
    research considerations, 82–85
    transition and college student evaluations, 70–77
  attributes, professional demeanor in, 9
  characteristics, professional demeanor in, 9
  direct student, patient, and client contact considerations, 24–29
  entry procedures considerations, 21–24
  log, 33, 34
  orientation to, 36–37
  placement, 4
  preparation for, 3–4
  professional demeanor in, 9
  professional issues, 17–18
  professional practice considerations, 29–35
  program structure, 4–6
  research considerations through practicum, 82–85
  security procedures, 13–15
  site placements, 6–7
  site supervisors, 14
  specialization, 69
  students, 86–87
  student liability insurance, 15–16
  surviving and thriving in grad school, 8–13
Practicum Competencies Outline, 40
practitioner/mental health agency interviews, format for, 197
Pregnancy Discrimination Act (PDA), 195–196
preintervention baseline measurement, 181

PREPaRE: School Crisis Prevention and Intervention Training Curriculum, 98
Principles for Professional Ethics (2010), 134, 145, 146, 183
professional dress, 9–11, 127–128
professional ethics, 143
professional image, building, 127–128
professional liability insurance, 16
professional practice considerations, 29
  Family Educational Rights and Privacy Act (FERPA), 31
  Health Insurance Portability and Accountability Act (HIPAA), 29–30
  log data and implications for internships, 34–35
  log records, 34
  record keeping, 33–34
  sexual harassment, 31
professional practice positions, practice interview questions for, 194, 196
professional practice, setting boundaries for, 125–126
professional role, 126–127
  association membership, 98
  audience and purpose of interactions, 128–129
  interpersonal skills and administrative interactions, 128
  publications and presentations, 97
  resources for communication with parents, 129–130
  transitioning to, 126–127
professional work products review, 42–43
proof of liability insurance, 15
proofreading, common writing errors, 64–65
Protected Health Information (PHI), 30
proximal data, acquisition of knowledge and skills, 39
PsycCareers webpage, 186
psychoeducational evaluations, 72, 79
psychoeducational report writing, 71
  goal of, 152
psychoeducational school-based assessment and evaluation reports, 157
psychological assistant, 187
psychological case reports
  clinic-based case reports, 182
  diversity considerations, 183
  legal and ethical guideline considerations, 182–183
  report writing, 151–181

232 • INDEX

psychological report writing, 152, 182
psychologist licensure, documentation and, 118–119
psychologists, unlicensed, 187
psychology, forensic. *See* forensic psychology
psychology postdoc opportunities, 186
PTA. *See* parent teacher association

quid pro quo, principle of, 32, 33

rapport building, 21–22
reasonable accommodations, 75
record keeping, 33–34, 117–118, 146
records retention, 121–122
recruitment process of graduate school, 8
Rehabilitation Act of 1973, 75
Rehabilitation Psychology, 187
relationship skills, 41
remediation, 44
remote supervision, 147
reports/publications
    assignments of, 151
    career interviews, 199
    school-based, 73, 184
report writing, 64, 65, 151–157, 183
    basics, 157–181
    guidance for, 182
    intervention, 184
    principles, 152
    psychological, 152
research-based postdoc positions, 188
research-intensive position, 185
research-intensive programs, 7
research positions
    interview format for, 197–198
    practice interview questions for, 194, 195
research postdoc, benefits of, 188
resource allocation, 188
resources, for communication with parents, 129–130
role definition, 135–138
rules and policies, 143

salaries
    entry-level salary, 201
    financial considerations for, 200
    for hospitals and agencies, 201
    negotiation for, 200–201
    for school-based positions, 200–201
    spousal hires, 201

sample university institutional review board study application, 83
school-based internship, 102, 106
school-based intervention, 182
school-based positions, salaries for, 200–201
school-based reports, 73, 157–181, 184
school psychologists, 6, 28, 30, 46, 70, 73, 77, 86, 125, 134, 143
    credentialing, 118, 128
    role of, 56
school psychology interns, 102, 115, 124, 133–134, 140, 143, 147
    practice within competencies, 134
    role definition and expectations, 135–138
    self-advocacy, 138
school psychology internship, 133
school psychology programs, 14, 16, 39, 54, 69, 71, 82, 137, 140
schools/clinics, hierarchy and culture within, 23
school setting, definition of, 100–102
scientific inquiry method, 3
scientist–practitioner model, 4, 82
    practica experience supports, 3
scoring protocols, 63–64
securing accommodations in classroom, 77
security procedures, 13–14
    drug testing, 15
    fingerprinting and background checks, 14–15
    identification, 15
self-care, time management for interns, 124–125
self-reflection, on performance, 49
sexual harassment in workplace environments, 31–33
shame-proneness, 45
shared-cost arrangements, 201
skills acquisition, 39–41
    measurement of, 42–43
socialization process, 3, 188
social network sites, 191
Society of Behavioral Medicine, 186
Society of Clinical Child and Adolescent Psychology, 187
Society of Pediatric Psychology, 187
special education classification, 23
specialization practicum, 69, 189
    clinic-based examples of, 70
    college transition evaluations, 70–71
    hierarchical infrastructure for, 190

spousal hiring policy, 201
Standards for Graduate Preparation of School
    Psychologists, 130
start-up packages, 201
statement of interest, internship, 106–107
   experiences, 107
   opening paragraph, 106–107
   style and length, 106
stipends, 104–105
stress management, 11
student evaluation forms, 42
student liability insurance, 15–16
   personal liability insurance, 16
   professional liability insurance, 16
students' cumulative files, 29
student-to-student harassment, 32
summative work products, 43
supervision, 41
   electronic, 147–148
   face-to-face individual, 148
   field-based, 148
   goals, 139
   logistics, 138
   peer. *See* peer supervision
   postdoctoral, 186
   remote, 147
   university-based, 148
   written electronic, 148–149
supervision alliance, student strategies for
   fostering, 45–46
supervision models, 57–58
supervisors, 22
   conflicts with, 44–48, 140–142
   e-mail communications between interns
     and, 148
   evaluation, conflict between students
     and, 44–45
   field-based, 137, 139
   interns, 135, 136
   personal conflicts between intern
     and, 140, 141
   responsibility of, 48, 49
   role as mentors, 46
   strategies for fostering trainee alliance,
     47–48
   university-based, 126

telesupervision, 147–149
testing, drug, 15
theft, risk for, 24

timeline, application process, 105–106
time management, 124
   electronic calendars for, 124
   for interns, 122
   prioritization, 122–123
   self-care, 124–125
   skills, 11–13
   tools for, 123–124
title conflicts, 146–147
Title VII of the Civil Rights Act of 1964, 194
tools
   for time management, 123–124
   visualization, 125
trainee alliance, supervisor strategies for
   fostering, 47–48
training programs
   formal and informal, 187
   philosophy of, 188
   supervisors, 48
transactional leadership, for mentor–mentee
   relationship, 57
transformative leadership, for mentor–mentee
   relationship, 57–58
transmission mechanism, 26

universities, spousal hiring policy, 201
university-based internship coordinator, 140
university-based supervision, 148
unlicensed psychologist, 187
U.S. Constitution, 143
U.S. Department of Justice, 13
U.S. Equal Employment Opportunity
   Commission, 197

web-based calendars, for time
   management, 123
WHO. *See* World Health Organization
WHO-Family of International Classifications
   (WHO-FIC), 87
working alliance, 140
workplace environments, sexual harassment
   in, 31–33
work products, summative, 43
World Health Organization (WHO), 87
writing errors, proofing, 64–65
writing skills, 174
written communications, 149
written consent, 122
written documents, internship plan, 140
written electronic supervision, 148–149

Printed in the United States
By Bookmasters